PRAISE FOR WHERE WA: ▮▮▮
NEEDED HI.

"Our path to healing might be quicker were our shepherds brave enough to reveal their wounds. Like a modern-day psalmist, Dr. Myers's vulnerability helps readers tow that all too familiar tension between our love for God and our frustration with Him when life takes its turns. If you've gone through pain—you need to hear what Dan has to say. If you've had the pleasure of a pain-free life, read this volume anyway. For as Mama said, 'If you've never known pain, just keep living.' Thank you, Dan & Dorene, for providing answers to the question we're all asking!"

—Ricky Jenkins
Senior Pastor, Southwest Church, Indian Wells, CA

"Dr. Dan Myers is a pastor with a unique blend of humor, practical living, and wise counsel. He demonstrates this in all he does as he reaches out to others, listens, and encourages people in every walk of life. Today, the concept of God's peace is often challenged; but Dr. Dan teaches that despite despair, we can know joy amid sorrow, anxiety, and loss. I am grateful that, in times of personal loss, he has conveyed some of that joy to me. Everyone will benefit from reading *Where Was God When I Needed Him?*

—Rosemary Jackson
Alumni Director, and Assistant to the President for Alumni Events, Vanguard University 1979-2007

"Dr. Dan Myers pulls back the veneer of glib spirituality in *Where Was God When I Needed Him?* to face the pain and bewilderment of unexpected tragedy and unanswered prayers. This book is not about providing an answer. It is a travel companion for those of us that are living the question—a must-read."

—Dr. Michael J. Beals
President, Vanguard University

"Have you have ever been on a mountain top, in a desert, in a storm, or on calm water? If you have ever wondered where God might be in the middle of the mess, or raised your fist or voice and yelled at God (like I have!) during your pain when the miracle did not come, then you will love this book. My friend Dan Myers is no "armchair quarterback" in the journey of well-earned faith. Dan has experienced the heights and depths of life and comes through them with a vibrant faith in God, His Word, and His goodness. Read this book and grow deeper; I know I did."

—Dr. John Jackson
President of William Jessup University, Speaker, Author of books on personal and organizational transformation

"If you already have all your faith questions answered, then don't bother reading this book. However, if you sometimes have nagging thoughts that things haven't turned out as you thought God might provide, then start reading. There is an excellent reason for me to endorse Dan Myers's journey as told in this book: my wife, Bev, and I traveled with him and Dorene through both the smooth and rough patches of their road. We have been close friends and fellow pastors for over fifty years. As I read Dan's manuscript, I thought of an alternative title for the book: *But Even if He Does Not,* in reference to the three guys headed for the furnace in Daniel 3). Dan Myers has shaped my life. I think he will yours as well."

—Steve Rumpf

"My friend, Dan Myers, has written a compelling work about real faith, the kind of faith for the most desperate of times. I believe this book can help provide hope for those who are just hanging on and wondering where God is. All of us need hope and faith. I am incredibly thankful to Dan for the read. I know God is going to use this book to encourage many."

—Jack Hamilton
Executive Pastor at The High Desert Church, and Mentor Pastor for Transformation Ministries

"How appropriate that this book, *Where Was God When I Needed Him?*, was written by a hang gliding enthusiast! All of us have felt the exhilaration of being lifted above life's mountain peaks to experience the "power of His resurrection." But we also have days when we lose our lift and fall back toward earth to experience "the fellowship of His suffering." This honest look at faith, hope, and love is not merely a theoretical exercise. These insights come from an early mentor of mine who has "slipped the surly bonds" of an earth-bound perspective to live out a life that is eternally significant."

—Dr. Gary Brandenburg
Pastor-at-Large, Fellowship Bible Church Dallas

"This is a great read for anyone who has/is experiencing the pain of unexpected trauma and tragedy. The author shares from personal experience the shock, the questions, the inner strength that comes from

God even when He seems silent and distant. The path to strength, power, and recovery is clearly defined for all who go through these times of emotional and spiritual distress."

—Dennis A. Davis
Pastor, Denominational Executive, former president
of Northwest University

"It was shortly after Renee's death that we had Dan speak at our couple's annual dinner for parents who had lost a child. He spoke on, *Where Was God When I Needed Him? The Question Everyone's Asking*. I remember at the time thinking how helpful it would be if all parents could hear his story, and now through his book, they can. At the beginning of our loss, we did not want to hear about Romans 8:28. The pain makes it difficult to absorb; but as you read Dan's book, you will see a purpose in your heartache and the good that can come from your loss."

—Daisy Catching-Shader
Founder and President of Umbrella Ministries

"Reading this gripping book will help you find 'how to turn an endless tragedy into a limitless future.' A must-read from start to finish. This book will demonstrate that He's really there all the time."

—Ronn Haus
Pastor, Evangelist, Telecaster, Musician

"All of us will experience a tragic loss. The question we're left to answer is how can our souls grow, and our lives move forward after that moment? *Where Was God When I Needed Him?* can walk with anyone who is trying to deal with the hand they've been dealt–especially when it's not the hand they would have chosen."

—Scott Hitzel
Executive Pastor at Fellowship Church in Los Angeles,
Southwest Church in Indian Wells, CA, and on pastoral staff at
Saddleback Church in California

"Dan Myers challenged my thinking the very first time I met him twenty-five years ago. He is still at it! *Where Was God When I Needed Him?* challenges us to face life's darkest places and hardest questions. You won't find cheap, easy answers here. But Dan will point you to the Lord of life, who will one day fill in all the empty blanks."

—George White
Iowa United Methodist Pastor, Author of Grubbing Hoes,
Bibles, and Gavels and Toxin 666: Terror in the Heartland

"As a Marriage/Family therapist, I am often asked this question by clients experiencing gut-wrenching emotional pain who are crying to God for answers. Often God's silence makes it appear as if He does not care. Dr. Dan Myers vividly and honestly expresses the pain, the questioning, and the despair he and his wife experienced after the accident and eventual homegoing of their precious daughter. He holds nothing back. This book is extremely well written, with the powerful use of scripture pointing people to Christ, and is one I will recommend to clients. A must-read!"

—Jeenie Gordon
LMFT Marriage/Family therapist, author, speaker

"What happens to our faith when the props that have always supported us give way and the ground beneath us begins to crack? When life unexpectedly dishes out pain so unimaginable that it threatens to undo us? Pastor Dan Myers and his lovely wife, Dorene, were forced to find out when the unimaginable happened. Following a sudden tragedy, Dan takes us on a transparent journey toward faith and a trust in God's love that was deep enough to not only survive, but recover and thrive in Christ once again. I wholeheartedly recommend this book! Sometimes funny, often sobering and painful, enormously encouraging, always profoundly insightful–this volume will be a truly valuable resource and blessing to anyone whose faith is challenged by the traumatic experiences of life. And, sooner or later, that will be *all* of us!"

—Dr. Clayton Ford
National Co-Director of Holy Spirit Renewal Ministries,
pastor, conference speaker, author of Called to High Adventure: A Fresh Look at the Holy Spirit and the Spirit-Filled Life, *and* Berkeley Journal: Jesus and the Street People, A Firsthand Report. *See hsrm. org and claytonford.net.*

"This book is a must-read for people going through any struggle that they don't understand. It will be such a treasure for those who are trying to weather their storm. Dr. Myers's deep understanding has been molded in the crucible of years of pain, prayer, and even disillusionment. Through it all, he realized and rested in the wisdom and faithfulness of a beyond-amazing God. Readers will vicariously experience Myers's most inner thoughts, fears, and victories. Such wisdom resulted! No doubt, you will find consolation and hope through your storm."

—Gerald R. Wheeler, Ed.D.

"I can't think of a person more equipped to write on why God allows pain and suffering. Dan Myers is the Pastor Emeritus at the church I currently lead, and the events he describes took place in our town and church. His deeply insightful meditations are grounded in biblical truth, yet confront the honest, heartfelt questions he had to process as he dealt with the tragic loss of his daughter. Myers's vulnerability, compassion, and deep-seated confidence in Christ will not only be a balm for the souls of those currently going through hardship, but prove a valuable resource for pastors and counselors as well."

—Chris Johnson
Lead Pastor of Grace Chapel, Lancaster, CA

"This book is a Christ-empowered book that can provide direction for each of us in our life's walk when things get tough and beyond our human understanding and control. The book reflects turning *all* our unexplainable adversities over to God and exemplifies how Dan, and the love of his life, Dorene, chose to cope with the realities of life's hard times, not chosen by them. This book can be summarized as a genuine, adventurous, surrendering, no-nonsense God-serving love journey. It's based on Dan and Dorene's unprecedented and unconditional faith, hope, and trust that God would provide both wisdom and answers for their questions. He did."

—Dick Williams
Business Entrepreneur, Past Chairman Southwest Church Elder Board

"On guiding Dan through his insatiable quest to master the sport of hang gliding, I was blessed to get to know one of those rare individuals that leave lasting impressions on all whose paths they cross. Just meeting him was a delight. Listening to him was always a gift; and now reading of his journey through some of the most difficult times one can imagine, is nothing short of a treasure. Dan's book is a treasure for everyone who is or has been lost, or in the future, finds him or herself helpless and short on hope. Thank you, Dan, for your gift."

—Joe Greblo
Professional Flight Instructor, Los Angeles, CA

"The book is a fantastic journey through tragedy, struggle, and ultimate victory. As I turned the pages, my own experience of loss echoed in my mind. Who among us has not asked, "Where is God?" when confronted with tragedy. Your deep dive into personal experience and biblical exploration brings comfort and peace. God's sovereignty can be perplexing when we are in the middle of a personal trial, but it is ultimately the hope that leads us to embrace an eternal perspective and knowledge of our Creator's great love."

—George Runner
Educator, a former member of the California House of Representatives and California State Senate

I know of no one better to help you navigate the times we all face in our lives when it seems that God has gone missing. The combination of caring for others as a faithful shepherd, his own deeply moving personal experience, and his faithfulness to Scripture and story will provide you with a trusted guide on your journey.

—Dr. Dennis Easter
Executive Minister for Southern California Four Square Churches

DR. DAN MYERS

WHERE WAS GOD WHEN I NEEDED HIM?

The Question Everyone's Asking

FOREWORD BY RAY JOHNSTON

HigherLife Development Services, Inc.
P.O. Box 623307
Oviedo, Florida 32762
(407) 563-4806
www.ahigherlife.com

Printed in Canada
10 9 8 7 6 5 4 3 2 1   25 26 24 23 22 21 20

Myers, Dan
Where Was God When I Needed Him?
ISBN: 978-1-951492-16-8

TO MY WIFE, DORENE

The man who finds a wife finds a treasure, and he receives favor from the Lord. (Proverbs 18:22, NLT)

An excellent wife, who can find? For her worth is far above jewels. (Proverbs 31:10, NASB)

I discovered a jewel my first day on the college campus of my junior year. In a rapid moment, I decided I had to meet this young lady. Of course, she was beautiful and engaging, but even though I felt so in control, I stumbled with the invitation, "Would you join me at Jolly Roger this evening?" Not knowing it was a restaurant, she replied, "Who is Jolly Roger?" She had the face of an angel, the innocence of a child, a voice that sounded like a breeze blowing though cool pines, and her conversation captivated this class president in hot pursuit. By the end of that first day and date, I was helping God to understand that this lovely creature needed to be my wife.

This beautiful young lady's name is Dorene. The name has an Irish, Celtic, French, English, and Gaelic (take your pick) connection meaning "gift." For sixty-four years she has been God's perfect gift to me.

From the moment we met on the steps of the university commons, she has been the delight of my life, making it exciting and worth living. Long before hearing Stevie Wonder, she was and continues to be the "Sunshine of my Life."

I could speak of her friendship, faithfulness, love and respect, and encouragement, but most of all, I will always remember her faith, strength, and character during those challenging years following the life-debilitating auto accident of our youngest daughter. Dorene's faith and love have provided the mortar for this husband, our family, and the encouragement for this book.

But to her, I now say, your beauty remains to this day, your friends delight in your wisdom, and *"your children rise up and bless you; your husband also, and he praises you, saying, 'Many daughters have done nobly, but you excel them all.'" (Proverbs 31:28-39, NASB, paraphrase and emphasis mine).*

CONTENTS

FOREWORD

Like most Christians, I go to church—almost every weekend. There is singing. There is praying. There is an offering. And there is always a sermon.

Unlike most Christians—I am the one speaking.

I am a pastor, and every weekend I have the privilege to speak to thousands of people. It's called a sermon. And all preachers and all sermons and all churches have one unspoken rule—during the sermon, *no one ever gets to stand up, stop the sermon, and ask a question!*

If that day ever comes, I am convinced the question would be: *Where* (in the world) *Was God When I Needed Him?* What do I do when the promises of faith collide with real life? What do I do when, no matter how many times I ask, pray, or beg for a miracle, nothing happens? What do I do when I need answers, and none arrive? And most frustrating of all, what do I do when well-meaning, religious *experts* deliver pat answers and none of them work?

God tells us there are secrets He is keeping, such as the date and time of Christ's return. Other secrets He has revealed to us, which we learn through prayerful study of the Bible. And yet people sometimes (often) claim to know every answer to every question, even the mysteries that have baffled philosophers and theologians for centuries. To state simplistic answers in complex situations doesn't meet a person's needs, and especially when those answers hurt rather than help. *Let's face it: sometimes there are no simple answers. And that's what this book is all about.*

When we are shocked by circumstances that we didn't see coming, when we face events that stretch our ability even to grasp reality, when life spins out of control, we generally search for a handle—a piece of information, a scrap of wisdom, to get some understanding. We look for things to tell ourselves about it, and ways to live through it. Lots of well-meaning people will provide all kinds of trite answers to try to help the situation. In the end, we're stuck with the dilemma: what *do* we do when God doesn't seem to be there for us?

In the following pages, Dan Myers generously shares his walk through the life and death of his daughter Renee. By so doing, he provides us with proof that we *can* live through the darkest valleys of life, even if we never understand them. We may never know exactly what happened from a spiritual point of view. We may never gain clarity on certain unknown and unknowable truths. And yet, there is a certainty of known truth to which we can cling.

There is a difference between certainty and clarity. When tragedy strikes, we want clarity. Why would God let this happen? Why me? Why my family? But what we often get is certainty. In Dan's case, this is what I know with certainty:

- Dan's daughter, Renee, was loved every second of every day of her life.

- God was honored and blessed by the kinds of decisions Dan and his wife, Dorene, made for Renee.

- Christ's love was evident through the support Dan's family received from relatives, neighbors, and friends.

- If every parent cared as much about their child as Dan and Dorene cared about Renee, we would live in a much better world.

- No life is ever devoid of meaning, and somehow God used and will continue to use Renee's life in ways we cannot comprehend.

- Renee's last breath here was followed by her first breath there in the arms of Jesus.

- The next time Dan sees Renee, they will both be more alive than they have ever been.

- God is close to Dan, because the God Christians worship understands what it means to lose a child.

In Dan's book, you will not read about the miraculous recovery of a child that came close to death. You will not read a phenomenal account of divine healing. What you will read is the story of parents who prayed for a miracle and never stopped praying, just because that's what the Bible said to do.

You'll read about a loss of life, but not a loss of love; about loving parents and a loving community that rallied around an ailing child who grew through her adulthood without ever being aware of it. And you'll read about how Dan and his wife, Dorene, came to understand that oft-quoted and just-as-often misunderstood passage was written by a man named Paul who knew firsthand the worst kind of betrayal, persecution, grief, and scrapes with death, and who inscribed the answer and the mystery: "We know that in all things God works for good with those who love him, those whom he has called according to his purpose" *(Romans 8:28, GNT)*.

—Ray Johnston
Lead Pastor, Bayside Church, Granite Bay, CA

INTRODUCTION

This is not a book about tragedy followed by intense prayer which brought miraculous restoration, after which everyone lived with joy and thanksgiving forever. Popular books about tragic accidents and near-death experiences are available through an unlimited number of authors and publishers. They do well because most have a happy ending. When we read them, we say, "If it can happen for them, it can happen for us." There is a common thread that runs through them: a phenomenal account about how God met their prayer of faith with an indescribable response of divine healing. Who would not rejoice and be inspired in reading such accounts of healing or restoration?

Christians and some non-Christians pray for miracles for a couple of reasons. First, Christians pray because they are instructed in Scripture to do that when there is a need that is beyond one's ability to perform. Secondly, some non-believers think there must be something mystical in prayer. They imagine that lighting a candle can, by some unexplainable means, carry the prayer into God's presence, making it possible for Him to respond. But, let's set aside the non-believers' prayer activity and reasons for now.

Nowhere does the Bible ask us *not* to proceed boldly to God's throne of grace with all our needs. In fact, the opposite is true! Believing that— then and now—we prayed for miraculous healing after our daughter's accident based on the biblical evidence that God continues to be the God of miracles.

No matter how often, how long, or how intensely we prayed, what we prayed for seemed more elusive than ever. Did God not come through for our daughter and us? Where does that leave us? Should I forget about praying for others?

Where Was God When I Needed Him? addresses that question, but it also raises another question: "What do I do when I'm praying for a miracle, and it doesn't happen?"

Usually, we try to understand why something happened. Those who are working hard to be helpful and with the best intentions try to ease the pain of those suffering from profound loss. Often these friends come up with comments that do not help. Here are just a few.

- It was just their time to go.

- God needed them more than you do.

- God just said, "No."

- God always takes the best. He gives and takes away.

- They are in a better place.

I understand that Christians seek to comfort those who have suffered a significant loss with a passage of Scripture. Romans 8:28 is such a promise from God, but it's very difficult to sort out, when you lose a child, a son in the prime of his life, a mother with small babies, or any loss that tears at the heart. In this verse, the apostle declares:

> *And we know that for those who love God **all things** work together for good, for those who are called according to his purpose. (Romans 8:28, ESV, emphasis mine)*

The book begins with the loss of life, but not love. It moves into the sport of hang gliding which became cathartic for me in many ways, helping this father and pastor to cope with a life I had not chosen. A significant portion of this book provides a theological understanding to the title question: *Where Was God When I Needed Him?* It will also address my emotional battle with Romans 8:28 and how I have been reconciled with the "all things" of that verse.

In the final two chapters, I'm dancing across the clouds in the freedom of unending flight. As we journey together, I'm hopeful Romans 8:28, one of God's great promises, will come alive, lifting you from despair to delight.

> *And we know [with great confidence] that God [who is deeply concerned about us] causes all things to work together [as a plan] for good for those who love God, to those who are called according to His plan and purpose. (Romans 8:28, AMP)*

Come fly with me!

CHAPTER 1

GIANT MOUNTAINS AHEAD

The Journey from Heartbreak & Hurt to Healing & Hope

—Dan Myers

A hundred years from now it will not matter what your bank account was, the sort of house you lived in, or the kind of car you drove. But the world may be different because you were important in the life of a child.

—Mac Anderson

Where Was God?

The phone rang. I tried to determine where the ringing was coming from. When I looked to the back of the hall, a man was holding a phone, pointing to me and then the phone.

I had just finished speaking to the Christian Women's Club in Boron, CA. The occasion was their annual Christmas dinner with husbands or special friends invited. When I reached the man in the back, he said, "You need to take this." On the other end of the line was an officer with the Los Angeles County Sheriff's Department. He was calling from Lancaster, our home city, about sixty miles away. He wanted to know if we had a daughter named Renee. I said, "Yes." He said, "She has been in an auto accident," and suggested we return to the Antelope Valley Medical Center as soon as possible.

Renee, our youngest fourteen-year-old daughter, had been to a Christmas party in a private home with several of her friends from our church. On the way home, a woman under the influence failed to stop at a stop sign, hitting the car Renee was in. She was injured from the severe force of her head hitting the window on the passenger side of the vehicle.

For more than ten years I had served as the pastor of The King's Place, a growing, loving group of people who had been a significant focus of my life. About seventy-five of our people had arrived at the hospital before we were able to get there from Boron. They were there to support us, and for the next three weeks, different ones from the church family met in the hospital chapel every hour around the clock. They petitioned God for a miracle that only He could perform. It was a remarkable demonstration of love and devotion that we will never forget and for which we will always be grateful.

The Family

When we arrived at the hospital, Renee was lying on a gurney, seemingly asleep, but we were soon to learn she was in a coma.

Immediately the hospital staff, many who were my personal friends, started moving her into the intensive care unit. Every piece of equipment known to the medical profession seemed to be employed. CAT scanners were relatively new then, and our hospitals in the high desert did not have one yet. Dr. Harvey Birsner's only option was to do a brain angiogram. He explained an angiogram presented a greater risk than a CAT, but since that was not available, it was his only means to discover where the damage to Renee's brain was. We agreed.

Only hours before the accident, the three of us had been in our kitchen: Dorene, Renee, and me. We were about to leave with another couple for my speaking commitment sixty miles to the north in Boron. I remember lifting Renee by her waist and sitting her on the kitchen counter. It was an unforgettable moment, one of her last conscious moments for the next eight to ten months. I told her I loved her, kissed her, and said, "Mom and I will see you when we get back."

When we walked into the emergency room, there was no reason to be particularly overwhelmed. Renee didn't have a mark on her body from the accident. Her injuries were unseen inside her head. The doctors had said something about a coma, but don't most people come out of comas eventually?

Dr. Birsner performed the angiogram. He was an excellent and skilled neurosurgeon, the only one in the valley at that time. He invited Dorene and me into a side room, so he could explain the results. He said, "I don't have good news. Renee has severe damage to her brain stem." He suggested we go downstairs and sign papers to harvest those parts of her body that could be helpful to others. Without any sign of emotion, he said, "She will not be alive when morning comes." His words felt like a sledgehammer striking a bowl of Jell-O. I looked at Renee's mother, tears were cascading down her cheeks. She held on to me and said, "God will help us through this, dear!"

I thought I was a person of considerable faith. I believed God not only taught us to pray for healing, but that He is the One who still heals today. I had not only taught that from the pulpit but practiced praying for the sick and injured as instructed in God's Word. But somehow, this test of faith, praying for the healing of our daughter's brain stem, didn't seem to be in the same category as praying for a person with the flu. Did I have the faith to believe God for the greatest miracle request of my life? Renee's mother did.

The events of that night unfolded so rapidly that I did not have time to doubt God's ability. No matter what Dr. Birsner reported, I honestly felt that God could do what the medical profession could not. A real encouragement to our faith came from the seventy-five-to-one-hundred people who had gathered at the emergency room that night, some remaining all night in the chapel praying for Renee, the medical staff, and our family. We had covered all the bases. We were now in God's hands. We just simply needed to be patient and wait for Him to honor our faith.

At that moment, we were not questioning one of the greatest promises in the Bible, but that would change.

> *And we know that in all things God works for the good of those who love him, who have been called according to his purpose. (Romans 8:28)*

It became increasingly difficult to understand what God meant by "all things" as we continued to pray without any evidence that God was hearing and responding to us. *Where was God when I needed Him?* That question was the result of God's silence. Did God's silence mean He was unconcerned or uninterested? Was there a better way to understand this verse? This book is written to reveal my understanding for the purpose and truth of Romans 8:28, especially when faced with tragedy.

Renee didn't die that night, or the next, or any of the nights that followed for many years.

Dana, Renee's only sister, had recently married and was living in the state of Washington with her husband at the time of the accident. When we called her from the hospital, she was devastated, unable to deal with this first major tragedy in her life. Since Renee was in a coma and not expected to live through the night, she decided to wait a few days before flying down. Theron, Renee's brother, was with Brian, one of his best friends, the son of a much-loved staff member at the time. Both sixteen, they had enjoyed a day at the beach, a stark contrast to our high desert climate. Returning that evening, they saw the flashing lights and heard the sirens of the ambulance taking Renee to the hospital. Theron did not know his sister was in it. When he got home, we weren't there, but he knew about my speaking engagement, so he wasn't concerned. One of our elders called Theron and told him what had happened. Since we lived only a few blocks from the hospital, he drove over immediately, and was overwhelmed to see his sister in a coma. Tragedy often brings people together. That would not be true for our family during Renee's hospitalization. Instead, it was the beginning of a dark night for all three of them: Renee, her brother Theron, and her sister, Dana. Our entire family would never be the same.

For the next thirteen months Dorene lived at the hospitals in a recreational vehicle endeavoring to help with Renee's restoration and healing. I was home consumed with my responsibilities as the pastor of The King's Place. At the time the choices we made seemed like the right thing to do. Looking back now, we would have made different decisions.

The rebellion of Renee's brother and sister added another layer of questions and guilt. This often happens when family members respond in a negative way when caught in circumstances that can't be explained or understood.

I was never a person who struggled with "false" guilt, feeling guilty for the behavior of others, especially those who tried to make me feel guilty for something they had done, but this was different. I was looking at our two teenagers, thinking: *What have I not done? What did I do that's causing them to move away from the Lord instead of seeking Him for help and comfort?*

Some might have considered my intense focus on the church as *noble and committed*. The truth was that my unreasonable "commitment" became cathartic and self-serving; it was my way of dealing with the pain. I quickly felt like a juggler unable to keep a single ball in the air. I had prayed, our family was engaged in counseling, and still, it appeared that God was like the image of Stonehenge—impressive, but without feeling. Admittedly my temporary attitude about God was conditioned by my expectations and personal desires for Renee and my family. It was difficult to believe that God would want anything less than what I wanted: the full restoration of my daughter, and now the family could be added to that request.

I knew all the instructive passages in the Bible that encourage us when we are in the middle of a storm. I had preached hundreds of times about such crises, yet every time I walked into her room her condition was overwhelming, and tears seemed to be the only release—tears that for the moment replaced everything I believed and had taught. It was a different kind of crisis. It was not limited to just Renee; it had become a family crisis. This would not be resolved in a quickie crisis management seminar.

What I thought was a core principle of my life turned out not to be. I had proclaimed from the pulpit, God first, wife second, children third, and church fourth. Somehow in the mixing bowl of chaos, I allowed a rearrangement of my priorities. If I had followed what I said I believed and taught, I would have taken a six-month sabbatical to focus on the family in search of a different kind of healing. The church would have agreed.

The process of healing began with the most humbling experiences of my life. The process continued because of a mother's unconditional love and because friends prayed with us. We were beginning to learn the meaning of "trust in the Lord with all of your heart" (Proverbs 3:5), even when we didn't see the results we wanted from the One in Whom we were trying to place our trust.

We discovered that God is not just a God of rainbows (promises), but a God of silver linings as well. We were beginning to see and feel how God heals hurting hearts, even when we did not get the desires of our hearts.

It seemed like the intensive care nurses had taken up residence in our daughter's room. The cadence of the breathing machine overwhelmed me. She looked so peaceful. There was no external physical damage. Even with all the tubes and equipment, she didn't look seriously injured. Could the doctor be in error?

In an accident that took less than a second, Renee fell into a coma, lost her gag reflex (which enables a person to swallow), and could no longer control the temperature of her body. A special blanket was placed underneath her to compensate for what the brain usually did. The blanket cooled her when she ran excessively high temperatures and warmed her when her body chilled. In spite of all the equipment, she looked like a sleeping angel ready to wake up—if only her pastor father could figure this out and find the right scripture, offer the right prayer, and say the right thing. Fathers often have the idea that they can make most anything right, but even fathers learn that some things are beyond their reach, no matter how much they love someone.

She looked like a sleeping angel ready to wake up —if only her pastor father could figure this out and find the right scripture, offer the right prayer, and say the right thing.

As we stood there in the hospital, I had no doubts. It seemed impossible that our vibrant daughter would be gone. Along with our friends who continued to pray and encourage us, we all believed that God would provide a miracle, but her coma continued.

It would not be long until I discovered there are times when great passages of God's Word are not helpful to a person. I am not suggesting that they are not true, but there are moments when a person is so cracked and broken that these truths cannot provide the comfort and help those around them intend. In my case, Paul's writing serves as an illustration.

And we know that in all things God works for the good of those who love him, who have been called according to his purpose. (Romans 8:28)

In that moment of severe emotional pain, Paul's words seemed less than comforting. I had just been asked to sign papers that would allow the medical staff to harvest Renee's body, so others would have a chance at life. In truth, I wasn't thinking about gifts of life for others. I wanted my beautiful daughter to live with all my being. How could I *not* cry out *against* what Paul had written?

I loved the Lord. I knew that I was called, but I couldn't process the *"all things."*

I looked at Dorene, her face awash with tears. She held on to me and said, "You have preached it, and I have said it before, God will help us through this."

I wanted to cry out, *Really?* But I didn't.

My conversations with God went something like this: "Father, I understand that I am not special or unique. *If* I once felt that way, I do not anymore. I know I can't avoid tragedy or loss. Other wonderful people have experienced excruciating anguish of heart and mind that exceeds anything I shall ever know, yet I plead my case before You. You know I love You, and You know I've committed my life to You. Not man, but You, have placed this calling on my life. Haven't I met at least the minimal conditions that would make it possible for You to come through with this promise about 'all things working together *for good*'? What am I not understanding about 'all things'? Is it realistic for me to expect that I should be able to understand every detail of my world when it was beginning to seem alien? God, I can't process all of this. I need Your help." Time seemed to have stopped or be moving in slow motion.

When we had first walked into the emergency room, I felt emboldened. I knew our friends were people of faith, and my faith at that moment was strong, but that changed when the doctor came back with his report, followed by his suggestion to sign the papers for harvesting our daughter's body. I felt like my friend when he described the fear that gripped him the moment when his hang glider broke in mid-flight and he pulled the ring and the chute didn't open. He knew he had a backup chute, but in those first moments while grabbing for that elusive backup ring, he nearly became a casualty. Like my friend, I needed a backup. Fear was leaving little room for faith. Dorene and I held one another; we talked, wept, and then simply prayed prayers that appeared to be trapped by the ceiling. In my own desperation, I nearly shouted, "God, where are You when we need You?"

After the Rain, the Tsunami

I wasn't doing well in finding an answer, and it wasn't going to get better. Within twenty-four hours of our daughter's accident, the question became even more intense when my former secretary's daughter was killed.

On that Sunday evening, Leslie, a young mother from our church, was working alone in a service station, hoping to earn a few dollars for that extra room to accommodate her young family of three young babies all under the age of five. Leslie was one of Pat Combs's four daughters, and had been a single parent, having lost her husband several years before. Now Leslie's young husband, Jim, was learning what it meant to be both a husband and father.

Sometime between eight and ten on that Sunday evening, two men ordered her to open the safe at gunpoint at the gas station in the Antelope Valley. After cleaning out the safe, they abducted her, drove eight miles to a desolate spot where they both assaulted her. Before leaving, they shot her five times and left her at the foot of a hill out in the desert. Jim, her young husband and father of their babies, was devastated.

Leslie's sister, Patsy, and her husband, Mark, took the children into their home, offering a priceless gift that has made all the difference in the lives of these three babies. They gave them their love and raised them with their own four children. Patsy and Mark were not only the aunt and uncle to these orphans, but now Mother and Dad as well. The Mark Longs have never considered what they did a sacrifice, but only an expression of their love. It was done not only for the children, but for their father too. The loss of his young wife and the thought of trying to be a single father to three small children caused Jim to fall into a dark place from which he never recovered. Unable to cope with his own grief, Jim lost his life in a motorcycle accident less than a year after Leslie's death.

On December 11, 1978, our church family gathered in the sanctuary for Leslie's memorial service. It had been only days after Renee's accident and Leslie's murder. Of the hundreds of memorial services, I've conducted, Leslie's was the most difficult. How do you tell a mother, sisters, husband, and other members of the family that their loved one is in a better place? You can tell them that, but their pain was multiplied by the unspeakable circumstances of her death that there was little immediate comfort. The children were not present, but Patsy and Mark had a host of challenges before them in raising them along with their own four children, and we all knew it. The adult Christian members of the family grieved, and their faith gave them the comfort to know that Leslie was in the presence of the Lord. They were thankful for that reality. Even so, their pain was still intense.

I found myself in a mixing bowl, asking my question with a greater sense of urgency and desperation: *God, where are You when we need You?* This was no longer just the piercing cry from my own family. Now my bowl combined with the Long and Comb families, who were all asking the same question. We all struggled with Romans 8:28 more intensely than before. It reverberated in our hearts daily, over and over again, louder and louder:

And we know that in all things God works for the good of those who love him, who have been called according to his purpose. (Romans 8:28)

We agreed we loved the Lord. There was no question that we were called according to His purpose and will. *There must be something we didn't understand about God's purpose. What was going on? God, help us understand!*

I continued to serve for another eight years at The King's Place. During that time and for many years after, the Los Angeles County Sheriff's Department and the Los Angeles County District Attorney's Office were diligent in pursuing every lead in Leslie's case, but it became a cold case. It took nearly forty years before Terry Moses, fifty-nine, and Neal Antoine Matthew, fifty-eight, were charged and convicted for her grisly murder. Both received life sentences without parole.

The case was finally broken because of the untiring efforts of three very special people who worked on it for nearly forty years: Tannaz Mokayef, Assistant District Attorney, Sergeant Brian Schoonmaker, Homicide Detective, and Steven Lankford, Deputy.

Brian Schoonmaker, the lead investigator, was (and is) a member of Leslie's church family. Eight days before his retirement he received a positive identification from the DNA. The Los Angeles County Sheriff's Department gave him special permission to postpone his retirement for one year so he could work the new lead. After a year, both suspects were identified, arrested, and charged with the crimes against Leslie. Then Sergeant Schoonmaker retired and Steve Lankford took over as lead detective. Lankford assisted Tannaz Mokayef in the trial.

After more than thirty-seven years, researching every lead and detail, Sergeant Schoonmaker and this team of committed professionals finally found a measure of justice and closure for Leslie and her family.

Singing in a Cave

In those desperate moments when I felt that God had abandoned our family and Leslie's too, I read a quote from Elisabeth Elliot. Elisabeth was the wife of Jim Elliot, one of the five men martyred as they tried to take the gospel to the hostile Auca tribe in Ecuador in 1956.[1] After losing her husband, Elisabeth struggled with some of the same questions I had. How she could find peace after God allowed the death of these five missionaries?

In 1976, nineteen years after Jim Elliot's death, Elisabeth was addressing the Urbana Missions Conference. She told of being in Wales, watching a shepherd and his dog. There she found a simple answer to questions that had troubled her. This is what she shared that day:

The dog would herd the sheep up a ramp and into a tank of antiseptic in which they had to be bathed to protect them from parasites. As soon as they would come up out of the tank, the shepherd would grab the rams by the horns and fling them back into the tank and hold them under the antiseptic for a few more seconds. Mrs. Elliot asked the shepherd's wife if the sheep understood what was happening. "They haven't got a clue," she said.

I've had some experiences in my life that have made me feel very sympathetic to those poor rams—I couldn't figure out any reason for the treatment I was getting from the Shepherd I trusted. And He didn't give a hint of explanation.

If you've been a Christian for very long, you've been there. You might have felt the Shepherd you trusted threw you into some circumstances that were quite unpleasant, and you didn't have a clue as to why He was doing it. David had been there. He wrote Psalm 57 out of the depths of just such an experience. When he was a teenager, David had been anointed as king to replace the disobedient King Saul. Then he slew the giant Goliath and was thrust into instant national fame, but King Saul's jealous rage sent David running for his life. He spent the better part of his twenties dodging Saul's repeated attempts on his life. The title tells us that he wrote this psalm "when he fled from Saul, in the cave." Caves are interesting places to visit once in a while.

Elisabeth Elliot had found peace with a shepherd and some dumb sheep. In 1993 she included this event in her lesson on Psalm 57. She titled it "Singing in a Cave." Her lesson from that great psalm seemed to be reserved for me. *If David could sing in a cave when his life was threatened, I could too! If Elizabeth Elliot can sing after watching her husband and friends brutally murdered, so could I.* With a brave heart calling for a song, I had no idea how that song would turn out.

CHAPTER 2

FROM MOUNTAINS TO DESERTS

"What makes the desert beautiful," said the little prince, "is that some-where it hides a well."

—Antoine de Saint-Exupery

Keep bubbling over with abundant joy, peace, and love. You may be the only well-watered oasis for someone going through a desert in their lives.

—Caroline Naoroji

A Beautiful Beginning

My parents were young and very ordinary. Both came from large families. At the time of my birth, my father was the headwaiter at Pick and Whistle, one of the most elegant restaurants in Los Angeles. Both were active and faithful members of Bible Assembly, my church until I was ten. My siblings and I were unique in that we had three grandfathers, all very committed Christians. My Grandfather Myers had been a farmer all his life. My maternal Grandfather Zahnter had been a blacksmith, and my Grandfather Gresham was my pastor. On many occasions, I bragged that I had adopted my Grandfather Gresham. He and his wife raised my mother during her teen years, so it was natural for my siblings and me to affectionately call the Greshams Grandpa and Annie.

To help my mother's family during the height of the Great Depression, the Greshams took her into their home. The Gresham and Zahnter families were very close since the entire Zahnter family were members of the same church. It turned out to be a wonderful arrangement. The Greshams helped my mother's family, and Mother helped the Gresham's with their two younger daughters and assisted with housework.

As my mother matured, she took on many responsibilities in the church in which my grandfather served. It was the church in which my parents (and most of my mother's siblings) were married as well. It was also the church where Dorene and I were married in 1957. Since Dorene's grandfather, Reverend Jerry Hauff, was her pastor, and Reverend Everett Gresham was mine, it was very special to have our grandfathers perform our marriage ceremony. As these men led us in making our promises first to God and then to each other, we sensed that what we promised that night was recorded in the eternal presence of God. That was sixty-three years ago, and we continue to follow God together.

During my early years, Grandfather Gresham spent a great deal of time teaching me the ways of God. That may have been due to the fact he had no sons or grandsons; and since I was the firstborn son of my parents, I became a very special person to these dear people, their only "grandson." Since they always thought of my mother as a daughter along with their own two daughters, it was natural for them to think of me as their grandson. My parents told me I would often mimic my grandfather's mannerisms: the way he prayed, spoke, and greeted people.

I was learning quickly from watching my grandfather. When I was very young, about three, I performed my first clerical act. One Sunday morning, my grandfather had baptized many who had recently declared their faith in Christ. When we returned home while Mother was preparing the noon meal, I filled a good-sized washtub with water. I felt it would serve excellently for what I had in mind. My next stop was my father's chicken pen. Dad had just bought three-dozen baby chicks. They were to provide many meals for the next year. Having that little stash of chicks was vital to our dinner table during the Depression. I rounded up all the little chicks and baptized them one by one, just like my grandfather had done with people: in the name of the Father, Son, and Holy Spirit. I was just a baby myself, so I really did not understand what I was doing or saying. It just seemed to be the right thing to do—even to baby chicks. When I finished with my most serious task, I laid them neatly and carefully in a row. Of course, I expected them to get with it and become the chirping little chicks I knew.

When my father called out to me to come in for lunch, he noticed the little chicks in a single row lying there on the grass. My father was very loving but a man of few words. I began to sense something was not quite right as he moved closer to me. The expression on his face was grim: one I had never seen before. I soon realized my father had a dark side which my backside was about to discover.

Grandfather Gresham impacted my life significantly. He took me to exciting places like camps and special meetings. In those days, many pastors went door-to-door inviting folk to the weekend services. He often took me with him. One Saturday afternoon, I was with him as he helped a stranger take his first steps as a Christian right there on the man's porch. At the end of the day, he asked me if I wanted to make the decision to accept Christ too. I did, and he baptized me the next day following the morning service. I was a very happy nine-year-old believer.

There was much that I did not understand at such a young age, but no one will be able to take from me the memory of my baby steps as a Christian.

My father moved our family to Eugene, Oregon where he felt he would have greater opportunities as a small building contractor. It was a great move and a beautiful place to grow up in as a teenager. In moving, I was leaving my grandfather, who was the second most influential male in my life. I would have little contact with Grandpa and Annie until my senior year in college when I lived with them and assisted my grandfather in the same church he had led from the time of his ordination.

A Life of Near Perfection

Only days before the accident our family drove to Big Bear, California, for some fun time in the snow. We all did our best on the bunny hill and even got a bit aggressive when we jumped on the lift to spend the afternoon over on the intermediate slope. Dana, Renee's older sister, wasn't with us that day, but her brother, Theron, and one of his friends were. That day will remain in our memories for life as it was our last family outing before the accident. With sweet memories, we have thanked God for His goodness and love.

Renee grew up loving every creature God created. She could have been a marvelous veterinarian. She had a mini zoo in her bedroom. Most anytime you could find hamsters, kittens, baby ducks, chinchillas, guinea pigs, tarantulas, and a whole host of insects to feed those hairy creatures.

The Elusive Miracle

The miracle of Renee's full recovery didn't happen, yet God's people continued to pray with faith. Often when we don't get what we pray for, we begin to rationalize this whole faith issue by suggesting that God is either saying, "Yes," "No," or, "Not now." I have never considered this a very satisfying concept. I generally see it as an inadequate answer, an effort on our part to provide God with some sort of excuse for not doing what He encouraged us to have faith for. While in this life I may struggle with the fact that God grants a petition to one and not another, it is essential for me to say that my need to know or understand is not as critical today as it was in the past, but that's because I am writing many years after the accident. When my questions get beyond my ability to understand, like David, it's time for me to find a cave and do some singing.

I will not say that God didn't hear and respond to our request on our daughter's behalf. He did, but His response did not seem to fit the petitions. I couldn't help but ask God about "rejoicing always" in the midst of terrible circumstances, and the longstanding question: "Why do bad things happen to good people?"

I believe God helped me understand that each of us has a different purpose for being on planet Earth. We have various opportunities and privileges. Some of us come to personally develop and strengthen the fruit of His Spirit: love, kindness, patience, joy, peace, goodness, faithfulness, gentleness, and self-control. Sometimes we come to help others develop the fruit of the Spirit, but we are all here to become more Christlike, as Paul describes in Romans 8. In the core of my being, I fought the thought that even in the most terrible circumstances, these events could stimulate great change in the lives of individuals. Without observing cruelty, we would not be moved to compassion. Without personal trials, we would not develop patience or faithfulness. At a moment of loss, it is hard to see that the recognition that our human issues matter little when compared to life eternal allows us to know joy in the midst of sorrow and worry. This truth does not come easily in the middle of pain. Could it be that while God did not cause Renee's accident, He was using this event to teach me lessons about life that could be learned no other way?

Two Special Families

In the mid-1970s we had an interracial couple invited to our church by the George Runner Sr. family. After visiting the church three or four times, the couple was a little concerned that I would be a good pastor for them, so they called and asked if they could visit with us in our home. Our congregation already looked a bit like the United Nations. We were a mix of different cultures, ethnic groups, and places, mainly because we were in a military-industrial complex with Edwards Air Force base to the north and Palmdale Plant 42 to the south. However, at that time we didn't have any marriages that were racially mixed, so they visited us, asking if we thought they would be accepted, and would they be free to serve?

When the doorbell rang, I answered the door. There stood Ray and San-dy Poe. Ray was a very handsome man of color holding a tiny white

Persian kitten, and Sandy was holding the littermate, a little black Persian kitten. Ray said, "Pastor, what do you think?"

I said, "Think about what?"

He answered, "The fact that we have a racially mixed marriage. Do you feel we can worship and be accepted at The King's Place?" I understood their concern. In the early 1970s, interracial marriages were not the norm.

I thought for a moment and then reminded them of Jesus. When Jesus was on His way to Calvary, after having been beaten within a breath of death, He stumbled, unable to carry His heavy cross. A man, many believe to have been a man of color, stepped to His side, picked up the cross, and took it the rest of the journey for the Lord and soon-to-be Savior of us all. I've never read that Jesus paused to recognize the man's color, so my question is, why should we?

Until this marvelous, godly couple retired and eventually moved, Ray's family were strong members loved by all at The King's Place. Some of their children and grandchildren are still there. Ray, a man with a beautiful servant's heart and a smile that could span the Grand Canyon, served as an excellent usher for years. He and his wife took four fatherless boys and raised them to become men of strong faith, one a pastor today.

While those kittens were a symbol of something beautiful, both past and future, they were the love of Renee's life. One of our favorite photos finds her sitting on our living room couch holding a kitten in each arm. Her smile could not be bought.

You may be wondering, what does this have to do with Renee's accident? It provided a precious memory of a child who didn't make judgments about people because of hair color or relationships. She received the gift of kittens and they received her love for the rest of her life. Her love and response to our new friends was a great lesson for me and has served me well.

In the twilight of my life, I have been honored to serve as an elder in our church family. For several reasons, those seven years were perhaps the most challenging in the history of Southwest Church. In the final two years of my eldership, I served as the chairperson; and during that period the congregation had the formidable task of searching, finding, and extending a call for our next lead pastor. There were many faithful people who served in that process. I would like to believe that on a night long ago, two beautiful people knocked on our door holding two tiny kittens, one white and one black, and that my daughter's response had something to do with my attitude when we eventually called an interracial couple to help us understand God's will and vision. Renee would never know how that visit many years ago, and her attitude would shape my thinking and heart for the rest of my life.

Challenging Medical Report

The day came when the medical staff called us in and explained that Renee could no longer remain in our local hospital. They were saying they had done all they could. They were ready to place her where she could die in comfort. This was a gentle way to say she would be warehoused till death. My immediate thought was: *How can one die in comfort in such a place?*

Within twenty-four hours after that conference, we received word that Renee had been accepted by the Children's Hospital in Los Angeles and then later to the Rancho Los Amigos National Rehabilitation Center in Downey, California. This meant that Renee would receive the best care possible at two of the most exceptional medical facilities on the West

Coast. Could this be a way that God was assuring us of His love and that He was aware of our circumstances? Renee was still in a coma, and thus far, improvement was invisible or non-existent. What were we to think?

My wife, one of God's angels and also Renee's mother, took up residence at the hospitals. I would drive her to the hospital each Monday morning and pick her up on Friday evenings. Friends from our congregation loaned us recreational vehicles that we parked in the hospital parking lots. During the day, from seven in the morning to nine at night, Dorene became part of the medical team committed to Renee's recovery. Friends continued to pray. Every technique known to man was employed to break into Renee's coma. Popsicles were placed on her lips to stimulate the mouth. Legs and arms were placed in casts to keep the limbs from posturing (twisting), a result of the brain injury. Her eyes were open, but they appeared to see nothing or little. If she wanted to speak, she was unable. Music CDs were played, hoping to resonate with something deep inside her subconscious, but the vicelike coma prevailed. The question kept raising its ugly head, "Where are the results of the relenting focus in prayer?" We even employed the biblical imperatives of prayer and fasting, anointing with oil, and lived with heartfelt prayer cascading from our hearts and lips.

Time to Go Home

After thirteen months in three hospitals, the medical staff brought us in for a final consultation. These patient evaluations involved twenty-to-twenty-five members of Renee's medical care professionals that represented every part of her recovery team. A representative from each medical discipline gave a brief report on progress, and then suggested what they hoped for until the next three-month evaluation. They would always conclude by explaining our options.

Upon the recommendation of the medical staff we made the decision to bring our fifteen-year-old daughter home. We knew she needed twenty-four-hour care. We knew it would take forty-five minutes just to feed her, since she could no longer swallow normally. We knew that everything of a personal nature would have to be done for her, but we still clung to a hope that while our daughter would never be the same as before, yet with God's help, we could make things better. We understood Renee and her girlfriend, Pam Goudy, would never ride their horses together again across the sandy beaches of Malibu with the wind blowing in their faces. We knew she would never be a debutante and dance with one of the young airmen from the air force academy when they made their annual trip to our valley. We knew she would not have a wedding or children that would mirror her indomitable, gregarious, fun-loving personality, yet we had this hope that we could help our daughter reach a level of recovery that would eventually enable her to live independently with a purpose for living.

Our Most Difficult Decision

After nearly three years at home we came to the painful conclusion that Renee would never be able to manage independent living; and so once again at the advice of her medical team, we made the most difficult decision of our lives: We placed Renee in a facility built and equipped to meet the needs of the brain injured and physically challenged. This decision went beyond the unthinkable. It was a horrendous choice to make. At first, it seemed like a final surrender. I had never raised a white flag to any challenge before. For the first time, I felt that I was being forced to do so. Many times, I had been with families when they had to make that hard and sometimes impossible choice to pull the plug. It seemed as though the same was being required of us. Once again, I was asking, "God, where are You when I need You?"

In such a moment, it is extremely difficult to separate the issues. On the one hand, we focused on what we wanted in having our daughter with us. On the other hand, we wanted the very best care for her, a place where she could make improvements, no matter how small. To spice up the recipe, we wanted God to do what we wanted. It was clear we couldn't have all of that at the same time, if ever.

We visited the recommended facility in the San Fernando Valley, Sylmar, California, about fifty miles from our home. The people were very kind and naturally caring, but it wasn't a Marriott overlooking the Pacific Ocean. The interior was gray, serious improvements were needed, and the employees appeared to be poorly trained and at the bottom of the pay scale. In other words, it didn't seem these employees had the educational credentials that would prepare them for work in such a place.

Dorene and I walked out to the parking lot, sat in our car, and wept together, feeling we were being forced to a decision we did not want to make. It was difficult to pray; we had been doing that for more than four years, so in silence we wept, through what seemed to be the longest trip home.

In a few days, we made the decision to place Renee in the Sylmar facility. In spite of the gray interior, we discovered that the employees were beautiful caregivers and did everything possible to make it better for Renee. Even so, we were still conflicted as we recognized they would never be able to offer anything more than a human warehousing environment.

Some were gently suggesting that my faith was weak, and I suspect they were right. What was becoming painfully apparent was that God's response was not what we had requested. It was clear that Renee's condition was not going to change because of my faith or anything I might do. It could only happen through a sovereign, gracious act of God.

When a pastor and his family are loved, and when that family experiences heartache and pain, the people feel that as well. No congregation could have been more supportive with both emotional and financial help. Their love was beyond anything we had ever known before or since. Recreational vehicles were offered for Dorene's stay at the hospitals, food was brought to the home, hundreds prayed for weeks on end, many fasted, and others offered to spend time at the hospital with Dorene. Trips to the different hospitals she was at were not short. The first one (Children's Hospital of Los Angeles) had been seventy miles from home and the Rancho Los Amigos Hospital was nearly a hundred miles one way.

This was a time when I had little to offer as their pastor, but they were a beautiful demonstration of Paul's exhortation in Romans 12:

> *Rejoice with those who rejoice; weep with those who weep. (Romans 12:15, ESV)*

In those days there was a lot of weeping and little rejoicing. As the body of Christ, could it be they were a part of the answer to our prayers, that we didn't recognize it at the time?

I remember many dear, loving Christian friends. Their desire was always to encourage me. One said, "Pastor, do you remember when you taught from Philippians 4:6-7? Do you remember this?

> *Do not be anxious about anything, but in every situation, by prayer and petition with thanksgiving, present your requests to God. And the peace of God, which transcends all understanding, will guard your hearts and your minds in Christ Jesus. (Philippians 4:6-7)*

Yes, I remembered it well. Of course, I remembered what I had preached and sincerely believed, yet the whole idea of thanksgiving was being crushed in the vice of life, and the concept of God's peace, which transcended all understanding, was being challenged in my despair. I would never be so disrespectful as to suggest that the apostle Paul was using hyperbole when he said, "But in every situation," but did he really mean *every* situation? What did the apostle mean when he said the peace of God would guard me?

While I knew the only answer was in trusting God, I was living and working as though it all depended on me.

Even though I felt I had met the conditions listed in the first part of the verse, I didn't feel like my heart and mind were guarded, and I was certain this was "transcending" my understanding. Whatever worth there may have been to feel at all seemed to have vanished.

When a man serves as lead pastor, it is difficult to separate what is personal from the concerns of the church. However, this is not an option, and somehow must be done. At times I failed in this. My way was to be so aggressive and "faithful" that somehow I could help God resolve my personal pain caused by Renee's accident. If I could study with greater discipline, preach with greater clarity, and love with a higher intensity, then surely that would be a recipe for climbing out of this dark hole. Ironically, it was during this time that many felt my preaching was more compelling and insightful than ever. Even so, none of this was producing the result our hearts longed for. I was living out one of the classic mistakes we make when caught in the conflicting maze of life. While I knew the only answer was in trusting God, I was living and working as though it all depended on me. Why wouldn't I feel that way when prayers seemed to evaporate when leaving my mouth? If God wasn't dead, He must be deaf.

As a family, it was difficult not to be shaped both mentally, emotionally, and financially by our daughter's accident. Our escalating debt from the accident and medical costs beyond insurance coverage was close to a hundred thousand in 1979 dollars. Added to the challenge of Renee was our need to meet the emotional needs of Renee's brother who was still at home.

There was one pesky proverb that kept demanding our attention:

> *Trust in the Lord with all of your heart and lean not on your own understanding; in all your ways submit to him, and he will make your paths straight. (Proverbs 3:5-6)*

What does that mean? Is the word "submit" important?

Hope from the Neurosurgeon

We received a call from the neurosurgeon that had carefully followed Renee's case. His call came nearly ten years after the accident. Renee was now twenty-four. He explained there was a remote possibility that he and his surgical team might be able to help. After meeting with him, it seemed as though the world was standing still. Could this be the answer to our prayers? Would it be too much to hope this would be God's way of restoring our daughter to some reasonable level of recovery, or maybe even *complete* recovery?

The doctor explained the surgery and was very careful to help us understand that the operation was experimental at best. It had never been performed on a patient with a brain stem injury but had been done many times on patients with Parkinson's.

He took us into a room where he showed us an excellent video of the procedure that was performed on a Parkinson patient. He said, "I can't give you a percentage of success since we simply have no supporting data. What I do know is this: we will have one of three results. First, Renee's condition will remain unchanged; second, she could show considerable improvement with body movement and speech; or third, it's possible she will not make it through surgery. Let me give you some time as you think and pray about your decision."

When the doctor said there could be an improvement in body movement and speech, it caught our attention. Since the accident, Renee had not spoken one word, and because she had severe ataxia on her right side, we were not all that hopeful we would see significant improvement in that area of her body. Ataxia makes it impossible for a person to manage any defined motion. If a person reaches for a glass of water, the likelihood is that the glass would be knocked over. If we could not see full use of the right side, perhaps we could hope for the ataxia to be eliminated. Renee was left-handed, but she had about an 80 percent paralysis on that side. We had hope for the left side much like our hope for the right. If we could achieve any improvement after the surgery, that would be a gift beyond measure.

Surgery

Ten years seemed like an eternity since the accident, but we were hopeful once again for some measured improvement or more. During that time there had been more than a hundred consultations and meetings with Renee's medical professionals. We were ready for any gift, no matter how small. We thought if only Renee could write again, at least we would be able to communicate. She would be able to express her desires and emotions, which up to now had been relegated to a very simple wheelchair tray. The tray had a series of graphics to which Renee could point. When she pointed to a particular graphic, she could let us know if she wanted to eat, use the bathroom, sleep, or have us pray with her. We called this Renee's communication board. You might imagine the excitement and hope we felt in imagining Renee being able to speak or at least write notes to us.

The morning of the surgery came. Since Renee would be completely awake during the procedure, we were allowed to view the operation from a balcony above the medical team. The gallery was filled with observing medical staff. Since this was our daughter, the surgery was not easy to watch. First, they shaved her head. Renee was a beautiful brunette, but who cared about hair when there was the possibility of speaking and writing again? The doctor took a hand drill like any you would purchase from Home Depot or Ace Hardware and drilled four holes in the top of her skull. These holes would provide stability for the rack that would be placed later. The next step was to cut a one-inch square hole in the top and center of the skull. Through this hole, a tiny pencil-like probe would be inserted into the brain. The rack fastened to the top of the head provided the necessary stability so the movements of the probe could be exact. TV monitors made it possible for the surgical team to see precisely where the probe was once it was inserted.

Because Renee's hearing was diminished from the accident, it was difficult for the surgeon to verbally communicate with Renee during the surgery which was absolutely necessary. The medical staff had large cards they prepared, so Renee could read and understand what the doctor wanted her to do. If the doctor wanted her to raise her left arm, the card person would show her the appropriate card, Renee could read the card to know what he wanted her to do. Her doctor first asked her to move her right arm. When she was able to move that arm without any shakiness, then he knew he was in the right place in the brain that controlled that movement. When he was able to eliminate shakiness in her limbs, he would freeze that tiny part of the brain. This was accomplished through the tip of the probe. This is not a technical explanation of what he did, but a simple explanation he gave us so we could understand what he was hoping to accomplish.

The surgery ended, and Renee was taken to a semi-recovery room and put into a mild sleep. It would be several hours before we would know the results of the surgery. We had waited nearly ten years, so what was a few more hours?

Renee was finally brought back to her regular room, completely awake, eyes bright, with that infectious smile we had loved in the past and missed since the accident. She managed to speak a few words, a sentence or two, and then she motioned for something to write on. We were prepared and gave her a tablet. She wrote for what seemed like an hour or two expressing her love. The joy, the weight of the world seemed to have lifted. I struggle to put in words what Dorene and I experienced that night; the word *euphoria* comes close. All the days, nights, and years filled with pain and disappointment seemed to vanish in those moments. It was a night for which we will ever be grateful.

The next day was a new day with hopeful expectations for a new normal, but that was not to be. Sometime during the night Renee had reverted to her condition before surgery. I must admit that if Dorene and I had a question about God's mercy before, we still felt strong in faith, but weak in spirit.

Let's move the calendar back to 1981. That would be three years after Renee's accident. Another challenge for family and congregation, a storm so powerful that appeared too strong to survive. This storm would have been less a problem had it not been for our daughter's accident; however, what we faced would be a defining moment for both pastor and people.

CHAPTER 3

PASSION

When you catch a glimpse of your potential,
that's when passion is born.
—*Zig Ziglar*

My Other Life

Until now I've said very little about our lives other than what happened to our family in the course of living. At the time of Renee's accident, I was the pastor of a congregation with a day school of approximately 2,000 students with a church family that was vital and growing. We had recently built and relocated on the other side of town at the cost of about $2,000,000 in 1975 dollars, which is $9,567,000 in 2019 dollars. We had made the decision to finance the new facility by creating what we called a Living Trust. It operated very much like any bank or savings and loan. People were able to make deposits and withdrawals as they would in their own banking or savings institution. We spent more than $40,000 with our attorneys to make sure that we met the requirements of the State of California.

When we received our certification from the California Corporation Department, we were the only church with a state-approved certified living trust in the State of California. Our attorneys informed us that more than 385 churches were operating with their own living trust within the state. The reasons for this are unknown to this day. According to the requirements placed on us by the state, we were allowed to use 80 percent of the funds for construction. We did that.

Our challenge came in 1980-81 when the interest rates rose to approximately 21 percent. According to the state requirements, we were unable to offer anything above 10 percent to our investors. At the time we had been in the new facilities for about two and a half years, following the plan and doing well; however, our problem came from two directions. First, 80 percent of the Living Trust had been used correctly as prescribed by the trust agreement with the Corporation Commission in the State of California. Like most banks and savings institutions, investors could invest and withdraw additional funds at any time, and that with the high 20-to-21-percent interest rates caused the second challenge: a run on our Living Trust.

Investors outside of the congregation began to withdraw their accounts to place their investments where they could earn double the interest. One could not be critical of these wonderful people since their investments were primarily a financial transaction, and we had promised and paid 10 percent until the markets torpedoed the plan. Very quickly we lost liquidity and were forced to close the Living Trust with an amount that would enable us to meet the emergency needs of the elderly until we could find a solution.

Finding a solution was not easy. Many investor meetings were held. Enormous pressure was placed on the executive staff of the congregation, as well as many who had invested. In many cases, people had invested for retirement. With rare exception, those within the church family faithfully believed that God would help us through this crisis as He had on other occasions.

While the general health of the congregation continued to remain good, there was little doubt it was the beginning of a dark cloud settling on God's people. That only intensified when we were faced with the prospect of bankruptcy or selling those beautiful three-year-old facilities at cents on the dollar.

The years before the accident and collapse of the Living Trust could not have been more encouraging. Growth was unprecedented, giving continued to increase, hundreds were being baptized, lives were changed for the glory of God, and our new facilities were meeting the needs of a growing congregation. Also, our Learning Tree (Grades 1-12) was increasing each year by an unprecedented number. It would eventually reach 2,200. It seemed like every piece in the orchestra was playing its part with near perfection. We had been the recipients of a symphony conducted by God. History became a focus for thanksgiving; it wasn't long in realizing that life could not be supported by the past. We were grateful for those times when the presence of God was felt every time we came together, but now it seemed that a dark cloud settled over the congregation. Every effort to reach back into our past and grab a handful of God's blessings seemed like sand slipping through our fingers.

We didn't have to be prophets to understand it would take something far beyond our gifts and ability to lift us in the words of the old gospel song: "He brought me out of the miry clay, He set my feet on the Rock to stay; He puts a song in my soul today, A song of praise, hallelujah!" [1]

If you have ever been stuck in quicksand, you know just how hopeless it feels and how impossible it is to free yourself. If you don't get help, you will die. Yet, the question persists, how would the God who opened the sea for the Israelites, who knocked down the walls of Jericho, who gave life to the woman at the well, who raised Lazarus from the dead, who provided a complete pardon and restoration for humanity—how could this magnificent God come face-to-face with us and our need?

Could God really take something that was stuck in the mud and make it fly again?

Could God really take something that was stuck in the mud and make it fly again? A clue was found in the Word of God spoken through His prophet Isaiah:

> *But they that wait upon the Lord shall renew their strength; they shall mount up with wings as eagles; they shall run, and not be weary; and they shall walk, and not faint. (Isaiah 40:31, KJV)*

Ever since Jesus read from the scroll of Isaiah in the synagogue of Nazareth, Christians have gravitated to this great prophecy as the interpretive center of the Old Testament. Historically Isaiah was telling the story of Israel, scourged by judgment and exile, yet hopeful of restoration. Isaiah spoke of Israel's world, framed by its witnesses, heaven, and earth. Apparently, there was a spiritual dimension to their recovery. The question for Israel was: How would they move through their school of suffering and be propelled toward divine destiny as the vanguard of a new heaven and earth?

That being true for Israel, could it be right for us? Could we mount up from despair and defeat to fly once again as eagles? My answer, or at least a part of it, would come from an unexpected place.

Lessons from Above: The Principality of Liechtenstein

The principality of Liechtenstein is a constitutional monarchy ruled by the prince of Liechtenstein. Liechtenstein is in the heart of the Alps between Switzerland and Austria. We were on the final leg of a twenty-one-day Holy Land tour that included not just the Holy Land, but Egypt, Lebanon, Syria, Greece, and Switzerland.

On this final day before catching our flight back to the states, our group was enjoying a delightful lunch in an outside Bavarian restaurant in the town of Balzers. As we looked up to the left, Gutenberg Castle was in full view, one of the most important historical landmarks of Liechtenstein with its natural beauty and centuries-old allure.[2] It was a magnificent sight. While Gutenberg Castle was such a handsome structure, which immediately caught our eye, something else caught our attention that was to change the course of my life. Dozens of colorful hang gliders were soaring back and forth in front of the mountain and castle. Our group sat mesmerized at the sight of what looked like live birds flying effortlessly in the clear blue sky. It was a sight most of our group would never forget.

I turned to my wife, and said, "When we get home, I'm going to find a place where I can learn how to fly a hang glider."

She nearly fainted, but smiled nonetheless, and patronizingly said, "Well, dear, if you insist, just make certain you find a school with qualified instructors."

Windsports International

After returning home, I investigated places where I could learn to fly. I discovered a Hang-Gliding School in the San Fernando Valley, a suburb of Los Angeles. Two young nationally recognized pilots, Joe Greblo and Rich Grigsby, created Windsports International in 1974. Windsports quickly became the leading training school for those who had a desire to fly with eagles with perhaps a crow or two tossed in.

I visited Windsports, then located in Van Nuys, California, and spoke with Joe. He explained what would be involved in the four phases of training: the ground school, beach training at Dockweiler State Beach, the intermediate training on a 300-foot hill in Simi Valley, California, and finally the 2,400-foot launch and flight off Kagel Mountain located in Sylmar, California.

First Level of Training: The Corporate Office of Windsports

With great excitement, I signed up for my professional training. The first phase was a breeze (no pun intended) that took place at the Windsports location at Van Nuys. This was classroom instruction, which informed want-to-be flyers of necessary flying skills, the dynamics of handling a glider, how to set up a kite, and how to pack it up once a flight was completed. We also learned how to correctly pack a parachute. Our instruction also included what to expect in the various final three levels of class instruction. There was a great deal of information about the second level of glider used on the Dockweiler State Beach sandhills.

Second Level of Training: Dockweiler State Beach, California

It was an exciting day as we made the twenty-five-mile trip to Dockweiler State Beach. This site is directly under the Los Angeles Airport take-off pattern when planes take off to the west over the Pacific Ocean. Dockweiler is the birthplace of hang gliding as we know it today.

This beach site is where first-time students get hooked into a glider for a five-to-ten second launch-and-landing flight. From a thirty-foot hill, we were given basic instruction for the launch and landing—hopefully just above the sand. This lesson is designed to help the student acquire a feel of what the glider feels like as the ocean breeze lifts both pilot and glider just two or three feet off the sand. The instructor expects that the student will gain confidence in both the launching and landing of the glider.

Third Level of Training: Simi Valley, California

The third level of training happened on a three-hundred-foot hill in Simi Valley, California, about ten miles from Windsports. Training at this site provided new pilots the opportunity of a much longer flight than possible at the beach. Even though this flight lasted only sixty-to-ninety seconds, we were able to refine our launch techniques, learn how to efficiently turn the glider back and forth while descending, and how to set up correctly for landing. After three or four visits to this site, we would receive certification for the Big One: the high altitude twenty-four-hundred-foot launch from Kagel Mountain at Sylmar.

Friends have heard of my terrific sport. The inevitable question is: "Have you ever had an accident?" While I have experienced a few blown launches, the most severe injuries were to my ego and broken-down tubes. For those not familiar with the structure of a hang glider, the down tubes and horizontal control bar form a triangle. This is located below the wing and provides the pilot with the one piece of equipment that allows him to control the glider. It's like the steering wheel for the glider.

I can't leave this launch site without admitting it was here that I did have an accident that could have been serious; however, it proved to be minor. I crashed and cracked my collar bone.

Two days later, Dorene and I with another couple flew to Tahiti where we celebrated our twenty-fifth anniversary. On the islands of Morea, Bora Bora, we dove for shells and enjoyed one of God's most beautiful oceans. I forgot the flying accident as we enjoyed the giant mantas. The tropical fish we saw there were breathtakingly beautiful.

Fourth Level of Training: Kagel Mountain, Sylmar, California

Standing on the top of Kagel Mountain, I was certified, but even more important, I was petrified. I had gone through my preflight checklist, making sure the glider was airworthy. It was. It is difficult to explain my emotions: raw fear since it was my first time standing at such a high-altitude launching ramp. More than twenty-four-hundred feet below, I could barely see the landing site. *Why am I here? What was I doing?*

On a first high-altitude flight with a wind blowing up the mountain directly into the nose of my glider at twelve miles per hour, the standard launch procedure is for three launch helpers: one on each wing tip and one holding the nose level. It could be catastrophic if the nose got blown up or either of the wings were elevated over the other once the launch began. Just before launch, you want every part of that glider level. When the pilot feels he is in complete control and the wind or updraft is in the right wind cycle, he will shout, "Clear!" The nose assistant is the most critical. When the pilot yells clear, he must immediately release his hold on the glider and fall away to either his left or right, but do it quickly, so he is not caught by one of the glider wires as the glider passes over him. From that point, it's all up to the pilot. First, he will make sure that he is flying as expected. Once stabilized in those early seconds of flight, he will then place his legs in his harness. When the legs are in place, the pilot pulls a cord that zips up the harness on the bottom side. These types of harnesses are called cocoon harnesses for a good reason. When soaring and flying the pilot is in a prone position completely encased.

The flight was uneventful for a first flight—not long, maybe thirty minutes. I flew back and forth across the face of Kagel Mountain several times and then decided it was time to head out for the landing. When I reached the place to set my approach, I was still too high to land, so I decided to fly another quarter mile away from the mountain beyond the landing area. I was now flying over El Cariso Community Regional Park. I made a couple of 360s to lose a bit more altitude and then set up my landing with a typical airport approach. The landing went well, even without the standard landing plastic wheels that were customary on the gliders of beginner pilots. In the event of a hard landing, these wheels would protect both pilot and glider, and especially the pilot's ego. I remember walking my incredible flying machine over to the area where a galley of fellow pilots and well-wishers were lined up to welcome me. Joe Greblo, my exceptional instructor, was there to congratulate me on a flight he said was "well flown." I considered that to be a compliment from one recognized as a hang-gliding master.

When I looked around the flying site, several other students had also made their first flight. I noted that many had a considerable amount of moisture below the belt. I can only speculate that most had difficulty with the one maneuver necessary to pass the flight test: You could not get your hang-level H1 license without successfully stalling the glider at about two thousand feet. This training maneuver is designed to prepare a pilot for a condition called falling off or falling over the falls. The result of such a stall is a steep dive, a straight down dive. Hang gliders are designed to pull out of the dive and level off between fifty-to-seventy-five feet; but when you are in that dive for the first time, you begin to wonder if the glider will ever right itself. That could well have been the cause of lower extremity wetness for some; it was a terrifying experience when you had never done it before.

To help you visualize what I'm describing it's necessary to know how a stall is initiated. The pilot must push out on the control bar which forces the nose of the glider up. That causes the glider to stop in the air, forcing it into a God-fearing stall. I remember when I initiated that first stall, the nose dropped dramatically like a rock, still flying. My head was down with legs and feet pointed to the sky, trying unsuccessfully to catch up with my head. In those two or three seconds, before the glider began to level itself, this thought pierced my mind: *If God had expected me to fly, I would have been born with wings. Why am I here?* But then I remembered, I wasn't born with clothes either.

When I was learning to fly, those were the good old days. In those years, all high-altitude training flights were solo. Today there is no such thing as a first-time high-altitude solo flight. They are all done in tandem with an instructor at your side, the two of you in the same glider. You can imagine how significantly that reduces the fear factor; at least if you die there will be someone with you at your side who knows what they are doing.

On my first high altitude flight, I was not yet the most accomplished pilot, but I was beginning to fly with a beautiful group of pilot friends. I was meeting and befriending some fascinating people from all walks of life, people that would probably never visit The King's Place, my parish and place of comfort. These flying friends respected me for my profession and what they called an "expert" on faith. I admired them as being expert flyers. It made for beautiful relationships.

Unusual Moments with the Flying Family

During my flying years, I had the joy of marrying several flying couples—sometimes on the top of a mountain and at other times in a traditional church setting. How well I remember one of my instructors and his bride. Beverly, Roger's bride, was in the same hang-gliding class with me in our pursuit of being part human/part bird.

The Lake Elsinore Flying Club and many flying friends from other Southern California clubs had made the trip with their gliders for the ceremony and the following reception. Together, we caravanned to San Mateo Peak, the highest peak in that Santa Ana mountain range just west of the lake. The ceremony took place with the couple standing together underneath the glider. The best man was holding the right-wing tip steady, and the maid of honor was doing the same on the left-wing tip. The father of the bride held the glider nose steady and served as the ring bearer.

The ceremony was not only a celebration of two people making their life promises to one another, they were also making promises before God. I pronounced them husband and wife. The couple kissed while attached to the glider. Instead of the usual first dance by a wedding couple, they were the first to launch in a tandem flight headed for the landing and reception below. As the presiding cleric, I was the next to launch. The conditions were not only beautiful for a wedding but perfect for flying. In just twenty minutes, forty-to-fifty pilots launched and flew for several minutes to celebrate our friendship with a couple of "love birds." After scoring back and forth across the face of San Mateo Peak, we landed right next to a beautiful restaurant where we gathered for the reception.

Phil Warrender was a significant contributor in the early history of the Southern California hang gliding community. Like so many in the first years of the sport, he was an entrepreneur and developer of various hang-gliding paraphernalia. Phil developed and produced one of the most excellent cocoon harnesses of the time. For reasons we may never know, Phil didn't pursue his line of interest. I have long suspected that a particular young lady he met while flying the skies of Sylmar may have had something to do with that.

After a great flight, Phil and Lynn waited for me to land in the Kagel landing area. As I walked my glider over to the side where we usually took them apart, Phil and Lynn said they wanted to talk with me. I could tell something was up. They had that glow about them that made no secret of the fact that they were in love. Since we had become flying friends, they wanted to know if I would help them plan their wedding ceremony and then perform it. I was more than happy to agree.

The wedding was in June 1983, and the reception was in one of the valley's most elegant restaurants surrounded by the San Fernando Valley Country Club. Because Phil and Lynn were so well-established in our southern California hang gliding community, the ceremony and reception were attended by many flyers and their friends.

Both Lynn and Phil had chosen Ephesians 5 for their ceremony, one of the significant passages of Scripture that provides God's blueprint for marriage. In pre-marriage counseling, we had worked through that rather carefully. There was also another piece they wanted included in the ceremony, believing it would be appropriate, not only for them but for all their flying friends. Read "High Flight" and see if you agree!

"Oh! I have slipped the surly bonds of earth,
And danced the skies on laughter-silvered wings;
Sunward I've climbed and joined the tumbling mirth
of sun-split clouds—
and done a hundred things You have not dreamed of—
wheeled and soared and swung high in the sunlit silence.
Hovering there I've chased the shouting wind along
and flung my eager craft through footless halls of air.

Up, up the long delirious, burning blue
I've topped the wind-swept heights with easy grace,
where never lark, or even eagle, flew;
and, while with silent, lifting mind I've trod
the high untrespassed sanctity of space,
put out my hand and touched the face of God."

Pilot Officer Gillespie Magee Jr.
No 412 Squadron, RCAF
Killed December 11, 1941[3]

A month or so after the Warrender's ceremony, Lynn called me and said, "We would like to see you." I have to admit my first thought dropped below the line, and I thought, *I wonder if there is already trouble in paradise?*

When we finally met, Phil said, "Dan, we can't tell you how much we appreciate your part in our wedding. We want to do something for you." Phil pulled out his measuring tape and began to measure me very carefully. He didn't say what they had in mind, but I knew he was measuring me for one of his finest-of-the-line cocoon harnesses. In a couple of weeks, they presented me with the best of the best. This investment of their love and appreciation was considerable, but more importantly, it became a treasure to me because they had personally designed and produced it together.

That harness had all the bells and whistles, including a special pouch for the parachute on the front. If it ever needed to deploy, it was an easy reach and a simple pull. I am fortunate that I never needed that protection. It was in this harness that I flew to an altitude of 17,200 msl (an msl is Mean Sea Level) and set the unofficial cleric record for a long-distance flight. This Warrender-perfected harness served me well for many years until I hung it up for the last time. It still hangs in my garage, next to my first knee hanger harness. It provided me years of protection and flying comfort that most hang-glider pilots take for granted.

I smile when I speak of my cleric personal distance record, a flight that began from Walt's Point just south of Lone Pine and terminated in Nevada. That flight was nothing in comparison to the flights of Larry Tudor, Steve Moyes, the late Mark Gibson, and so many others. Tudor, now retired, is recognized as the greatest hang glider pilot ever to parse the clouds and top out the highest thermals.

Tudor had set the distance record of 221.5 miles just three years before my longest flight. Tudor was limited only by the hang-gliding technology of his day, not his lack of ability, but even Tudor's record (that stood for thirty years) has been broken by more than 254 miles, more than double Larry's record. Larry's record was erased by a dynamic duo of young pilots, Australian Jonny Durand and the American Dustin Martin, flying together across the state of Texas with gliders that are sophisticated flying machines compared to the gliders of Tudor's time. It is difficult to imagine records much beyond the current 475 miles; however, we know current records will be broken with advanced technology and pilot skills.

The Sylmar Hang Gliding Association: My Flying Home

The Sylmar Flight Park or Sylmar Hang Gliding Association was my home club, and it was at this site that I enjoyed most of my hang-gliding friends and flying. Here I regularly soared with a resident red-tailed hawk. He was magnificent. This beautiful bird often joined me shortly after takeoff and flew for several minutes at a time about ten-to-fifteen feet off either of my wing tips. He seemed to prefer the right side of my glider. He had a rather strange in-flight behavior. When flying we usually kept our eyes focused ahead, but the hawk often cocked his head toward me, so that he was looking directly at me, as if to say, "I can help you find that next thermal if you will just pay attention and follow me." I miss my flying friend since retiring my wings.

I had another very unusual feathered friend but saw him far less often: a California condor. When this fellow came near, he looked like a Boeing 747! A majestic bird, he seemed far more cautious and less friendly than my hawkeyed mate. At that time, California was seeking to reintroduce the California condors back into our skies. I'd flown with this fellow a couple of times at Sylmar, California, and with other members of his flock in the Big Sur area on the California coast.

Big Sur was a favorite flying site. A laminar wave (a smooth flow) of air coming in off the ocean made for unforgettable flights. It was thrilling to be able to fly a quarter mile or more out over the Pacific before returning to the level landing site, at perhaps a hundred feet above the surf. Coastal flying had its romance because of that very smooth air coming off the water. Beach flying did not provide the excitement of distance flights or the sense of power I felt when caught by a monster thermal, but I could fly back and forth across dunes for as long as the onshore breezes prevailed. Such a memory remains to this day.

As I became more skilled, I purchased gliders that were more sophisticated, gliders that had a far superior glide ratio. This meant that in the right conditions, I could fly for more extended periods of time and at a greater distance. Like golf or any other sport, the technical equipment becomes the X-factor for the committed pilot, and most can't wait for the next great flying machine that would add another mile to a flight.

With a much higher skill level and experience, I began to travel to other sites that were either more exciting or more challenging. In California, I have flown in La Jolla, Torrey Pines, Palmdale, Crestline, Lake Elsinore, Seaside, Sylmar, Ventura, Santa Barbara, the Big Sur, and the Sierras, west and east. I have also flown in Lake Chelan, Washington; Lakeview, Oregon; Maui, Hawaii; Sun Valley Arizona; Telluride, Colorado; the Nevada Whites in Nevada; and Mexico.

During my years of flying, two sights will forever be etched in my hang-gliding memory: The Eastern High Sierras (Owens Valley) and Telluride, Colorado. How beautiful!

The Telluride International Hang Glider Fly-In

In 1984 my wife and I packed our four-wheel-drive Blazer with my Dawn glider on the top rack. When we arrived at Telluride, Colorado, we met hang glider pilots from around the world. The sky was filled with a kaleidoscope of color. It was a fantastic event, filled with several days of superb flying. It was not difficult to fly more than a hundred miles or more from Telluride when the conditions were right.

I had flown with the big boys: the young aerobatic daredevils that pressed the limits in competition provided fantastic entertainment. It was simply amazing to see what some of these young flyers could do with a hang glider. The ability of these young pilots to handle those gliders in tight loops and tiny landing areas almost defied belief. I was not in their class, but I was beginning to put together some impressive long-distance flights of my own. When we returned from Telluride, my hang-gliding friends started calling me "The Flying Parson." Although they had never heard me preach, on many occasions they had witnessed me bow my head on launch just before embracing the sky.

The High Sierras World Class Hang Glider Venue

Owens Valley located on the eastern side of the California High Sierras is world renowned for both hang gliding and paragliding. My first long-distance flight in the Sierras launched twenty miles north of Bishop on the Nevada Whites and ended in Lone Pine, California. Such a flight was not more than sixty miles, but it achieved an altitude far higher than any of my other flights before or after. My second significant flight would prove to be both my longest and final long-distance flight in the Sierras.

My First Long-Distance Flight

I had flown many times in the Sierras but tried never to push myself beyond my level of experience or confidence. I'm not sure there is such a place where one can fly and always feel entirely comfortable. When flying in the Sierras, I believe it is still best to heed the words of Joseph C. Lincoln, from his book, *Soaring for Diamonds*. He is speaking of the sky when he writes, "The sky, to which some men are drawn like lost children going home, the sky, sometimes lover, sometimes the mother, sometimes savage master."[4] After reading that I never stood on a launch site without recalling Lincoln's words along with a prayer to my Father in heaven, and as you can see, I'm still here to write about it.

I had owned three previous gliders, and they were all appropriate to my level of experience. My first two gliders were created and built by Wills Wing and were excellent pieces of equipment. My third glider was a Dawn built by Progressive Aircraft. The designer and owner of that company was Richard "Dick" Boone. The glider was on the cutting edge of technology. Instead of the two wires that connected to the leading edge and the two ends of the control bar, Dick had developed two struts that could be packed into the sail without detaching them. This made setup at launch faster than other gliders, and many believed provided additional strength. The Dawn went into production in 1984 but never competed with other glider manufactures that were able to produce exceptional gliders for the competitive flyers.

My fourth and final Glider was a UP 185 Comet, built by Peter Brock and designer Roy Haggard, out of Salt Lake City, Utah. This glider revolutionized hang gliding during the early years of its production. Today, it would not be a competitive glider; but when first produced, it was at the top. It was an excellent glider for long distance flights; this is the gilder I flew in the Sierras.

On most days we flew north from Walt's Point, just south of Lone Pine. On this day, the conditions were not right, so we decided to head for the launch site about twenty miles north of Bishop on the Whites side of the valley. Once we were finally able to launch, we expected a casual descent down the face of the Sierra Whites landing somewhere near Bishop. That proved to be true for my three flying friends, but I was fortunate enough to catch a significant thermal moving up the face of the Whites at about 800 fpm. When I reached the northern side of Westguard Pass, I was flying three thousand feet above the top. I was confident I would be able to make this five-mile crossing and pick up more thermals once I reached the Inyo side of the pass and then be on my way to Lone Pine.

Unfortunately, I hit massive sink while crossing. I soon realized that Lone Pine was probably out of the question and that if I didn't head back west for Big Pine, I might have to set down in a tight spot. I was sinking fast, much too soon. I did a quick visual sweep, looking for a place, any place, to set down. As I flew back in a northwest direction, my eye caught a narrow spot with fewer boulders. It seemed that God had emptied the last sack of His divine rocks east of Big Pine, and they were all in front of me. I set up to land and unzipped my harness to allow my legs and feet to swing down. I was about 125 feet off the deck, ready to take a semi-vertical position behind the control bar, and then it happened. I flew into a massive thermal. The nose of my glider pitched up. I pushed out hard on the control bar and moved into a tight 360. In a matter of moments, my little vario-altimeter was screaming, telling me that I was rising at 2,100 fpm. I was drifting slightly to the southeast, and when I looked down the valley floor, the mountainside seemed to be disappearing below. The huge boulders I had seen only moments before when setting up to land were already almost invisible. When I flew over Waucoba Mountain at 13,079 msl, I was about two thousand feet above the top and still climbing. Since I had never been in a thermal with such power and lift, I decided to stay with it and continued to circle above Waucoba. I was carrying oxygen with me for any eventuality, never expecting that I would need it. However, over Waucoba I found considerable relief in sucking tiny inhales, as. I was now flying at 17,200 msl! I was not an experienced pilot, and had never flown at that distance or height, so I felt it wise to pull the bar in and head downrange to Lone Pine. To my surprise, I was not losing altitude as I passed to the east of Tamarack Canyon, Water Canyon, and Kearsarge.

Still flying at 17,100 msl east of Independence, I noticed what looked like a plane coming directly toward me. He must have been three or four miles ahead but closing rapidly, and it appeared that we were on a collision course. I knew I was flying just north of the restricted zone for the military aircraft coming out of China Lake, but had been told they would be flying above 18,000 msl feet. As a precaution, most hang glider pilots placed tinfoil on the inside tips of their wings; this helped pilots see us on their radar long before we could see them. Whatever was approaching me was coming at a very high rate of speed, and there was little I could do, hanging in a glider and flying no faster than forty to fifty mph. I realized I had to make a decision. I didn't have time to circle the table and get everyone's opinion. If I didn't perform some evasive maneuver, my next great adventure would be standing at the celestial gates in the form of an Italian sausage. And then it happened! In a moment I could see a flash about two hundred feet below and perhaps fifty yards to my right. It was a high-performance sailplane dancing across the peaks of the eastern Sierras. Talk about relief. Quickly I checked to see if there was moisture below *my* belt. Fortunately, I was as dry as a freshly changed baby, and ready for the next thermal.

I continued on my southerly course but noticed my vario-altimeter beginning to sing again indicating a gradual lift. I was now back to 17,200 msl. I decided that I must be in a Sierra wave, but I wasn't sure. At any rate, I was not descending as intended. My little attached temperature gauge was telling me it was minus twenty-five degrees. My goggles provided some protection, but I wasn't sure my frozen nose and ears would make it to the ground with the rest of me. I'm not sure what I would have done if I hadn't been wearing an excellent pair of gloves and thermal flight apparel under my regular flying suit. The same clothing that made this flight end well, cooked me at the lower altitude. Even with my great cocoon harness, it didn't take me long at this high altitude and low temperature to recognize that I had flown from one climate zone into another.

I was now flying over Beveridge, a little northeast of Lone Pine. The elevation of Beveridge is 5,587 msl. However, I was still flying at 11,400 msl. I was much more comfortable than before, but still shivered like I was inside a freezer. I was still cold from the 17,000 msl part of my flight.

The lift continued to be strong. It took incredible strength to circle down even a couple of hundred feet. I had to pull in my control bar with all my strength, and in some cases, that was not enough. I couldn't relax even for a moment. If I did, the glider would once again begin to ascend, and that was not the direction I wanted.

Seeing the Lone Pine Airport, I was very careful to keep out of "regular" pilot take-off and landing patterns. I was fortunate there was no airport activity during my descent. I was still flying too high and too far to the east for that to be a problem though. The challenge was mine, not that of other pilots. I was not descending as needed. I decided to fly directly over Lone Pine crossing Highway 395. My thought was that if I could fly far enough away from the Sierras on the eastern side of the valley and fly out of the wave that was not allowing me to descend, I could descend. That proved to be the right decision; and after many more 360s, I was eventually able to land on the edge of the Lone Pine Airport.

Fortunately, I was able to keep radio contact with my three friends who were now in Independence making their way to Lone Pine by car. They couldn't wait to retrieve this exhausted, but euphoric, pilot and hear first-hand about my incredible flight. When my experienced flying friends arrived, they could hardly believe that an admitted novice had enjoyed the flight of his life. The question is often asked, "Would you like to make that flight again?" The truth, if I weren't in my eighties, I would do it in a heartbeat.

That flight happened on a Friday in July. According to one of my parishioners, I preached well the following Sunday. After the third service that morning he said, "Pastor, you were on it today. You sounded higher than a kite." Little did he know. He knew nothing of my flight two days before.

Going for the Unofficial Long-Distance Cleric Record

Rick Masters, published his classic piece titled, "Racing for the Record—221 Miles Without an Engine!" in many countries and magazines, not the least of which was *Whole Air Magazine USA*, Sept/Oct 1983. With permission, I quote Rick's introduction to "Racing for the Record" from *Glider Rider Magazine* of December 1983:

> *Hang Gliding has always been a sport associated with danger, pursued by adventurous souls seeking the freedom of the birds and the exhilaration of the gods. But contrary to popular opinion, hang gliding is now as safe as other forms of sports aviation. Today's hang glider pilot is better trained, flies a certified glider and carries a backup parachute. Modern hang gliding has finally outgrown its daredevil image. Except in the Owens Valley.*

Renowned for its fabulous thermals which lift hang gliders to more than two miles above the earth's surface, the Owens is the premier site for hang gliding world records. Rising to the top of these updrafts of air, a hang glider pilot can glide great distances in search of the next thermal, and thereby repeat the process, flying farther and farther.

But the pilots and the machines pay the price for the free ride: the Owens is feared (and not just by the hang glider pilots) for its bone-jarring turbulence. And turbulence isn't the only danger. Sometimes reaching altitudes of 18,000 msl (and above), hang glider pilots attempting records risk hypoxia—oxygen starvation—if they fail to carry supplemental oxygen with them. The thin air and bone-chilling temperature at such elevations slay the strength and endurance needed for flights lasting six to 10 hours (necessary) for world-record distance.

For officially recognized records, witnesses must verify both the launch and landing and a barograph must document the flight's changes in altitude (the same method used with sailplanes).

The Owens Valley is indeed the mecca for world-record hang gliding flights. But it is as far from normal recreational hang gliding as the Indy 500 is from a Sunday drive.[5]

My second and final long-distance flight was without question my greatest flying experience. Never did I consider myself in the class of flyers that Rick Masters was referring to in his introduction; however, for my age and time constraints, I was somewhat above the casual flyer who enjoyed less demanding flying conditions.

I was standing on what is known as Walt's Point, close to Horseshoe Meadows, just southwest from Lone Pine, elevation 9,175 msl. Walt's

Point is a mega-classic launching site for epic XC flights and advanced pilots. For many years this is where hang-glider pilots from all over the world came to fly the "big air" and most of the stories and wild tales that have come out of this place are true. Giant thermals, extreme turbulence, very high climb rates, and maximum altitudes, long-distance flights: this launch provides it all. Many times, I have flowed this ultra-classic route from Walt's Point to Big Pine, approximately fifty miles somewhere just north or south of Big Pine. Usually, I would terminate my flight without an attempt to fly further.

On this day I had long ago circled Mt. Whitney and carried on a brief shouting conversation with campers on the ground. I was flying quite well and moving with good speed toward Big Pine. West of Big Pine is where you decide to either go for it—by crossing the Owens and try for the long distance up the Sierra Whites —or after assessing the conditions, you decide to land and call it a day. I decided to go for it. Flying above Kid Mountain (11,680 msl), I was a little over 14,000 msl. As I headed out across the valley floor, I hit considerable sink because of the lava rock on the west side of Highway 395. Even though I was not dangerously low when I flew over Crater Mountain, I hit a bump, the edge of a pretty significant thermal. My confidence was building since I realized I would easily be able to make the east side of Highway 395 where possible landing sites were much friendlier. If I had to land, the only real concern was missing the cows in one of the landing sites. My confidence for a long flight was not great, but at least I knew I would be able to land safely and not on sharp, craggy lava rock.

I had attempted three or four valley crossings in the past: none were successful, but this flight was showing promise. A lack of experience was my number one problem. I had never been beyond this point in a flight for distance while flying north. I was now relying on information from other pilots and my feel for flying.

I was also losing altitude rapidly and still flying northeast. It appeared that my flight would end before I reached the southern tip of the Whites. Currently flying low, very low over Soldier Canyon (4,750 msl) six hundred feet above, I was looking to the left for a suitable landing spot when suddenly and unexpectedly, I was hit with a thermal that pushed me slightly to the northeast at a rate of six hundred feet per minute. That soon increased to nine hundred fpm. Very quickly I was looking down on Black Mountain. I thought, *Wow! Now that I've made it over Black Mountain, I might have a chance to top out the range!* In a few miles, I got to the mountains that lifted me toward the heavens at twelve thousand msl. Since my thermal was still pushing me up above Black Mountain at a surprising rate, so I went with it, hoping I could top out and find something less stressful flying up the Whites.

I was now flying about eight miles northeast of Bishop airspace where I had never been before. This is where the Whites reach twelve thousand msl feet and a little beyond. I was flying a very similar route that Larry Tudor, John Klaus, Steve Moyes, and John Pendry had flown while flying for a record, a record set that day by Tudor of 221.5 miles.

Approaching the Pellisier Flats, which were 13,031 msl on the White Mountain side of the Owens Valley, I had heard other pilots speak of these canyons where many flights had ended. They were a series of canyons that often terminated once promising long-distance flights.

When I reached the southern end of the Pellisiers, I was experiencing some beginner's luck as I flew along at 13,800 msl. It wasn't long until my optimism evaporated with the loss of lift. I was now below the Flats, wondering if I too would find this as the end of a great flight. I had just flown beyond the canyons below but was still sinking rapidly when

I caught a weak thermal. I had read about Tudor's flight of three years before and mine was following a similar pattern except my thermal never reached the 1,200 fpm of Larry's. I either flew out of that thermal, or it merely said goodbye.

The Flats were now high above. Expecting to rise above them once again did not look like a card the wind gods would deal me that day. I no sooner filed that thought away when a 1,300 fpm thermal lifted me well above Pellisier Flats. I was now looking north, trying to decide the direction I should take. It wasn't a difficult choice. Boundary Peak was directly ahead, Nevada's highest mountain. While still in the thermal, I noticed a stretch of clouds with rather flat bottoms between Boundary Peak's 13,129 msl and me. From everything I had studied and heard from others, this had to be a cumulus cloud streak in the sky just for me. I gladly accepted and headed in a straight line for Boundary. I may have been in a cumulus streak once before on that high-altitude flight ending in Lone Pine, but this was a bit different. I didn't lose a foot of altitude on my way to Boundary. When I reached Boundary, I was flying at 13,993 msl.

Between the top of the Flats and Boundary, those wind gods were at my back, and I could fly forever. So far on this flight, I was learning that once a thermal and glider get connected, it was a simple matter of discovering a whole string of cousin thermals flying north. I was hopeful this would hold true beyond Boundary, but my questionable skill and luck may have been sinking with the sun.

On this last long-distance Sierra flight, I flew well into Nevada. By the time I landed, I had been in the air about eight-and-a-half hours hours and had flown 153.6 miles (unofficially). That was indeed not the longest recorded flight, but it was a cleric record. It wasn't a record all that difficult to set because as far as I knew I was the only cleric flying a hang glider.

As you know, Nevada is known for her business that caters to a *particular* male clientele. My flying friends tell me it's not uncommon for flights to begin losing altitude and lift near one of these places of business. Friends who never thought I would fly such a distance had warned me. Nonetheless, I was prepared for any eventuality since it was my practice to carry with me a couple of copies of Bill Bright's *Four Spiritual Laws*. Unlike so many of my friends I didn't land close enough to such a place, so I was not able to share my laws with the ladies.

Most seasoned pilots have a safety net built into their flying; mine was my wife. She faithfully served as the driver of our chase vehicle, but on this flight, she was not my chase driver. For my retrieval, I was able to get the help of others who were also flying north that day. When in the air, flyers have consistent contact with a chase crew. There were times when I would be so high or far from the highway that they couldn't see me, but in most cases, I could see them. Chase crews always had a map in the event that they lost sight of their flyers, and in most cases, they studied those maps very carefully the night before. Both the pilot and the chase crew have two-way radios for near perfect communication. This was especially helpful when a pilot had to land in a somewhat remote area, some distance from a major highway.

On this particular flight when I realized I was beginning to lose altitude, caused by less thermal activity and a sun that was rapidly setting, I told my crew my position and where I thought I would be landing. After I landed, they were there within minutes to gather both my glider and me and make the long trip back to Bishop for the night. You can imagine that I was still feeling pretty high-in-the-sky, even though my feet were back on the ground.

In the years that followed my epic flight, there would be many other pilots who would fly further and higher, but none would provide greater excitement and accomplishment for this pilot than on that day when I flew 153.6 miles.

Flying Like Eagles: Your Question

By now you may be wondering: "What's this got to do with God, Renee, and Romans 8:28?" I love this sport; it's a free, unfettered form of flying. I'm grateful for the unparalleled challenge and lessons I've learned about discipline, faith, and trust in others; and what may be most important, the mental strength and confidence I've gained in my own abilities and those of my teachers. The many lessons and experiences in my years of flying made me stronger. These lessons became friends in my journey. Let me speak of just one: faith.

Faith is a friend that many never seem to grasp. They struggle with the idea that faith is not a "reality" that can be known or proven empirically. You can go to the laboratory and mix specific ingredients in a test tube, but you will never prove faith by the scientific method. Faith is something that you know intuitively before you see the evidence. Once it is understood, you don't need faith.

As a beginning hang-glider pilot, I had to have faith that the designers of my glider had the technological expertise to create a glider that would enable me to fly safely. To use it, I was exercising faith. When my instructor was providing me with explicit instructions on how to handle the glider when launching, turning, and landing, I had to apply faith once again. I had to have faith that he knew what he was talking about. He warned me of flying situations that could be life-threatening if I didn't carefully follow his instructions. I didn't debate his knowledge of the sport; I was a receptive learner and glad to be. Later in my flying experience, there were many times his instruction saved my life.

For some, faith feels like a high hurdle, but the truth is we practice it every day. When you take your seat in a commercial plane, you have the confidence the pilot is competent, and the aircraft is airworthy. You are hoping that is true. You have faith in that system. When you pick up a prescription at the pharmacy, you have confidence in both the prescribing doctor and the competence of the pharmacist. Again, you are hoping

For some, faith feels like a high hurdle, but the truth is we practice it every day.

this is true. These are invisible realities in which we must exercise faith before the evidence is revealed. You hope the pilot knows what he is doing and where he is going. You hope the plane is safe. You hope your doctor has the knowledge to prescribe the right pill, and you hope the pharmacist knows the difference between aspirin and Ramipril.

If you are a person who struggles with expressing faith in what God says, while at the same time you have faith in just about everything else in His creation, it may be you are trying to understand Him with the wrong tools. Could it be that you are trying to force Him into a lab when He wants you to trust Him in what He says even when the reality of what He says may be invisible to you at the time?

We forget this, but the things we cannot see are the most fundamental realities in God's universe. *Love* is invisible, but it turns the wheels of life. *Personality* is invisible, but it has a magnetizing effect on others. *Conscience* is invisible, but where conscience reigns, the kingdom of God is present. *Truth* is invisible, but still, it haunts men to invest their lives in search of it.

In the New Testament, God makes a profound statement that summarizes this thought concerning the indivisible reality of faith. The Bible says:

Now faith is confidence in what we hope for and assurance about what we do not see. (Hebrews 11:1)

And so, what is faith? Faith believes God for what He says—even before you see the evidence. For example, the Bible says that upon His death, Christ entered the gates of death (Hades) and came back triumphant, breaking once and for all the bonds of death. The apostle Paul believed that. Believed what? He found that through His death, Christ broke the bonds of death for mankind forever. Because Paul understood that, he was able to write for God in his letter to the Christians in Rome,

For I am convinced that neither death nor life, neither angels nor demons, neither the present nor the future, nor any powers, neither height nor depth, nor anything else in all creation, will be able to separate us from the love of God that is in Christ Jesus our Lord. (Romans 8:38-39)

Like Paul, I believed, exercised faith, and trusted God's Word.

But still, like many, we stumble over the reality of faith, and say, "That's the problem! Faith is not a reality since I can't prove it in a laboratory. I need something concrete that I can reach out and touch, something I can hold in my hands."

Do you believe that Bonaparte Napoleon lived? Do you believe President George Washington and President Abraham Lincoln were real people? Since you are not a fool, your answer will be yes. Why do you believe these three men lived and were real? Recently I had this conversation with a friend. His answer was, "I believe that because of the record of history."

My response was, "Do you understand there is more historical evidence for the person of Jesus Christ than for any of the three mentioned above? Your answer to my question proves that you are putting your faith in the hope that the writers of history got it right."

Here's another invisible reality for you to ponder. It takes as much or more faith for the atheist to believe in a negative (that God doesn't exist) because he has far less evidence to support his faith than a Christian has in believing in a loving, living God.

Let me share one more evidence of faith. It comes from my flying experience. When you are standing, ready to launch on Glacier Point in Yosemite National Park, you best have faith in those who taught you to fly and your training. You must also have faith in those who built your glider. It is true that God gave us life without wings, but He smiled when man provided us with wings to become part bird and part man. By the time you stand on that first high altitude launch site, you will have learned many lessons—lessons about hang gliding and lessons about life. What you have learned will possibly save your life, and may even determine where you spend eternity.

The sport of hang gliding, along with my faith in Christ, has taught me much about faith, hope, discipline, preparation, teamwork, love, and consideration for others. None of these attributes are strangers to my sport. I would like to believe I'm a more responsible person today because of these disciplines, and that I am better prepared for what comes next. Ah, we continue to fly.

CHAPTER 4

THE PIECES BEGIN TO FALL IN PLACE

Why not go out on a limb? Isn't that where the fruit is?

—Frank Scully

Call from a Stranger

Early one Monday morning I had just finished a time of devotion and prayer in which I was seeking God's guidance. My plaintive cry was simply, "God, I need help, and I need it now!" I had just finished when the phone rang. A man who I had never met introduced himself. He asked me if we had a financial problem in the church. I said, "Yes, I believe we do." The word was out, and The King's Place's predicament was known. The caller said, "I'm working with one of your sister churches in the Bay area. May I fly down, take you to breakfast, and explain how I believe I might be able to help?" He arrived the next morning. We had breakfast, and he shared ideas I found difficult to believe. He said, "With God's help, we should be able to raise approximately three times your annual income over the next three years, and your people will never be the same."

As I contemplated what this stranger had shared with me, it seemed like the odds and risk were considerable. Still, I realized we were in a seemingly impossible situation. We needed to find God's will for the people of The King's Place. Is it possible this stranger was God's way of getting our attention?

Even so, my faith and confidence in such a program were not all that great. My attitude was the same as many of my clergy friends who had great skepticism about anyone claiming to accomplish what seemed unbelievable. What I was hearing sounded to me like the mother of all sales pitches. Many thoughts were running through my mind: *How could a man who knew little, if anything, about our people make such a claim? Let's get real. I have been with "my" people for more than twelve years, and I am convinced of one thing. I know I'm incapable of raising that kind of money above our regular income over three years. I think this "friend" is on the other side of reality, and besides, he's from another part of the county that's culturally out of step with those of us who live in California. He hasn't even seen our financial statement.*

After our breakfast meeting, my thought was, *How do I back away from this gracefully?* Still the question about whether this was God's way to capture my attention nagged at me. What should I do? I knew well the instruction of James 1:

> *If any of you lacks wisdom, you should ask God, who gives generously to all without finding fault, and it will be given to you. (James 1:5)*

Didn't it make sense that in asking for wisdom or direction from God, I should actually partner with Him, assuming that I first listen and then take His counsel? I still had a problem. Asking for wisdom and direction is different sometimes. *How was I to know God's perfect will right now? The Bible didn't deal with "capital stewardship programs" in churches?* There had to be another way of knowing.

The Bible didn't deal with "capital stewardship programs" in churches?

I remembered another biblical principle. When we lack the wisdom to make a decision, we have the confidence that God will give us the understanding needed, and there are times when He uses others to participate with us in the process. Many instructions in the Bible encourages the wise counsel of others.

> *Surely you need guidance to wage war, and victory is won through many advisers. (Proverbs 24:6)*

This verse seemed appropriate. We were definitely in a war, and we were losing.

I explained that our board of elders would be meeting that evening and if he were willing, I would invite him and allow him to share what he had shared with me. We met that night; the gentleman made his presentation. After an engaging discussion and several pertinent questions, we excused our guest, had further conversation, prayer, and then made a decision.

That evening we entered into an agreement with this stewardship consultant who would become a dear friend and eventually a colleague. He helped us with what proved to be the most successful debt-liquidation capital stewardship program in history. Through that effort, God enabled The King's Place to return to its mission. It wasn't a total solution, but it was a significant step in the right direction. We gladly gave up our interest in the banking industry.

In most capital stewardship programs; the senior minister is invited to give a commitment testimony. I understood the reason for this, and I was not opposed to the need for modeling stewardship for the benefit of our people. However, while the congregation did not know the exact amount of personal debt we had incurred in medical and doctor bills, they knew it was considerable. To suggest publicly that we were making a significant commitment in the campaign when we owed nearly a hundred thousand dollars seemed like a hollow testimony that could be misunderstood by many as a disingenuous effort to motivate the flock. After my wife and I prayed earnestly about our commitment, I shared what that would be with our consultant. I explained that not a penny would be given toward it until every dollar of our daughter's accident debt had been paid.

Author Barry Webb calls Isaiah the "Romans of the Old Testament"[1]: where all the threads come together, and the Big Picture of God's purposes for His people and His world is most clearly set forth. Attuned to the magnificent literary architecture of Isaiah, he escorted us through this prophecy and trained our ears and hearts to resonate with its great biblical-theological themes.

Webb helped us understand that in difficult times Israel was able to rise up from defeat. I began to teach from Isaiah. As we studied God's purpose for Israel and Israel's response, we understood this had application for us today too. We began to rise from depression to faith, from despair to hope, and from defeat to victory. In the words of Isaiah 40:31, we had waited on the Lord, and our strength was being renewed. We were flying again on wings like the eagles.

We called our stewardship program "Flying Like an Eagle," and it was a major step toward solving our financial crisis. When people began to express their love to the Lord through sacrificial commitments, God began the process of restoring our collective spirit. When our consultant asked me if we had a financial problem at King's Place at that first breakfast, I knew the answer immediately. Churches don't have financial problems unless there is also a spiritual problem. Once the spiritual issue is resolved, the financial crisis disappears.

However, while God was helping us be His church once again, my personal conflict from Renee's accident only increased. I felt like I was living two separate lives. It was much easier to enjoy God's presence when I was with God's people, but much more difficult when I tried to face the enormous disappointments of Renee's lack of improvement. We had been so hopeful. I was not giving up, but personally I was in a valley, unsure how or where I could find help.

The Mission to India

Another thread in the tapestry that God was weaving happened through a uniquely gifted man that I had never met until we invited him as a special guest of our congregation. His name was Dr. P. N. Kurien. He had been the Minister of Education in Gandhi's government. After his conversion to the Christian faith, he created the All-India Prayer Fellowship. For many years, Dr. Kurien invited between 150-200 American pastors to India to conduct crusades.

In 1983, he invited me to join many other American pastors to do several crusades in different parts of south India. It was an invitation I took seriously, but there was a problem. The time I was to depart for India came when we were in the middle of our stewardship campaign. While both the India crusades and stewardship program were important, I had to give my energy and precedence to the campaign and decline. Regrettably, I had to delay my invitation to India for at least a year.

In 1984, Dr. Kurien extended the invitation a second time, this time for five weeks instead of the original four. Our stewardship program had gone very well—far beyond anything I might have expected and certainly far beyond my level of faith. With helpful instructions from Dr. Kurien, I began to prepare myself for what would prove to be the most significant ministry experience of my life. This experience would build the foundation for my restoration.

For two days and nights, I flew and traveled to Trivandrum in the state of Kerala, on the very southern tip of India. Dr. Kurien met me at the airport in Mumbai, where we stayed that night. The next morning, we flew to Trivandrum. Dr. Kurien made sure I got to my hotel, and then served as my interpreter for the next five weeks. He explained that the Trivandrum hotel would be our home, but it would be necessary to be driven by taxi each afternoon to the place of our brush arbor meetings, usually between a three-and four-hour drive one way each day. A brush arbor meeting was one held in an open-sided shelter with only a roof to shield the participants from the weather.

Dr. Kurien gave me a two-hour briefing on what to expect since this was my first visit to India. He explained that the Indian people I would be speaking to would not understand many illustrations and idioms that my people at home would, so I had to adjust that to make myself clear.

On that first night, as we neared the village, we saw people walking on either side of the road a mile out in single file singing songs I had never heard, but beautiful to the ear. Since the British Empire had colonized so much of India, most of the people spoke with a beautiful clipped English accent. When singing, they sang in English as well.

They were all making their way to the place where they could listen to this man who had come from America. To suggest that this was a brush arbor setting is a bit misleading. When I arrived, there was a simple elevated platform with a thatched covering for the speaker and Dr. Kurien, my interpreter, but not for the people listening.

We took our place and more than five thousand people, all sitting on grass mats, much like we might see on American beaches, gathered to hear about the God of the Bible. The children were seated in the front. Dr. Kurien introduced me and invited me to speak. There was no singing since they had done that as they walked to get there.

As I began to speak, the clouds broke apart. The rain fell in torrents. It was difficult to see those more than forty feet away, yet not a person moved. I spoke for thirty minutes and then sat down, and still not a person budged. I turned to Dr. Kurien and asked him why they were not leaving. He answered, "Most of these people have walked fifteen to twenty-five miles to hear about this Jesus. They want to hear more. You must continue!" I spoke for another thirty minutes and sat down again. For a second time, they insisted that I continue preaching and so I did for more than two hours that night. If I ever felt anointed, it was that night in India.

After two hours I was finished; at least I thought I was. When I sat down for the third time, the people remained on their grass mats. I asked my friend once again, "What should I do?"

He said, "The Holy Spirit has spoken to me and confirmed that this is to be an exceptional night. These people believe in their hearts that you can do what you have spoken about tonight and that you have a special gift to pray for the sick." As Dr. Kurien spoke I knew I didn't *possess* a gift; that belonged to God, but God would have a willing vessel. We invited those desiring prayer to move to the very front and about four hundred people flooded to the front. One by one we placed our hands on them and prayed a simple prayer of faith for their healing. Many were visibly healed. I was in awe.

The Bible is filled with accounts of such healings, but when you are in the mix of such an outpouring of the Holy Spirit today, it leaves you speechless. I knew there was nothing in my words, hands, or heart that could produce what was taking place. It was the power and sovereignty of the Almighty God that healed so many that night.

I shall never forget a twelve-year-old girl who was deaf from birth. We placed our hands on her head over her ears, and as we prayed you could hear a snap like a clap. She was healed! Something miraculous had just happened. As a sovereign work of God's power and grace, she could hear. I will never forget the look in her eyes and the glow on her beautiful face when she heard sounds for the first time. The next night the crowd swelled to twenty-five thousand from the five thousand that attended the night before. There had been no television cameras, flyers, or any other kind of media promotion. It was merely God doing what only God can do.

After the meeting, it was a four-hour taxi ride back to the hotel. At first, I was euphoric—like I was in those pages of Scripture turned by someone else. Next, I was exhausted from the travel to India, and spent from the trip and the meeting that had just concluded. I believed the enemy knew I was weak and tired from the journey. He was not willing to stand by while God had such a night of victory. I remember thinking how wonderful it would be if my church back home could be here, sitting beneath this waterfall of God's unrelenting presence. How could I ever explain what God was doing? I would soon find that a very challenging task.

In the back seat of that taxi during the long drive back to the hotel, I went through a struggle of gigantic proportion. Before I knew it, an oppressive wave of anger enveloped me. I wanted to shout at God: "God, where were You when *I* needed You? You bring me to India, and I pray for an Indian child I have never met and will never see again, and *she* is healed. I pray and plead for my daughter, and *she is not.* Is this some kind of cosmic joke? Do you prefer to operate in India, but not America?"

I conducted five crusades in Kerala. When we finished, Dr. Kurien asked if I would stay a week longer and hold two campaigns in New Delhi. He explained that there would be far less interest to the Christian message there than there was in Kerala. I found that to be accurate. The people were very kind and gracious, and we saw evidence of God's blessing on our effort, but New Delhi was different than Kerala. In the seven crusades I held in India over a period of weeks, I saw thousands more converted to faith in Christ compared to my twenty-seven *years* of serving three churches in America. I saw an exceptional hunger for the liberating message of Jesus Christ. It changed my life.

The impressions I brought back from India were remarkable. I will never forget the children with their beautiful complexions and dark eyes, the people sitting transfixed in the rain intent on meeting Jesus above anything else. They always sat right in the front and never felt the need for potty breaks during services that lasted more than two and a half hours, sometimes in driving rain. Simply amazing. The people were very poor, but did well with what they had. They had very little, but insisted on sharing—even if it was the last food they had.

Once I was the guest of a single family consisting of a mother, father, and two young children. There was little furniture in their two-room home. The larger room had a table with two chairs in it. Since Dr. Kurian and I were the guests, they insisted we sit on the only two chairs. The family members each sat on what appeared to be boxes that looked like apple crates to me. In the center of the table was a very plain dish with enough cookies for each of us to have one. As the father prayed for that simple provision, I wept. This family was so grateful for these few cookies—the only food they had for that day. In our country, those cookies would have been the dessert after enjoying a large meal—something this dear family may never have known. That did not matter to them. Instead they were grateful for something else. That became clear as the father prayed. They were grateful that they had been chosen to be the host of this pastor who had come from America to tell them about Jesus! I was thankful and humbled by this family's faith and kindness. I will never forget that moment.

Aside from the scheduled crusades, I was invited to speak at several other places during earlier hours before taking the taxi to the campaign for the evening. On one occasion I was the speaking guest at an all-girls school. More than twelve hundred girls sat before me on colorful mats that provided little comfort from the cold cement under them, yet they just glowed in their expressions of love to this visitor they had never met. Their singing was like a choir of angels.

While in Trivandrum, I was invited by the Vilathivilai, Church of South India to deliver their annual convention lecture on January 20-21, 1984. That was also a humbling experience with some of God's people. They walked in great love and humility toward me.

After our two crusades in northern India, near New Delhi, it was time to make certain all our paperwork was in order. Our flight back to the states left the next morning. Before I left, I purchased several beautiful carvings and portrait inlays that continue to bless our home today. I also bought several pieces of embroidery to give to staff members and friends. They were a win-win situation. Buying them supported the young women in southern India who made them. This was their only source of income. And I could give these beautiful pieces to particular people for whom these lovely dresser doilies could be a daily reminder to pray for those with so little. It was time to get a little sleep before my early wakeup call to catch that first flight out of New Delhi for Hong Kong.

A First Century Saint Flying First Class

When I returned home from India, I was utterly exhausted, yet emotionally higher than a kite. After an overnight stop in Hong Kong, I spent most of my long return flight to Los Angeles writing pages of notes on what I wanted to share with my congregation.

I remember wondering what it would be like if the apostle Paul could have enjoyed the luxury and convenience of my United Boeing 747 dancing its way across the Pacific. Can you imagine what he might have accomplished with a tablet or smartphone? That was a delicious thought, and when the three babies in the seats behind me stopped crying, I must have fallen into a deep sleep.

I began to dream and because I had been thinking of Paul earlier, there he was! Several of us, not a full flight, had boarded our Corinthian Air 747 just outside the city limits of Corinth. I had just settled in when I noticed a rather short, elderly man coming down the aisle. He took a seat in the same row as mine but across the aisle next to the window. As he settled in, he pulled a couple of items from his well-worn leather pouch. It was difficult to see what he had and what he was doing, but fairly quickly I realized he was writing, although I had never seen a pen like his before.

I noticed the two seats next to him were unoccupied, so I asked if I might take the aisle seat. (My ulterior motive was to escape from those little screaming heads who had just awakened again behind me. They were beginning to screech like girls at a rock concert.)

He glanced up and said, "I would love that. Young man, you look tired, what have you been up to?" I began to tell him about the greatest month of my life and how God met us in India, how people flooded our outdoor cathedrals to find Jesus, and how many were healed, and how several new churches were birthed. And then I said, "But I didn't ask to sit here to dominate our conversation. I'm interested in you. Who are you and what do you do? You seem very different from everyone else on this flight. Tell me about yourself!"

He looked at me and said, "You say your name is Dan. That's a good name. Do you know the meaning of your name?" Before I could answer, he said "It is of Hebrew origin, and means 'judge, God is my judge.' In what you refer to as the Old Testament we read about Dan. He was the fifth son of Jacob and founder of one of the twelve tribes of Israel. Then there is that 'other' Dan, usually referred to as Daniel. Perhaps you remember him too? He was the fellow who spent the night in the den of lions?"[2]

"Well, you know a great deal about my name," I replied, "What is yours and what does it mean?"

He smiled and said,

The truth is that I have been known by two names. The first was

Saul. Many referred to me as Saul of Tarsus. You mentioned you were returning home from a great series of crusades in India. That sounds like a great missionary journey. Knowing that, I suspect you know as much about me as I know about myself. You probably have already figured it out. My second name is Paul, and I'm often referred to as the apostle Paul. My earliest name, Saul, is also of Hebrew origin, and means 'asked for, prayed for.' When used of a boy, the name is pronounced Sahl.³ But as you know my name was changed to Paul after a once-in-a-lifetime experience on the road to Damascus. If you recall, I was on my way to gather up those pesky Christians and stamp out their challenge to the faith of my fathers.

My journey to Damascus was a trip the world will never forget. I was blinded and fell to the ground. I heard this voice asking me why I was persecuting the person speaking. After realizing it was Jesus, He told me to get up and go on to Damascus where I would receive further instructions. For three days I sat there in the city, blind as a bat, and finally, this fellow named Ananias visited me. He seemed to be trembling a bit. He told me God sent him, placed his hands on me, and said:

"Brother Saul, the Lord—Jesus, who appeared to you on the road as you were coming here—has sent me so that you may see again and be filled with the Holy Spirit." (Acts 9:17b)

My second name, the name given to me by God is from the Roman family name Paulus, which meant "small or humble" in Latin.⁴ That seemed very fitting since my life and ministry would have a greater impact among the Gentiles than the Jews. Even so, I have sought to become a servant to all.

The flight was not all that long, and there were many questions I wanted to ask. In some detail, Paul began to tell of his journeys and writings as well as the churches that had been birthed, and the trouble among some of the saints. He spoke of his trials, the miracles of healings, demons cast out, and much more. Finally, he said, "I'm on my way back to Jerusalem now where I will speak to the leaders about this most recent journey. Even there I will find two groups of believers. One group will find it difficult, if not impossible, to believe my accounts of God's miraculous acts of grace among the Gentiles. They want to believe, but I think they are still wondering if they can trust me. The second group is already anticipating my return and preparing a celebration to rejoice in what God is doing—especially among the Gentiles."

I noted a couple of the flight attendants whispering to one another and looking our way. Soon, one stepped back to our aisle and addressed my friend. He said, "Sir, are you Paul, known as the Apostle to the Gentiles?"

My new friend said, "Some have called me that."

"Sir," the young attendant said, "We are privileged to have you with us on this flight to Israel. Would you honor us by joining us in first class?" At first, Paul was reluctant, but finally agreed. He gathered up his belongings and followed the attendant.

The restrooms in the back of the plane were out of order and so when I needed to use the facility, I had to walk through first class. There was my new friend in an aisle seat, with a beautiful meal displayed on his tray. He was finishing a tasty bit of caviar washed down with a glass of wine, one saved for just such an occasion when Jesus performed his first miracle in turning water into wine. I asked him if he enjoyed the wine. His reply was, "You do remember, my son, that I'm the one who wrote:

Stop drinking only water and use a little wine because of your stom-ach and your frequent illnesses. (1 Timothy 5:23)

"I was writing to my young friend, Timothy, at the time, but I've often said, 'If it's good enough for Jesus, it's good enough for me.'"

A voice spoke over the intercom, instructing all passengers to take their seats since we were about to begin our descent. My new friend smiled at me, and said, "Son, when you get home, don't worry about those with little faith. Focus on those who will rejoice with you and our Lord for the victories that have been won."

I returned to my seat, and as we landed, the little ones just behind began wailing because of the sudden change of pressure in their ears. I was im-mediately brought back to the reality of my century, but now I was confi-dent that I had both a plan and the passion to share my five great weeks in India with my people back home.

CHAPTER 5

GREATNESS

The price of greatness is responsibility.

—Winston Churchill

Visitors in My Office

After the triumphs of India, this old eagle was about to fly once again—that is, until two of my young men asked if they could meet with me. These were not casual members of our church family. Both of these men and their families had found faith and relationship with the Lord at The King's Place. They were speaking for themselves and a small group in the congregation—people who agreed with them. To my knowledge, in all my years of ministry I had not lost any people who complained they were spiritually malnourished, but all that was about to change.

Both of these young men were very aggressive in their pursuit of Christian growth. Both worked at Edwards Air Force Base. One was an executive with the Jet Propulsion Laboratory of California Institute of Technology. For decades they were leaders in our national space mission and exploration.

They wasted no time in speaking about the reason for their visit. It was to announce their decision to leave The King's Place and begin a new congregation. They announced that this new congregation planned to start in the building that used to be The King's Place before we constructed our new facilities.

I need to be clear about this. These were not men who only attended on a Sunday morning and were not to be seen the rest of the week. Both had served in leadership capacities. Both had demonstrated considerable growth. They were young in their faith, but Christian growth in their minds was not an option, it was a command. They were fruit from the Jesus Movement, perhaps the most significant revival any of us have known during our lifetime. We were about to discover that if there wasn't a balance between one's quest for truth and obedience to the Word of God, chaos would prevail.

They wanted me to understand that I should not take their decision personally—an understanding that could only rise from a position of Christian immaturity. It immediately became very personal as I tried to process the turkey they had just dropped on my plate. As these men spoke, my countenance remained unchanged, but my heart sank.

I made what must have been a feeble attempt to help them appreciate the calling the Lord placed on every pastor. We are referred to in the Bible as under-shepherds. We are not to be dictators, telling people what to think and do, teaching them how they should live according to the blueprint from God's Word. We have the responsibility and privilege of caring for the sheep.

Of course, the elephant in the room was the question in my mind: *What is it that brought you to this decision?* These were not ordinary members of the church, but they were suddenly displaying an enormous degree of immaturity. I couldn't figure it out.

I was still in the dark as to why they were acting this way. After all, they had been the organizers of a three-week, around-the-clock prayer vigil in the hospital chapel immediately after our daughter's accident. There was no doubt in their minds that God would heal our daughter based on their interpretation of Scripture. When that didn't happen, they immediately felt it imperative to do what made sense to them. It would not be long before I realized that their interpretation of Scripture was in error. However, before explaining that, it might be helpful to understand a couple of critical events in their lives.

Clearly, these men had not been satisfied with the menu from the cradle of their faith. Their zeal and hunger for growth caused them to pursue shepherds of another flock—well, not exactly a flock. They were very impressed with this man in the Los Angeles area—a man with a nonexistent congregation. He was best defined as a freelance speaker, accountable to no one—only himself. They told him about our daughter's accident, the faithful prayers of thousands from around the world, yet without the results they felt could be demanded by the authority of God's Word. They were careful to explain that our daughter was still held in the grip of a coma. It had been more than seven months since the accident and her limbs had continued to posture in spite of the casts placed in an endeavor to avoid that. This itinerate "shepherd" needed to hear nothing more.

This "prophet's" conclusion and recommendation was immediate. He had a "word" from the Lord for my men. For Christians in a *particular* theological camp, this was a bit like a trumpet sounding from heaven accompanied by the voice of God Himself. This man's supposed "word from God" directed them to respectfully withdraw from The King's Place and create a whole new wineskin where God's will could be accomplished.

It was interesting to me that this man had never met or spoken to me, the under-shepherd of my men. He had never visited our congregation, nor had he ever visited the Antelope Valley, where The King's Place was located. Yet he had the final word from God Himself about what needed to happen in a place he knew nothing (or very little) about.

This self-proclaimed "prophet" was a disciple of two very popular teachers at the time. One has died, and the other continues his ministry, while living an extremely opulent lifestyle, flying from place to place in his private jet. While these men have done much good, they have also done great harm in the church. I am not questioning their faith, but I am questioning much of their teaching.

These men had significant influence among a small but aggressive part of our congregation. Significant themes in their teachings were the prosperity gospel, and the idea that Christians are immune to sickness. If a

Christian got sick or felt sick, he was supposed to recognize it as an attack by Satan. The solution to such an attack was to just "name it and claim it": meaning that you simply acknowledged the problem and then claimed the power of God's Spirit over the enemy. I once heard one of these teachers claim that he never feared flying. In his corrupted understanding of God and His Word, he actually believed that God would not let anything happen to a plane on which he was a passenger. He thought that because he was a child of the King, he was immune from such a tragedy. I've never quite figured out what happened to all the thousands of Christians who died in planes—apparently because they did not know how to exercise this protection. (I'm intentionally oversimplifying these important issues to avoid a lengthy exposition of God's Word about this for the moment, so bear with me.)

But back to my question for these two men. "What is it that brought you to this decision?" I asked.

Their answer was a little like an elephant walking through tall grass. When the old bull moved through the grass, nothing was left standing. "Pastor," they said, "we believe that God has not healed your daughter for two reasons. First, we believe there is sin in the congregation, and secondly, there must be sin in your life. It's because of this unconfessed sin that your daughter has not been healed. Once this sin is recognized and confessed, then God will be free to heal your daughter."

Well, they were right about sin. It didn't take a prophet to declare the reality of sin. What they were mistaken about was their conclusion that it was because of some hidden sin that God had not healed Renee. Even though I endeavored to help them understand that I didn't wake up each morning trying to determine just which sin I would choose to perform that day, they were not convinced. Any sin in my life wasn't intentional or premeditated.

I wanted to help them see that when I became a transformed child of God, receiving the grace of God through Christ, my sin was forgiven and dealt with, no matter what decade the sin was committed. They found it impossible to wrap their theological understanding around that fact.

Sickness and Death Comes to All

It wasn't long after my friends visit with me that they withdrew from The King's Place. They took a small group of about forty people with them—people of the same mind and theological interest. In the beginning, they thought of themselves as a remnant, a place where the truth of God could be proclaimed. The leader of this group, an exceptionally gifted teacher, had become a disciple of men whose teaching was tenaciously popular, but cultic in its understanding of the New Testament.

Paul once wrote to Timothy who was like his son in the ministry, warning him:

> *For the time will come when people will not put up with sound doctrine. Instead, to suit their own desires, they will gather around them a great number of teachers to say what their itching ears want to hear. (2 Timothy 4:3)*

Clearly, Paul referred to people who were just not satisfied with a straightforward and credible interpretation of God's Word. Because of "their own desires," some people become prey to teachers that mix some truth with teachings that are in error (or cultic) about the life and ministry of Christ.

The men who visited me eventually became under-shepherds, even though they were babes themselves. They were the good seed that had been planted, yet they had not matured because they were seeking "their own desires." They were like many great athletes that are unable to develop to their full potential because of improper nourishment and training.

They made a choice to put aside the teaching from the place of their spiritual birth and decided to follow the teaching of others. In their quest and excitement for the "greater things of God," they plunged ahead, not realizing they had "itching ears." They loved hearing about this "gospel of prosperity." They liked the idea that as a believer they could deny sickness. They were over the moon with the idea that a faithful believer could name it and claim it, a particular device making it possible to manipulate God for most anything one might desire.

My experiences and expositions of God's Word failed to resonate with these men since they saw me as a sinner. This was a logical conclusion in their minds. How could they possibly rely on my explanations of Scripture while I was practicing this assumed sin? It is of interest to note that they were never able to articulate what my transgression was.

In the beginning, their little flock had a remarkable launch. There was a great deal of excitement—particularly from the teacher and teaching. However, it wasn't long until cracks began to appear in the foundation of this group. Within the first year, the primary under-shepherd had cancer. Another three of the leading men died within the first two years. For Christians that didn't believe it was God's will for His people to be sick, a whole new revelation was unfolding before them. Their corrupt theology was not standing the test of time. These were the same friends who tried to help me understand why our daughter was not being restored.

Their blemished theology was beginning to crack. When the pastor and other members within their newly formed fellowship started to die, that just wasn't consistent with their teaching. If their theology had been correct, it would have been necessary for them to view themselves the same way they had regarded me when my daughter was not healed: There was either sin in the camp or there was sin in the pastor's life. Of course, we know that neither of these accusations caused God to withhold His hand of healing for my daughter or these friends. They were beginning to understand that praying for someone else is entirely different than praying for oneself. If you are praying for someone else and you don't see the desired result, it's easy to place a heavy burden of guilt on that person or group. Doing this allows you to keep your questionable (and contemptible) theology intact and avoid any responsibility, personal blame, or weakness.

However, this pastor was still my friend, and he was dying. He was slowly slipping away, day by day as the cancer was taking its toll. It is true that we understood parts of Scripture differently, yet our friendship remained. I visited him on many occasions in the same hospital where our daughter was first taken. In our last visit only a couple of days before his death, we wept and prayed together. I will not forget some of his last words to me. "Pastor," he said, "I was wrong. Had I been right, I would not be here at death's door today. Will you forgive me?" Of course, I did! I don't remember the precise wording, but I asked him to forgive me too— for whatever it was that he and his friend were referring to in my office. He said, "I do," but died without ever explaining what that was. I live yet for a season, and he died for an eternity, but we both understood that our gracious God does not hold a club over our heads when we come to Him as a child with his Father, nor should we. Even though we understood some parts of God's Word differently, I'm confident of that day when we shall fellowship in perfection before the throne of God's grace.

As you might expect I have had considerable time to contemplate the cultic aspects of my friend's misunderstanding of Scripture. It is not enough to simply tell a story of loving, aggressive, and energetic believers who had it wrong when it came to God's truth.

I am quick to make the point that while my friends' theology was contemptible, they possessed a desire to grow in their walk with the Lord that was commendable. Their mistake was to follow a teacher that was out of order, unorthodox, and cultic in what he taught.

Two critical passages of Scripture are often misunderstood. When they are, this creates unintended consequences, and severe harm to the body of Christ. This is especially true when these teaching texts are manipulated in the hands of false, cultic, or simply misguided teachers.

A Classroom Text: 1 Peter 2:23

Let's visit the classroom for a moment and seek a higher level of understanding as we look at 1 Peter 2:23-25. I want to look at this passage because it deals with one of the critical areas of confusion today. Peter wasn't confused, but many force an incorrect interpretation on what Peter wrote. The NIV has one of the most beautiful translations of this passage which speaks of the life and ministry of our Lord:

> *When they hurled their insults at him, he did not retaliate; when he suffered, he made no threat. Instead, he entrusted himself to him who judges justly. "He himself bore our sins" in his body on the cross, so that we might die to sins and live for righteousness; "by his wounds you have been healed." For "you were like sheep going astray," but now you have returned to the Shepherd and Overseer of your souls. (1 Peter 2:23-25)*

One of the primary principles of biblical interpretation that must never be violated is *context*. What is the context of this passage? The answer is salvation. There is no other way to interpret the statement Peter is making. The passage is talking about Jesus on the cross—dying for us—not opening His mouth, but enduring punishment and bearing our sin: That, my friend, is *salvation*. This is so pure, simple, definitive, and clear that you can't miss it.

Yet, when some teachers seek to break this verse down, they change the context from salvation to healing. They ignore the primary rule of context, simply because the word *healed* is present. Every time they see this word (in their thinking), it refers to the miracle of divine healing for the body. That is simply not true!

They are ignoring the Holy Scripture itself! Psalm 103 says that God heals the soul as well as the body. In the context of that psalm, God heals the soul *and* He heals all your diseases. That is Psalm 103. But what is Peter talking about in 1 Peter 2? When you note the background, it becomes clear that Peter is referring to one's soul. There are diseases of the soul that must be healed, and what is the primary condition of the soul in an unregenerate state? *Being lost!* So, what happens? God heals your soul, God heals your spirit, and God heals your spiritual nature, first and foremost.

Healing of the soul is what Peter is addressing in his first letter. He is not saying that Jesus *guarantees your physical healing*. If Jesus were making such a guarantee, then every Christian who is sick would be healed after being prayed for immediately.

Again, to be clear, I am not saying that God has not provided for our physical healing. What I have said is that 1 Peter 2 is not a passage you can wave in the face of God, telling Him, "You must heal me on the basis of my faith and my understanding of what You have said in this passage!"

We need to understand what God really means, and not demand anything from Him based on what we believe or have been taught.

Healing for the body and mind is a benefit, a provision of Christ's death on the cross, a benefit for the church. It is not and has never been in the history of the church a *guarantee* of healing in this life. God never promises that He will heal your body in every case. Healing your body is within the sovereignty of God, and we are encouraged to pray for the healing of the body. We will explore that later.

God says He will graciously entertain our prayers. He also says that if we exercise our faith (or if someone else exercises faith on our behalf) and if it's per His will, He will hear us and often He will heal us. God says that He delights in our being healthy and a favorable witness, but He never promised that the mark of one's spirituality would be that you will never sneeze. This idea is utter madness spreading like wildfire through segments of the church today, telling you that God's perfect will is that you are never going to be sick.

This priming the pump of people's faith and making guarantees the Bible doesn't make is false teaching. We have no biblical promise that God will heal based upon our faith demand. When we don't consider the sovereignty of God, we desecrate God's Word.

We have no biblical promise that God will heal based upon our faith demand.

There are times when we suffer a *No* from God, a benevolent *No*, a kindly *No*, a protective *No* perhaps, but a *No*, nevertheless. The next move on the part of these teachers is the one that levels those who are hanging on by a tiny thread of faith: It's when these self-proclaimed teachers have the colossal gall to tell people that if only they were more spiritual, had more faith, or believed as they believed, they would be well. The result of such nonsense is that whatever faith these people had is crushed. In that process, we hurt the whole body of Christ. Consider my friends, Bob Whittington, Dave Hawley, and Butch Smith. They were all wonderful men of faith, great men of God. Please do not tell me that they would be alive today if they had listened to "creditable" teachers. That would be arrogant in the extreme and only serve to hurt the body of Christ more.

Since none of us can heal, we need to embrace the sovereignty of God, and leave the healing to Jesus.

- Believe Him for healing.

- Trust Him for healing.

- Come to Him for healing.

- Pursue Him for healing.

- Search your own life to see if anything is standing in the way of that healing.

We trust His sovereignty by coming to Him and laying ourselves before Him on His conditions. The Bible says that if we follow His will, He will raise us up. If He desires to teach you something in the meantime, He may not heal.

If you are not healed, don't fall into the trap of believing the Holy Spirit is neglecting you. Avoid the suggestion that the Lord has a hard line on you or that He is on your case. Don't believe you have a lack of faith or no faith. Refuse to accept that God turns His back on you because some past sin is a dark chasm in your life. Remember that if you have sin in your life, God has provided for that. It's called forgiveness after confession.

When James, believed to be the brother of Jesus, wrote this:

> *And the prayer offered in faith will make the sick person well; the Lord will raise them up. If they have sinned, they will be forgiven. (James 5:15)*

In the next verse, James provides additional insight related to healing:

> *Therefore, confess your sins to each other and pray for each other so that you may be healed. The prayer of a righteous person is powerful and effective. (James 5:16, emphasis mine)*

There are many books based on what authors believe these verses prove and promise. When the sick are prayed for, and all of the conditions of James 5:14-16 have been met, and still the person is not healed, what happens then? Some teachers immediately fall below the line by criticizing either the lack of faith in that person, or by suggesting that sin is present in the person who needs the healing. What may be equally insulting is to suggest that "the prayer of the righteous" is apparently not so righteous. This is an example of arrogance and certainly reveals the kind of judging that belongs only to God. It would be well for such teachers to read verse 16 again and again until they recognize one tiny three-letter word: *may*. James, who was a far greater authority on God's intent than any of us, wants us to understand that not all will be healed when anointed with oil and prayed for, but they *may* be healed.

When we come to God's table for nourishment, let us feed on the bounty of His banquet, rather than scrambling through the garbage presented by false teachers. They will take you on trips of guilt while God will take you by the hand and allow you to walk by faith, trusting Him for whatever the outcome.

Remember, God is the One who heals, and there are times when He will permit things in our lives, using them as teaching moments. We see clear examples of this in the lives of Job, King David, and Paul to name a few. Let's rejoice in that, and live life by giving thanks in everything, for this is God's will.

Still in the Classroom: Isaiah 53:4-5

Thus far we have learned that 1 Peter guarantees salvation, and while providing healing, it is not a guarantee for healing in every situation. Now, let's move to the critical text many use to try and prove that God guarantees every believer good health just as He guarantees eternal life through the sacrifice of His Son on the cross. Isaiah 53:4-5 is a giant, prophetic jewel that foretells what Christ accomplished on the cross. It is for this reason we deal with this passage here.

We briefly have spoken of principles of biblical interpretation, and in the previous chapter, we affirmed that all Scripture must be interpreted by the context in which it is found.

Howard Marshall identifies three principles of biblical interpretation:

> *The first is that the Old Testament is always to be interpreted in light of the New, as the New Testament interprets the Old in light of the revelation of Christ. The second is that because Jesus' teaching was before Easter, it has a limited range of application. The Easter-event changes how we interpret Jesus' words in the gospels. Finally, Marshall contends that the concept of the gospel becomes fixed by the early Church—there is a real "apostolic deposit" that is used to detect and root out error. This is clear in Paul's letters, and becomes explicit in the Pastoral epistles. The Marshall plan is twofold: (1) use this*

"apostolic deposit" as an interpretative grid for doctrinal develop-ments...The "apostolic deposit" is teachings about Christ, and hence Christ becomes the "canon within the canon."[1]

Marshall's first principle of biblical interpretation is the principle we reference here. It is accepted by the vast majority of biblical scholars. For the sake of clarity, let's go over it again: The Old Testament is always to be interpreted in the light of the New Testament and never the reverse. The New Testament is the doorway into the Old. This means we do not begin with Isaiah 53; instead we start with Matthew's quotation from Isaiah 53. The reason is simple. Matthew gives the divine interpretation of the text of Isaiah 53 in the Old Testament. This is the only way that you are going to find out what Isaiah 53 means to the church. We know that when the Jews read Isaiah 53, their understanding of who or what the Messiah would be was very different from a Christian knowledge of this passage. I use the word *knowledge* to describe what Christians know. Christians are able to see the fulfillment of Isaiah's prophecy, a prophecy those in the Old Testament could not yet understand.

In the New Testament, Matthew declared what Christ had accomplished on the cross and correctly interpreted what Isaiah's prophecy was all about. This is a classic example of the New Testament interpreting the Old Testament. Matthew was a tax collector, a mathematician, and His entire book reflects the fact that he was a bug on details. If you doubt that, I suggest you get a commentary on Matthew and read it through. He had a mind like a steel trap. He was a member of "Caesar's Infernal Revenue." Being a tax collector, he was despised by everyone. If you ever want to meet a nitpicker down to the last dot, make friends with a tax auditor or an IRS agent. They are programmed to find it all.

Matthew wrote that way; he was extremely precise. Therefore, his choice of words under the inspiration of the Holy Spirit must also be considered divinely exact. Once we understand what Matthew really says about Isaiah 53, we should be able to deal with false teachers who are forever jerking this text out of its context.

A helpful place for us to begin is Matthew 8:

> *Then Jesus said to the centurion, "Go! Let it be done just as you believed it would." And his servant was healed at that moment. (Matthew 8:13)*

Pretty amazing! This is an example of divine healing. Jesus doesn't even touch the servant! He just speaks the Word, and the centurion's servant is healed! It's noteworthy that there was no anointing with oil, confessing of sin, or praying in faith. There was faith expressed on the part of the centurion, but the healing happened when Jesus spoke the word. Make no mistake: The Bible teaches divine healing. The Bible sometimes teaches it is in response to faith, but sometimes there isn't any faith. Sometimes God refuses to heal, and there are various reasons why. We will come to some of those reasons a bit later.

For now, this is the critical text that is continuously belabored. Do you see what Matthew wrote and what he means, so that you don't get yourself pulled out of proper order in your thinking?

Look carefully at verses 14 and 15.

> *When Jesus came into Peter's house, he saw Peter's mother-in-law lying in bed with a fever. He touched her hand and the fever left her, and she got up and began to wait on him. (Matthew 8:14-15)*

Here there is no indication of any faith whatsoever being exercised by Jesus at all. He came in, she had a fever, was sick, He touched her, and she became well.

Verse 16 is also noteworthy:

When evening came, many who were demon-possessed were bought to him, and he drove out the spirits with a word and healed all the sick. (Matthew 8:16)

This is divine healing in its perfection. The unique person who has the power to heal all the people all the time is Jesus. This is not to say others never exercised the gift of healing when praying for the sick. This is merely to make the point that Jesus had a 100 percent batting average when it came to healing folk, which was not the history of His apostles then or His followers at any time.

The apostle Paul prayed for Epaphroditus who was sick to death, and he left him at Troas for three months because God said no. Three months later God said yes and healed him.

Paul had a thorn in the flesh. Call it a demonic attack, call it whatever you want, it had physical ramifications, a thorn he carried. As far as we are able to determine, he had it to the end of his life. Three times Paul asked God to take it away because it was an affliction. In 2 Corinthians 12, three times God said,

"My grace is sufficient for you, for my power is made perfect in weakness." (2 Corinthians 12:9)

As far as the record goes, Paul was never healed.

Matthew 8:17

Now, let's return to this very intriguing passage in Matthew 8:

> *This was to fulfill what was spoken through the prophet Isaiah: "He took up our infirmities and bore our diseases." (Matthew 8:17)*

Let's focus on the word *bore*. It is the key to understanding Matthew's interpretation of Isaiah 53. Teachers that insist this passage teaches that Jesus, on the cross, vicariously *guaranteed* not only your salvation, but also provided complete healing for all your physical diseases, often quote this passage. They believe this text proves their position. I do not agree. It is not difficult to understand the error of their interpretation or the reason why they embrace it.

When they teach that Christ provides forgiveness and salvation through His death and resurrection, they are 100 percent correct, but when they teach that healing is *guaranteed* as a result of Christ's death on the cross, they are wrong. The key word is *guarantee*. God *provides* physical healing but does not *guarantee* it in every case. There is a substantial body of biblical scholars and knowledgeable writers of many commentaries that explain that Christ, through His death and resurrection, *ensures* salvation and *provides* healing. There are two questions I will endeavor to answer: First, what does Matthew say, and second, who are we to believe? My response to these questions rely on an understanding of Koine Greek, the language most used in the writing of the New Testament and Hebrew, the primary language of the Old Testament.[2]

I have already stated that I believe teachers who teach that physical healing is *guaranteed* in the here and now because of what Christ accomplished on the cross are teaching in error. The reality of their faith in Christ is not in question, but their theories are. Theories are dangerous because ideas have consequences. If these theories cause people to believe something that doesn't work when tested, the believer can become disappointed or depressed, and feel as though something has happened to interfere with their relationship with the Lord. For many, this creates an enormous guilt trip.

I know people who were not healed physically and were told they were not healed because of their lack of faith! Instead of driving a stake into the heart of the sick person, we should take a hard look at the teacher and their teaching. If a teaching *guarantees* physical healing through Christ's atonement because Isaiah 53 says so, it is wrong. It is also cruel because there are a myriad of Christian people suffering in the world today. I cannot imagine anything more brutal than to tell a person who has genuine faith in Christ that he wasn't healed because his faith was weak (worse, absent). The real problem is the teacher who is misinterpreting the Bible.

Actually, it is beyond cruel to tell people they have secret sins, and that's why they have not been healed. How do they know that? On what authority do they base such a judgment? Who made them God for that person? Who gave them the qualifications of the Holy Spirit to pronounce with such assurance and dogmatism that somebody else's disease is the result of sin on their part?

When it comes to judging the sin in another's life, the apostle Paul wrote:

> *You, then, who teach others, do you not teach yourself? (Romans 2:21a)*

Jesus also has a word we should consider and follow when He speaks in Matthew 7:

> *"How can you say to your brother, 'Let me take the speck out of your eye,' when all the time there is a plank in your own eye?" (Matthew 7:4)*

I believe in divine healing, and God knows that. For a variety of reasons, I am convinced that James 5 is still valid for today. When we see a person miraculously healed, we know it is by the hand of God. I have nothing to do with it other than to obediently pray for the sick.

There are times when I pray for someone, and I am impressed to the point of knowing God is going to heal them, but there are other times that I touch them and sense He will not. However, I do not presume to say that I understand how divine healing works. I can only tell you what it is not. I can also speak affirmatively about it from God's Word. Understanding how divine healing works and what it is are two different things, but there is much we just don't understand. We should leave those areas to the Holy Spirit.

As we consider our part in ministry to those who are sick, how should we respond?

- We should pray for the sick.

- We should pray to believe.

- We should encourage the faith of others.

- We should confess our sin.

- We should study the testimonies of Scripture and see what God has said and done.

- We should help people trust Christ for healing, but we should not humiliate or cause them to feel guilty if they are not healed.

- We should not relegate them to second-class Christian citizenship just because they don't have the same experience we may have had.

There is a better way.

- We are to love each other.

- We are to care for one another.

- We are to build each other up in the faith.

To summarize what we have learned from 1 Peter 2:23-25 and Matthew 8:17 as it relates to what Christ accomplished on the cross, physical healing is provided but not guaranteed; while healing for our souls is provided *and guaranteed*. Not only do we see that in these two passages but in many other New Testament passages as well. Nowhere does God say that because you were born again, He was bound to heal you anytime you asked Him. The benefit is there, but the guarantee is missing. When physical healing is made the key to this passage and a teacher tries to make that stick on our theological walls, it won't.

We have looked at the original language, in this case, the Greek, which sums up very well what we have learned in the New Testament, but the question remains, what about the Hebrew of Isaiah 53? While the New Testament was written in Greek, the Old Testament was written predominantly in Hebrew and Aramaic. To carefully understand the meaning of Isaiah 53, it would seem reasonable to see if we might discover something from the original language Isaiah was written in.

Esteemed Old Testament Scholars: Keil and Delitzsch

Now I can imagine that when you see the words "scholars" and the names "Keil" and "Delitzsch," you may be thinking, I prefer the stuff about flying hang gliders in the high Sierras rather than these boys. Yet, this is one of those times when we need to return to a safe landing spot to find our bearings.

I hold in my hand perhaps the single most significant commentary on the Old Testament ever written. It's by these German guys: Carl Friedrich Keil, a nineteenth century German theologian, and Franz Delitzsch, a converted Jew who became a vigorous Christian scholar. This is not a lightweight scholarly work. This four-volume commentary spans the entire Old Testament and goes over every single word, taking into account all the rabbinical commentaries and the Talmud, as well as all the essential writings on the subject of Old Testament word studies. This is not to suggest their work is infallible, but I can say they were light years ahead of whatever was in second place. Not only do they still have other scholars backing them up, but very few take issue with them today, and that includes the Jewish scholars. Since the vast majority of pedigreed scholarship accept their work as authoritative, what they have to say about Isaiah 53 should be of interest to any serious student of God's Word today.

What do Keil and Delitzsch say about Isaiah 53:4?

> *The meaning is not merely that the Servant of God entered into the fellowship of our suffering, but that He took upon Himself the sufferings which we had to bear and deserved to bear and therefore not only took them away (as Matthew 8:17 might make it appear), but bore them in His own person, that He might deliver us from them.*[3]

Many stop quoting there. They say, "See, according to these scholars Matthew 8:17 agrees with Isaiah 53." They never continue reading, and they should. It continues:

> *But when one person takes upon himself suffering which another would have had to bear, and therefore not only endures it with him, but in his stead, this is called substitution or representation—an idea which, however unintelligible to the understanding, belongs to the actual substance of the common consciousness of man, and the realities of the divine government of the world has brought within the range of our experience, and one which has continued even down to the*

present time to have much greater vigor in the Jewish nation, where it has found its true expression in sacrifice and the kindred institutions, than in any other.[4]

Keil and Delitzsch go on to quote Leviticus to make the point, saying that these verses define the word translated as *bore* as "to carry as one's own, to look at, to feel like one owned the agonizing, the unity with the person." This would seem to be rather clear. The idea here is identification. On the cross, Jesus took our *sins* vicariously.

The greatest Old Testament commentators agree that Isaiah 53 is vicarious, and that Matthew makes his point when he emphasized the idea of identification. It seems clear that Jesus did not provide a guarantee for our physical healing through His atonement on the cross. The weight of New Testament scholarship is against that interpretation of 1 Peter too. That position just doesn't work. Again, Keil and Delitszch have this to say about Isaiah 53:5 which states that "with his stripes we were healed":

The justice of God, this satisfaction procured by His holiness, had His love for its foundation and end. It was our peace, or, what is more in accordance with the full idea of the word, our general well-being, our blessedness, which these sufferings arrived at and secured. In what follows, "and by His stripes we have been healed," shâlōm is defined as a condition of salvation brought about by healing.

This refers to a healing of the soul, a condition which mankind could not remedy. We needed God to step down and rescue us from this deadly situation which would have killed each and every one of us for all of eternity. Jesus did that.

A person can claim God guarantees to heal because of the atonement, but it will be a claim in vain. God is never bound by people's incorrect interpretations of what He has said. He always acts according to His will, not our misunderstandings of His will.

God has promised a continuing ministry of the Holy Spirit to the church. That began on the Day of Pentecost and will continue throughout the church age. The gifts and the call of God can never be revoked; therefore, they are with us until the kingdom of God arrives in its fullness in the second advent of Jesus Christ.

With that thought in mind, what is a Christian to do when sick? James 5 provides explicit instruction.

> *Is anyone among you sick? Let them call the elders of the church to pray over them and anoint them with oil in the name of the Lord. And the prayer offered in faith will make the sick person well; the Lord will raise them up. If they have sinned, they will be forgiven. There- fore, confess your sins to each other and pray for each other so that you may be healed. The prayer of a righteous person is powerful and effective. (James 5:14-16)*

James's instruction is clearly conditioned by Christ's own teaching that whatever we ask of the Father in Christ's name will be given *if it is the will of the Father*. The Scriptures are clear in explaining why we often do not receive what we pray for. James continues to be our teacher in chapter 4:3, when he says,

> *When you ask, you do not receive, because you ask with wrong mo- tives, that you may spend what you get on your pleasures. (James 4:3)*

What is it that God wants us to understand? He wants us to hear this from Him: "*Yes*, I'm in the healing business. I have never closed the shop. The door is always open, and I love to hear from My children. When it agrees with the purpose best designed for their lives, I heal them. Sometimes I delay that healing, and sometimes I don't give it at all." (*the Dan Myers Version*)

The final decision rests with the Lord. You cannot compel Him with your understanding and faith to do what you want Him to do *if it is not His will*. That would not be an expression of faith since the evidence of what you hoped for would be non-existent. The Bible says in Hebrews 11:

> *Now faith is the substance of things hoped for, the evidence of things not seen. (Hebrews 11:1, KJV)*

Nowhere does it say in the Scripture that it is the will of God for everybody to be healed all the time every time.

In the first chapter, I spoke of our daughter's accident. She was not expected to live through the night and see the next sunrise, but she did and lived significantly disabled for the next thirty-one years. No matter how aggressively we prayed and expressed our faith, even joining many friends around the world praying for her, she was never healed. If we had listened to Job's friends, our faith would have been destroyed.

One might say her life after the accident provided the incentive for this book. I needed to discover what God said about life and not what others were saying who had never lived through such a trial. Living through such an experience is not a requisite for understanding the truth of God's Word, but it is a help.

The challenges of life demanded that I understand God's Word. Realizing it was not God's will for everyone to be healed in every situation, what then should my response be? Consider my list of three Christian answers:

First, we should be continuously positive, knocking on the door of our heavenly Father.

Second, we should believe that the Holy Spirit will confirm the message with signs and wonders in our own day.

Third, we should engage in teaching people how to strengthen their faith through the disciplined study of God's Word. This will enable believers to call on Him with confidence and trust, causing them to be willing to take from Him *whatever He gives.*

People that are forever talking about disease as a great evil have forgotten that it is through suffering and diseases that often God wins people to Christ who would not be won in any other way. There are times when God permits some to suffer for His own glory. You may be asking, "How can that be?" In John 9, there is an interesting exchange between the disciples and Jesus. In these verses, the disciples asked Him,

> *"Rabbi, who sinned, this man or his parents, that he was born blind?"*

> *"Neither this man nor his parents sinned," said Jesus, "but this happened so that the works of God might be displayed in him." (John 9:2-3)*

We all know people who have suffered terribly. Faith has nothing to do with their plight. Their suffering in Christ has been a testimony to others who have marveled in what Christ could do and have come to Him because they were overwhelmed by the grace that could make it possible for a person to suffer or die. When Jim Elliott and his fellow missionaries were massacred by the Auca Indians, the world was appalled by such a barbaric act. However, those very men who killed Jim's missionary group came to know the Lord, partly because of that horrendous act, and partly because members in Elliott's original group returned years later to demonstrate the love of Christ.

Don't ever tell a cancer victim, a Christian, dying in a hospital that he should and could get up out of that bed and walk out of the hospital if he only had enough faith. None of us are God. We must never be presumptuous in instructing the Lord. He is Lord, and He alone makes the decisions. As His children, we are to trust Him and move forward by faith that His knowledge is perfect, leaving the outcome to Him.

There is a final thought I leave with you as you seek to discover the truth as it relates to divine healing. It will help you understand the possible consequences when we demand something from God that may not be His perfect will.

King Hezekiah is portrayed in the Bible as a great and good king. When he came to the end of his life, he asked God for fifteen more years. It was not God's perfect will; however, he granted the king's request. During his extended life, he had a son named Manasseh who destroyed every single thing the king had accomplished. Manasseh also lost the treasures of the house of God and brought all the Jews into captivity. If King Hezekiah had been willing to die for the glory of God, Manasseh would never have been born.

Instead King Hezekiah said to God, "I want to live, I have been a good king."

God answered, "I will make you an object lesson for the whole world." Note the lesson here and learn from the wisdom of God. Hezekiah should have submitted to the will of God, but he didn't. Hezekiah learned the lesson, but only after he insisted on his will rather than submitting to the will of God.

Hezekiah finally said, "Better I should have died, so it shouldn't have been a total loss."[5]

So, let's look at divine healing as a beautiful gift, something the Christian may receive and experience. Let's look at it in faith, believing God, and then let's claim and accept whatever God by His Holy Spirit informs us is His will so we are in agreement with His Word and will.

On the other hand, let's not be presumptuous in claiming and demanding something from God that He has never promised.

Above all, please bury the false interpretation of Matthew 8:17 that tells you that Jesus took your diseases in His body. In truth, the context and meaning of the actual language do not support that rendering. Anyone pressing that interpretation is demonstrating a misunderstanding of the New Testament Greek, and especially the theology of the Gospel of Matthew.

If the atonement included physical healing for all Christians in every circumstance, we'd never die. The fact that all Christians aren't healed, and die of sicknesses and diseases just like everyone else, should tell us something. And please don't trot out the old "they don't have enough faith" card because that's pure theological nonsense.

CHAPTER 6

KNOWING GOD

*All my knowledge of Him depends on his sustained
initiative in knowing me.*

—J.I. Packer

How Am I to Understand God?

I was not able to forget my friend and son in the ministry, one of the two who visited my office many years before. The death of a well-meaning and godly man was painful to process. Even though he had explicitly rejected my leadership, he had to follow what he believed was God's will for his life.

At the time of his death, I had no sense of vindication. Who cares about being "right" when a friend has died? I felt more like the shepherd who found all the sheep safely protected except one. Jesus searched for His lamb and brought him back; I felt as though I had failed. However, I knew the Good Shepherd had done for me what I could not accomplish when He received my friend to a place where there was no more heartache, sickness, or death. This brother who had prayed so faithfully had preceded our daughter in death. In 2009, she joined him in God's presence. One day soon, I too will be added to the grand celebration.

The Final and Absolute Test

When pastors face a severe challenge to their teaching, they respond in a variety of ways. Some dig in their heels and claim they speak without error for God, while others are forced to an even deeper study of God's Word to find the truth. I chose the latter. The following are the results of my research and what I believe God's Word teaches.

Teachers of Confusion and Error

I had been a lead pastor in two churches for twenty years, and I realized I had not done a thorough study of God's Word about faith, prosperity, and healing. There was a need to be clear in my own understanding, but the greater need was evidenced in the congregation. The people of The King's Place were being pulled in different directions by teachers who articulated their positions well. They knew what I had taught among them for more than ten years, but some were impressed and, frankly, excited by these new teachings on faith, prosperity, and healing that they heard at seminars or on TV.

As you might expect, my task was enormous and consumed the next year of my life and ministry. In the beginning I prayed for two things: first, that God would enable me to speak the truth lovingly, and second, that hearts might be softened to receive God's Word as I sought to make it clear. Before going back to the classroom, let me share the story of one of the great theologians from the early years of Christianity. While the story is apocryphal, it makes the point that some mysteries of God were both difficult to understand and explain even for one of the early great Church Fathers.

Saint Augustine and the Little Boy at the Beach

Saint Augustine was walking on the beach one day, contemplating the mystery of the Holy Trinity when he saw a little boy running back and forth from the water to a spot on the seashore. The boy was using a shell to carry water from the vast ocean, pouring it into a small pit that he had dug in the sand.

"What are you doing?" Saint Augustine asked.

"I am going to pour all the sea into the hole I have dug," the boy replied.

"What?" said Augustine, "That is impossible, my dear child. The sea is so great, and the shell and the hole are so little."

"That is true," the boy said. "It would be easier and quicker to draw all the water out of the sea and fit it into this hole than for you to fit the mystery of the Trinity and His divinity into your little intellect, for the mystery of the Trinity is greater and larger in comparison with your intelligence than is this vast ocean in comparison with this little hole."

And then the child vanished.

Because of this story, the seashell has become a symbol of Saint Augustine and the study of theology. The account above is based on the story found in the "Golden Legend" written in AD 1275 by Jacobus de Voragine, Archbishop of Genoa.[1]

Saint Augustine of Hippo spent over thirty years working on his treatise *De Trinitate* ("About the Holy Trinity"). His goal was to produce an intelligent explanation for the mystery of the Trinity. In Saint Augustine's *De Trinitate*, he provides one of the most careful presentations of this Christian doctrine. His source is the Bible, and his exegesis (or explanation) of the Scriptures is impeccable.

Saint Augustine's struggle for clarity related to the doctrine of the Trinity. We too continue to have many different opinions about other core values and teachings of the Christian faith. However, for teachers today, we would do well to follow the example of St. Augustine in our pursuit of understanding truth, and dig deep and study long.

Let's consider the question of healing alone: we pray with faith, confess our sin, and then pray that God will heal. More often than not we don't see the healing for which we prayed. That usually sets off a massive campaign to help God out by providing all kinds of explanations for the unsuccessful attempt to crack these mysteries. This effort to find the answers we seek may be just as elusive as Saint Augustine's search for the explanation of the Trinity. I suspect that we feel like the little boy who dug his small hole and attempted to empty the ocean into it too. It doesn't take a great intellect to understand that this would be impossible for a boy (or a saint)! But we still try.

The Problem Stated

Today, perhaps more so than ever, there are gifted and articulate teachers who have majored on the subjects of *faith, prosperity*, and *healing*. Their teaching often marches under the banner "Word of Faith."

They teach that when the Son of God died on the cross, His sacrifice provided both salvation as a gift of God, and also, the guaranteed freedom from *all* diseases. Along with these two significant benefits, they also believe Christians have assured prosperity as well, as long as those Christians have the right kind of faith (whatever that may be). They manipulate passages such as 1 Peter 2:23-24, Galatians 3:13, Matthew 8:17, and Deuteronomy 21 and 28 in support of their position and teaching. Not surprisingly their prosperity teaching has not gained popularity in Third World countries.

For the record, let me be clear of what I believe is the truth:

- I believe in *biblical* faith,

- I believe that God is pleased to prosper *some* Christians according to His will, and

- I believe healing is available, but not *guaranteed*, because of the cross. This means we *ask*—but do not *demand*—healing from God.

In previous chapters, we have examined passages of Scripture that provide understanding and teaching related to divine healing. For the rest of this chapter, we will turn our attention to teachers and the test of Scripture.

We will discover that what men say, no matter how clever or exciting, is to be rejected if it contradicts the Word of God.

What men say, no matter how clever or exciting, is to be rejected if it contradicts the Word of God.

God's Warning to Teachers

God allows a great deal of freedom even among those who teach. He also allows us to be wrong. When our teaching begins to create fear or destroy faith within the body of Christ, then we will answer to God alone.

Not many of you should become teachers, because, you know that we who teach will be judged more strictly. (James 3:1)

James is making the point that to desire this gift of the Holy Spirit is to take on an enormous responsibility. Let me endeavor to remove some of that responsibility by saying that we should put everything to the test—everything spoken or written by me or any other teacher and allow the Scriptures to be the final test.

Satan Is Real

Most writers understand Satan does not sell books unless he's written as a fictional character. Many Christian writers realize the biggest sellers will be about God's love, hope, and joyful living. There can never be too many of those. By comparison, there are few books written about God's sovereignty, holiness, judgment, justice, and commandments. These have a lesser appeal with the general public.

Is there something wrong with writing and preaching about God's love, hope, peace, and joyful living? No, of course not, but perhaps another way to get to my point is to ask a different question. Is there a danger to only studying these happier subjects? If we only read and hear about God's love and never about His sovereignty, justice, and the fact that He is all-knowing, we will never understand how deplorable our sin is and how great His love is in comparison. Without realizing what God did on the cross, it would be impossible to ever understand the breadth and depth of His love.

Since God, by His nature, is both sovereign and holy, it is impossible for Him to allow man with his sinful nature to stand before Him. The very nature of God required a way for sin to be atoned for and forgiven. The question has nothing to do with God's love. God proved His love by providing His solution without any cost to us. The problem is the sin of man. The holiness and perfection of God, when confronted by man with his sin, is like trying to mix water and oil. Yet, while the problem is enormous, God's solution was perfectly completed by Christ when He died sacrificially on a cross, and then came back to proclaim what He had accomplished.

What Christ provided while on that barbaric cross was the forgiveness of sin; and since sin carried with it the eternal penalty of death, a fearful monster, death was forever destroyed. But that's not all.

The good news is that man is now able to stand before a holy God, forgiven, to take his place within the family of God *forever*. Through the cross, God provided what His sovereignty, perfection, and holiness required: the justice that only Christ could provide through His sacrifice on the cross. It took the perfection of Christ to satisfy the internal structure of God's requirement for the forgiveness of our sin. Today He still stands ready to forgive us from our rebellion and sin.

And so, on that day of crucifixion, evil men thought they had won the victory. What they didn't know or understand was that it was God's most significant of all victories. On that day, God destroyed death and provided forgiveness and life. On that day, Christ spoke for the ages, when He said:

"It is finished." (John 19:30)

For the first time in history, man had free access to the Father through His Spirit.

Not only did God meet the demand for His own justice, but that act also became translated into the most significant gift known to man. We call that the gift of salvation. Only God could give it, and only man can receive it when he lifts both head and heart to receive God's gift. Without man's response to God's gift, the cross would have been without any purpose. Without God meeting His own requirements and demands necessary to meet His justice, we would never know and experience His love.

What response must man make? Perhaps we can understand it better with a simple illustration. When a person desires to open a safe deposit box, it is necessary to do so in the company of a bank employee. Apparently, there is something in that box the patron wants. While the patron has his personal key, the bank employee has another key. Both keys must be used to open the box. Even though the bank employee is willing to provide his key, the patron must make his request to open the box and prove his intention by inserting his key. Receiving salvation is a bit like that. God has provided His side of the solution, but as a seeker, we alone have the key that will complete the transaction. It is this very willingness that the apostle John addressed when he said,

Yet to all who did receive him, to those who believed in his name, he gave the right to become children of God. (John 1:12)

To demonstrate the need for man to initiate a desire for God's forgiveness, the same writer makes clear that salvation is not global, but requires an individual response expressing both confessions of sin and desire for salvation.

> *If we confess our sins, he is faithful and just and will forgive us our sins and purify us from all unrighteousness. (1 John 1:9)*

While it is necessary to speak of God's love and hope, we need to balance that message with God's sovereignty and justice. To emphasize one part of His nature at the expense of what may seem uncomfortable is to deny the totality of God's character. In the final analysis, God is sovereign and unchangeable. He will never change, no matter what direction our perceived notions may take us. If we are repelled by some aspects of God's justice, our ideas about that will never change His righteousness in any way. We need to change for God, not the other way around.

You have heard some say, "I believe in the Golden Rule: to treat others as I want to be treated." These people may do good things, but this idea denotes a complete ignorance of their own sinful nature and what God has done about it. In truth, to rely on the Golden Rule as a basis for our salvation is to believe one of Satan's lies, a lie that sounds noble, but is not. Our actions cannot save us. People who live thus often believe that God is pleased with their stance. That is true. God will always be pleased with our loving acts to others, *but that is not the criteria by which our sins are forgiven.* And sin is the issue. When Paul wrote to young Timothy in 1 Timothy 2, he said:

> *For there is one God and one mediator between God and mankind, the man Christ Jesus, who gave himself as a ransom for all people. (1 Timothy 2:5-6a)*

Many are repelled by the fact that God says that people cannot get to Him in any other way than through His Son. We may not like that, but it's God's plan, and He isn't about to change it to another method just to suit any of us. His plan was flawlessly performed through the cross. He has closed discussion on the method. We don't do things to earn God's forgiveness, we do good things as an expression of our new life in Christ.

In the minds of many, Satan is an uncomfortable topic. Many even suggest that he is a figment of the imagination. The denial of Satan's existence is one effort to replace what God says about this creature. Conservative Christians are much more confident in the wisdom and truth of Scripture when compared to the understanding of men. In 1 Peter, we read,

> *Be alert and of sober mind. Your enemy, the devil prowls around like a roaring lion looking for someone to devour. (1 Peter 5:8)*

When Paul wrote in 2 Corinthians, he warned them,

> *The god of this age has blinded the minds of unbelievers, so that they cannot see the light of the gospel that displays the glory of Christ, who is the image of God. (2 Corinthians 4:4)*

"The god of this age" is an explicit reference to the devil, God's archenemy. Paul is teaching the Corinthians that the devil is an unseen power behind all unbelief, death, and anything that opposes God. There are hundreds of references to Satan and the devil in the Bible. That being the case, it would seem reasonable for men to recognize that he exists and see his influence in the world. We see his influence even in governments and wars. Hitler was a very bright person, yet, like many, he became controlled by a power that was beyond him. Believe me, Hitler did not sit around with his generals, singing "Kumbaya" and from that, develope plans for the Holocaust. Are we not able to see the influence and activity of Satan in the massacres of Christians and others by radical Islamist to-day? What about the beheadings of the Christians by ISIL after they refuse to abandon their faith and convert to Islam? Can we not see the influence and carnage of Satan in our own country with the mass shootings that are occurring so regularly that we hardly take notice? Sadly, there have been atrocities by professed Christians too. The point is that Satan is alive and well, but he no longer has the power to control the destiny of men when they respond to God's love and grace through His gift in Christ.

Why all this talk about Satan? Whenever God speaks truth through His Word, you can be sure that Satan will rise up with a counterfeit that opposes God's truth. Satan did it in the garden when he promised man that if he ate of the fruit, he would become like God. How did that work out?

Satan is a master at speaking the truth and mixing it with a lie to create his traps. When Satan was tempting Christ in the wilderness (Matthew 4:1-11), that temptation came after Jesus had been fasting forty days and forty nights. When Satan spoke, it was mockingly,

> *"If you are the Son of God, tell these stones to become bread."*
> *(Matthew 4:3)*

Satan must have thought, He's *vulnerable because of hunger and thirst. This is a good time.* But to be tempted does not equate with sin. To "tempt" is to try to get someone to do wrong. So, to "be tempted" means someone is trying to get you to do something wrong. Satan failed, even though he spoke the truth about Christ. Jesus met the challenge of Satan's temptation. Consequently, He was able to make His journey to the cross sinless, the perfect sacrifice to satisfy the just demands of God's perfection and holiness.

On the other hand, we must be careful to avoid the mistake of believing that every difference of opinion is caused by Satan, or that every negative thing that happens in life is the result of the evil one. Much of what happens to us is due to our own ignorance, and sometimes our own disobedience. Once we understand this, the reasonable person will look for an authority that is above himself, and I submit that to be the Word of God. The Bible gives us God's blueprint for living, and at the same time warns us against the deception of Satan.

The deception of Satan and Satan's broadside against the church is expressed in many forms. Many believe it is a fact that Satan accomplishes his greatest work through the church and that highly esteemed Christian teachers are often in error. This brings us back to the main point. When we hear what appears to be false teaching, how do we determine whether or not what is taught is in error compared to the truth? God in His wisdom has provided us with the answer.

The Test of Scripture

If you have something that is bothering you as a Christian, something about doctrine or teaching that affects your life, something that is confusing, what test should you use to test it? Along with the biblical blueprint, one must also pray for the guidance of the Holy Spirit.

The apostle Peter instructs us in his first letter to see what the Holy Spirit has said, not what some "faith healer" or influential person doing deliverance ministry, speaking from his experience.

If you allow your life to be controlled by your experience on spiritual matters, rather than a mature understanding of God's Word, you will never learn the truth. Instead, you will end up more and more confused.

After our daughter's accident, we read every book we could find written by Christian parents of children who had similar brain injuries. Some were exciting and even entertaining to read, and often ended well. When the healing didn't happen for our daughter, our friends, who had placed their trust in false teachers were devastated, which brings us back to the question: What should we do and to whom should we turn?

When Paul wrote Timothy, he instructed him thus:

> *Do your best to present yourself to God as one approved, a worker who has no need to be ashamed, rightly handling the word of truth. (2 Timothy 2:15, ESV)*

Clearly a casual reading of God's Word is not sufficient. Why must we be so serious about studying the Bible? The following ten thoughts provide a clear blueprint from God's Word that answer that question. The names following each point identify the writer.

* Because God Wrote It! 2 Timothy 3:16 (Paul)

> *All Scripture is God-breathed and is useful for teaching, rebuking, correcting and training in righteousness. (2 Timothy 3:16)*

Also, Jesus spoke only those things the Father had given Him. See John 1:50; 5:19; 8:26-28, and 14:10.

* David prophesied through the Holy Spirit according to Acts 1 (Luke)

> *Brothers and sisters, the Scripture had to be fulfilled in which the Holy Spirit spoke long ago through David concerning Judas, who served as a guide for those who arrested Jesus. (Acts 1:16)*

And Peter wrote:

> *For prophecy never had its origin in the human will, but prophets,*

though human, spoke from God as they were carried along by the Holy Spirit. (2 Peter 1:21)

Without question, God spoke through Paul's writings:

God spoke to our forefathers by the prophets. (Hebrews 1:1, ESV)

Scripture can be verified by other Scriptures, which means it can be understood as though God had picked up a pen and written it Himself.

- To Obtain Hope: Romans 15:4 (Paul)

For everything that was written in the past was written to teach us, so that through the endurance taught in Scriptures and the encouragement they provide we might have hope. (Romans 15:4)

Undoubtedly, we cannot be recovered without hope, for Paul also wrote:

We are saved by hope. (Romans 8:24, KJV)

One way that faith comes is through the patient study of the Scriptures (Romans 15:4), so how can we mentally confirm our salvation if we don't study the Word of God?

- To Avoid Deception: Mark 13:5 (Mark) and Colossians 2:8 (Paul)

Jesus said to them, "Watch out that no one deceives you." (Mark 13:5)

See to it that no one takes you captive through hollow and deceptive philosophy, which depends on human tradition and the elemental spiritual forces of this world rather than on Christ. (Colossians 2:8)

There are many warnings in the Word of God to guard us against deception, and it is clear from Scripture that if we fail to recognize error and follow false teachers, we can indeed lose our way or be led astray.

- To Obtain Faith: Romans 10:17 (Paul)

So, faith comes from what is heard, and what is heard comes through the message about Christ. (Romans 10:17, HCSB)

Studying the Word of God is not the only requirement for increasing our faith, but it is the first essential step.

- To Obtain Answers to Prayer: Proverbs 28:9 (Solomon) and John 15:7 (John)

If anyone turns a deaf ear to my instruction, even their prayers are detestable. (Proverbs 28:9)

"If you remain in me and my words remain in you, ask whatever you wish, and it will be done for you." (John 15:7)

Obtaining answers to prayer are vital as this gives us an assurance of the reality and presence of God in our lives. One of the conditions to obtaining answers is that the words of Jesus abide in us (John15:7). This will not happen unless we absorb them through a disciplined study of the Bible.

- To Please God: Hebrews 11:6 (Paul)

And without faith it is impossible to please God, because anyone who comes to him must believe that he exists and that he rewards those who earnestly seek him. (Hebrews 11:6)

We know that:

Faith comes by hearing, and hearing by the word of God. (Romans

10:17, NKJV)

If we don't have faith when hearing the Word of God, our initial excitement will die out; and since we cannot please God without faith, how can we please Him without studying the Word of God?

- To Show Ourselves Approved to God: 2 Timothy 2:15 (Paul)

    Be diligent to present yourself approved to God, a worker who does not need to be ashamed, rightly dividing the word of truth. (2 Timothy 2:15, NKJV)

The Greek adjective *dokimos* is translated "approved" meaning to be proved, or tried, just like metals are purified by fire. The same Greek word is used by James when he writes:

    For when he has stood the test, he will receive the crown of life. (James 1:12, ESV)

This shows that if we are approved or tested, we will be saved.

- To Obtain the Knowledge of God: Hosea 6:6 (Hosea) and Proverbs 2:1-6 (Solomon)

    For I desire mercy, not sacrifice, and acknowledgment (knowledge) of God rather than burnt offerings. (Hosea 6:6, addition mine)

    My son, if you will accept my words and store up my commands within you, turning your ear to wisdom and applying your heart to understanding—indeed, if you call out for insight (knowledge) and cry aloud for understanding, and if you look for it as for silver and search for it as for hidden treasure, then you will understand the fear of the Lord and find the knowledge of God. For the Lord gives wisdom; and from his mouth come knowledge and understanding. (Proverbs 2:1-6, additions mine)

However, as it is written: "What no eye has seen, what no ear has heard, and what no human mind has conceived"—the things God has prepared for those who love him—these are the things (all the knowledge of God) God has revealed to us by his Spirit (1 Corinthians 2:9-12, addition mine).

God wants us to receive this knowledge. Solomon made it clear that we need to diligently seek to obtain knowledge by studying God's Word in Proverbs 2:1-16. If we want to understand what Jesus taught, we need to study the Bible and learn about Him.

- To Understand God's Will for Our Lives: Romans 12:2 (Paul)

Do not conform to the pattern of this world, but be transformed by the renewing of your mind. Then you will be able to test and approve what God's will is—His good, pleasing and perfect will. (Romans 12:2)

God's will is revealed through God's Word through a process the Bible calls "the renewing of your mind." When we diligently study the Bible, we soon discover that it gives us a firm foundation, like an unmovable rock. This provides grounding, so we can grow with our spiritual feet firmly planted on God's Word. The Bible enables us to test whoever and whatever comes our way.

Furthermore, when we study God's Word, allowing it to saturate our whole being, we are inviting the Holy Spirit to guide us in our understanding. This understanding helps us discern the difference between credible and false teachers.

Scripture puts great emphasis on the Holy Spirit's ability to teach all of God's children. Here are a few passages that support that:

John 14:26: (Jesus)

"But the Helper, the Holy Spirit, whom the Father will send in My name, He will teach you all things, and bring to your remembrance all things that I said to you." (John 14:26, NKJV)

Matthew 10:19-20: (Jesus)

"But when they arrest you, do not worry about what to say or how to say it. At that time you will be given what to say, for it will not be you speaking, but the Spirit of your Father speaking through you." (Matthew 10:19-20)

It's encouraging to know that when you find yourself between a rock and a hard place, the Holy Spirit will give you words that cannot be resisted. In Luke 21, he writes,

"For I will give you words and wisdom that none of your adversaries will be able to resist or contradict." (Luke 21:15)

1 John 2:27: (John)

As for you, the anointing you received from him remains in you, and you do not need anyone to teach you. But as his anointing teaches you about all things and as that anointing is real, not counterfeit—just as it has taught you, remain in him. (1 John 2:27)

The Bible consistently advocates teaching, and John is not ruling out human teachers. The *NIV Study Bible* provides a helpful note in understanding this point: "At the time (John) wrote, however, Gnostic teachers were insisting that the teaching of the apostles was to be supplemented with the 'higher knowledge' that they (the Gnostics) claimed to possess. John's response was that what the readers were taught under the Spirit's ministry through the apostles was not only adequate but the only reliable truth…The teaching ministry of the Holy Spirit (what is commonly called illumination) does not involve revelation of new truth or the explanation of all difficult passages of Scripture to our satisfaction. Rather, it is the development of the capacity to appreciate and appropriate God's truth already revealed—making the Bible meaningful in thought and daily living. *All things*: All things necessary to know for salvation and Christian living."[2]

1 Corinthians 2:9-10: (Paul)

However, as it is written:

"What no eye has seen, what no ear has heard, and what no human mind has conceived"—the things God has prepared for those of us who love him—these are the things God has revealed to us by his Spirit. The Spirit searches all things, even the deep things of God. (1 Corinthians 2:9-10)

John Gill in his *Exposition of the Bible* wrote "God has made a revelation of them (*doctrines of the gospel*), not only in his word, which is common to men, nor only to his ministers, but to private Christians and believers, "*by his Spirit*"; which designs not the external revelation made in the Scripture, though that also is by the Spirit; but the internal revelation and application of the truths of the Gospel to the souls of men, which is sometimes ascribed to the Father of Christ. Matthew 16:17 sometimes to Christ himself, Galatians 1:12 and sometimes to the Spirit of Christ,

Ephesians 1:17 and who guides into all truth, John 16:13, and here to the Father by the Spirit"³ (parenthetical addition mine).

The Christian who finds it inconvenient to search and rely on the Word of God leaves himself defenseless to false teachers. They are unable to tell the difference between the wolves of destruction and the sheep of God's sheepfold. If a person can't tell the difference between fleece and fur, look out! He just became a prime candidate for doctrinal corruption.

I have no axe to grind. I have never engaged in public debate with others about faith, money, and healing, and I have no intention of doing so now. However, whenever something surfaces that is going to hurt the body of Christ, it is the responsibility of the under-shepherds in the church to speak and teach clearly from the Word of God.

God Doesn't Ordain Overnight Specialists

God doesn't set people in the church overnight just because they are called as evangelists or some other special ministry, or because they graduated from a quickie eight-week Bible course online. God doesn't raise people up quickly and make them the supreme teaching authority for the church. Many teachers of error have huge followings, personal assets that range in the millions, massive printing facilities, several homes, expensive automobiles and private jets that cost more than fifty million dollars. Of course, all of this is justified according to their interpretation of God's Word, by which God supplies their every desire. Their "prosperity gospel" has a tough curtain call in all Third World countries. I find it difficult to believe that the apostle Paul would collect money from the saints to buy the latest fast ship and then justify his purchase by suggesting how it significantly enhanced his ministry.

When Jesus moved about the countryside, it was never in anything comparable to Rome's finest chariots. No, He merely walked, and relied on the Holy Spirit entirely. When He rode into Jerusalem on what we call Palm Sunday today, He was mounted on a donkey, not a tremendously strong white stallion. When Jesus taught, He did not amass personal wealth. When Jesus taught, He merely spoke the truth.

All teachers should be tested by each other in the light of one thing—the Word of God. They are to be examined by the history of the church and her pronouncement on the great teachings of Scripture. People are to conform to Scripture, not the other way around. Scripture will never submit to the culture of any given time or generation.

In the church, there is no such thing as instant teaching authority. The Bible tells us never to lay hands on someone quickly to ordain them for ministry, nor exalt a novice. Every new candidate for ministry must serve in some kind of apprenticeship in which they can be observed, to be sure they meet the qualifications for their position as outlined in the Bible. Deacons and elders are described in 1 Timothy 3 and Titus 1. Both Moses and Paul had their time in the desert before they became useful to God in ministry. Most heresy and false teaching reported in the New Testament (and today) was the result of people who refused to be accountable to anyone other than themselves. These false teachers produced impaired Christians then and now. Any evangelical Christian organization unwilling to partner with the Evangelical Council for Financial Accountability should be suspect and unworthy of your support.

CHAPTER 7

HUMILITY

As long as you are proud you cannot know God. A proud man is always looking down on things and people: and of course, as long as you are looking down you cannot see something that is above you.

—C.S. Lewis

A Second Couple Visits My Office

On a Wednesday afternoon, two of my cherished friends came to see me. They said, "Pastor, we don't know exactly how far in debt you are from Renee's accident, but we suspect it's considerable. Bill and I have an idea that we think might help, but first, we want to ask you a question. Do you have any kind of investments?" I had to think hard before I remembered that several years earlier Dorene and I had made a forty-five-hundred-dollar investment in a limited partnership in an office building that was later exchanged for an apartment complex in Oklahoma. The current value of that investment was approximately twelve thousand. They asked me if we would be willing to sign that over to them. I thought to myself, *These are my friends*?

Smiling, Fred said, "Let me explain what we have in mind. We are building what will be the most beautiful apartment complex ever here in Lancaster. Together with our wives, we would like you and Dorene to become a one-third owner of those apartments."

That proved to be the best investment we ever made. Actually, it could be considered a gift rather than an investment. To this day I have not heard what happened to the Oklahoma apartments that we gave to our friends for apartments that were of a much higher value.

Eventually, we sold our interest in those quality apartments. Once the IRS was satisfied, we were able to pay every dollar of the nearly one hundred thousand dollars of medical bills from our daughter's accident. Additionally, we were able to complete that earlier stewardship commitment we had made only to the Lord and revealed to our consultant. It is difficult to comprehend how we could ever have satisfied that twenty-five thousand dollar commitment without the divine intervention of God through the kindness of our friends.

Before that experience, I never thought of myself as proud or humble. I just saw myself as an average guy trying do the right thing. Yet, the partnership with my friends was a humbling experience. It didn't happen because of my ability, and I felt a strong gratitude for their kindness. Frederick Buechner, an American Presbyterian minister and author, wrote something about humility that resonates with me:

> *Humility is often confused with the gentlemanly self-deprecation of saying you're not much of a bridge player when you know perfectly well you are. Conscious or otherwise, this kind of humility is a form of gamesmanship.*

> *If you really aren't much of a bridge player, you're apt to be rather proud of yourself for admitting it so humbly. This kind of humility is a form of low comedy. True humility doesn't consist of thinking ill of yourself but of not thinking of yourself much differently from the way you'd be apt to think of anybody else. It is the capacity for being no more and no less pleased when you play your own hand well than when your opponents do.[1]*

In my case, the hand I played was simply making the decision to accept the generous offer of my friends.

The name for our "Flying Like an Eagle" stewardship program was taken from Isaiah 40.

> *But those who hope in the Lord will renew their strength. They will soar on wings like eagles; they will run and not grow weary; they will walk and not be faint. (Isaiah 40:31)*

Isaiah, speaking hundreds of years before, was undoubtedly prophetic for our church family. Was there something in all of this for our personal family as well? Was this a different way for us to understand the "glory of the Lord"? At a time when we were asking God where He was in the solitude of our hearts, was this a different way for us to understand that He cared for us and He loved us, even though we didn't see the specific answer we wanted and had asked for? The skeptic will answer: "These questions are just the crazy crutches that prop up your insane explanations for why bad things happen to good people. You are just looking for an excuse for the silence of your God. You're just trying to help people cope with their repeated pleas for help, when the reality is that your God is absent (or non-existent) and you just don't want to deal with that!"

We preferred to see that Isaiah was right, and that God was enabling us to lift in flight from the shackles that had bound us to a barnyard of despair. Like our congregation, some of our family members were beginning to fly and soar again.

Through our people, God not only provided funds to save the tent, but He also provided some exceptionally gifted people. Steve Rumpf, our executive pastor, was one of many gifts to our church family during those challenging years. Through the gifts and energy of this man, the congregation was able to once again celebrate in The King's Place, where the King of kings and Lord of lords continues to reign.

One Door Closes, Another Opens

In 1986, after eighteen years serving as the lead pastor there, it was time to leave the people we loved, people who to this day remain in our hearts. Many have already transitioned from this life into the eternal presence of our Lord.

For several years the consultant who helped with our "Flying Like an Eagle" stewardship program had made regular visits with us, extending the invitation to join him and his business partner, Doug Laird. I eventually accepted that invitation, and for the next two years I worked with a very competent group of men who were committed to helping churches discover the biblical principles of stewardship. It was one of the great experiences of my life.

In 1988, I started Master Plan Ministries and for the next twenty-seven years, worked with more than 326 churches helping them raise just under a half billion dollars. Dan Jackson who succeeded me at The King's Place joined me at Master Plan in 1996. His contribution to the churches and to me personally is without measure. He was truly a man after God's own heart and is now enjoying his eternal day with the Lord, missed here by so many, yet finding himself in an unending eternity with his Master, Friend, and Savior. I cannot imagine his delight in meeting so many who have also made that journey because of his faithful teaching of the gospel of Jesus Christ.

God's Care and Love Evidenced by His Provision

The year 1996 would prove to be a pivotal year. We received a call from Harbor View, a state-run facility for people with devastating physical disabilities, and Renee's home for the past several years. They informed us that Renee had been approved for the Russell House, one of the Angel View homes near Palm Springs, California. We believed this to be an answer to what we had prayed for, and yes, it was! This meant that Renee could be moved from an institutional setting to a home that was built and staffed with people for those with her type of disability.

The downside for us was that it would be much more difficult and costly to see her regularly. Even so, we managed the necessary six hundred miles each week to pick her up on Friday evenings and return her on Sunday evenings. Making that trip from the Antelope Valley to the Coachella Valley twice each weekend eventually got to be more than we could handle. In 1998, we sold our home in the Antelope Valley and moved to the Coachella Valley so we could be nearer Renee. After the move, our weekends were far less stressful, and more time could be spent with Renee. That also meant that after living on the High Desert for thirty years we would be living now in the Low Desert near Palm Springs. Another great benefit was that we had a new church home, one of America's great churches, Southwest Church in Indian Wells, California.

At the time I was still working with churches through Master Plan Ministries. This made it difficult to become active in our new church home since I was still serving churches across the United States. I was often away for seven to ten days and then home for a few days before flying again. When I reached age seventy-eight in 2012, it seemed like a good time to retire from such an exhausting schedule and ministry, even though it was very satisfying.

During the last half of my ministry as a stewardship consultant, I was asked by former parishioners, "Now that you are no longer in the ministry, how do you feel about that?" I usually smiled and tried to explain that I never left the ministry, only the role of serving as a lead pastor. The truth is that I preached and taught more frequently as a consultant than I did when serving as the pastor of a congregation.

As I look at my life in the rearview mirror, I would say my most enjoyable years came from serving as a pastor to God's people. A man who has a pastor's heart will never be able to replace that once it is gone. Even so, God has been gracious in allowing me to serve for the second half of my active ministry in an area I would have never chosen. In God's wisdom,

He realized that our financial needs would be considerable in caring for Renee's special needs, so He made a provision for that. My work with churches made that possible. While that was not the total answer to the "all things" Paul speaks of in Romans 8:28, it certainly was a part of it.

In my work with churches across America, I have been able to enjoy God's blessing and sense of accomplishment to the kingdom. For this ministry to be successful in helping churches raise three to four times their annual income over three years in addition to their regular budgeted giving, they have to embrace the biblical teachings on stewardship. They need to have a pastoral relationship with the stewardship consultant too, believing he is credible and has their best interest at heart. When that happens, people change, and that is most satisfying for any who proclaims the truth of God's Word. Giving to God for causes that please Him from hearts overflowing with thanksgiving and love are the critical building blocks to Christian growth.

Giving to God for causes that please Him from hearts overflowing with thanksgiving and love, are the critical building blocks to Christian growth.

CHAPTER 8

GOD'S KNOWLEDGE
IS PERFECT

To say that God is omniscient is to say that HE possesses perfect knowl-edge and therefore has no need to learn. But it is more: it is to say that God has never learned and cannot learn.

—*A.W. Tozer*

Knowing a God Who Knows All

Dr. David Jeremiah recently published *The God You May Not Know.* The purpose of the book is to enable the reader to *know God* instead of just knowing *about* God. While his book may not satisfy every question raised by the honest seeker, each of his twelve chapters deals with a different attribute of God. At the end of the book, most readers will have the sense that God has been unwrapped, not for intellectual pursuit only, but for a connection on a personal level. We might compare that to a child receiving a gift. Not only is there the incredible excitement of receiving a present, but there is also a different relationship with the giver, engagement on a personal level. Thanksgiving and joy become a part of that developing relationship.

Even so, we struggle sometimes, most of the time in understanding God. There are some pretty big words to describe God's attributes: sovereignty, immutability, holiness, omnipresence, omnipotence, omniscience, self-existence, and many more.

We may struggle in our understanding with some or all of these words used to paint pictures for us of God's nature. It is not my purpose to dissect each of these attributes. This book is about a God we believe to be loving, faithful, holy, and sovereign, a God who is not limited by time or space, the One who encourages us to pray in time of need, which includes praying that we might be healed from disease or infirmities. We asked the question and used it as the title of this book: *Where Was God When I Needed Him?* We are moving closer to the answer.

Is it possible to believe and then trust that God is all-knowing? If there really is no beginning or end with Him, then where is He and why does He not respond to the very thing He instructs us to do?

In my search for answers from God's Word, I read Isaiah 55 where the Lord is speaking:

> *"For my thoughts are not your thoughts, neither are your ways my ways," declares the Lord. "As the heavens are higher than the earth, so are my ways higher than your ways and my thoughts than your thoughts." (Isaiah 55:8-9)*

Could it be that God's celestial Internet has a bandwidth that far exceeds mine? Dr. Jeremiah states, "When it comes right down to it, we must confess that God simply has more information than we do, and we have to trust Him with the margins that exist between our knowledge and His."[1] But can we do this and rest our case in the all-knowing power of the living God? Is it possible to believe, express faith, act in obedience, and still trust God, even though we do not see or receive the result for which we prayed? As Dr. Jeremiah stated, can we trust Him with the margins?

After some time of seeking the answer to my question, I came across a book by David Needham called *Close to His Majesty*. Needham, along with God's Word and prayer, has given me a different perspective. The story is not historical, yet it contains truth like the parables of Jesus. This is Needham's story:

> *Imagine with me—two farmers: One raises wheat, and the other, down the road, raises tomatoes. Both farmers have balloon payments coming up on their mortgages, everything hinges on harvest. A crop failure would mean the loss of the farm. Let's complicate things a bit more, let's put into each farm this fact: that the farmer's wife is very sick and is in need of expensive surgery and without it there is little hope of improvement. And one more thing, both families are faithfully walking with God.*

It's evening. Each family listens intently to the weather forecast. There is a 50/50 chance of rain this particular night. The wheat farmer is well aware that his fields need one more heavy soaking rain to bring the grain through to harvest. With that the farm would be theirs and his wife would be able to walk again. Down the road, the other farmer knows that his tomatoes are right at their prime. Ready to be harvested. But if the rain comes, not only will his fields become a muddy bog making it impossible to harvest, but also the moisture could trigger a blight that could destroy the entire crop. Without the harvest, they could lose everything. After the weather report, each family gathers around the bed in the room where mom is resting, and each family prays, mom and dad and a couple of the children. One by one they lift their hearts to God: "O Lord, prays the wheat family, You know what is at stake. Please, Lord, send the rain. You know how much we want to please You. If only You would bring the rain it would mean so much to us and we would give You all the praise in Jesus name. Amen."

And down the road, equally earnest prayers ascend to God. "O Father, please, please keep the rain from falling. Everything depends on this harvest. Thank You for listening, and we trust You in Jesus' name. Amen." And as the younger child slides off the bed, she turns to her mother and says, "Don't worry, Mommy. I know He will answer our prayers. Good night!"

It is silent now, except for the wind whistling around the corners of the farmhouses. The hours pass. What will happen? Here's where we play God. We could arrange to have the rain follow the fence line between the two farms: wet on one side, dry on the other. But that is not the way things usually are. What will we do? Let's find out.

Suddenly, the wheat farmer wakens; He hears a sound on the sheet metal roof of the garage. He holds his breath just one drop. Is that all? No! In moments the drops multiply until they sound like thunder on the roof. Two children come running down the hall, they have heard it too. Bouncing on Mommy's bed, they shout, "God heard our prayers! He heard them! Isn't it exciting?" Once again, the family gathers with tears of joy praising the Lord.

But down the road, the other farmer also hears the first raindrop. Sitting up in bed he too holds his breath. Perhaps it will stop. "Please, Father, oh please!" But no, louder and louder the sheets of rain sweep over his home, splattering against the windows and he sees in his mind those fields of tomatoes beaten down and drowning in the mud. Quietly he slips back beneath the blankets. There's no sound of children's feet running down the hall in this home. But in the darkness, he feels the gentle squeeze of his wife's hand on his shoulder as she whispers, "Sweetheart, it's all right. He knows. God cares."

Next morning, it's breakfast time with the wheat family and what a breakfast it is: Mom scurries around the kitchen in her wheelchair. Everybody is so excited. "Daddy," one of the children says, "Everything is all right, isn't it? We can pay off the farm, and Mommy will be well again! Isn't God wonderful?"

And the tomato farm: There's breakfast there too, but it's very quiet. Father says he will ask the blessing. But instead, there is a long, long pause. Finally, unable to hold back the tears, he speaks between his sobs. "Lord, we prayed. We really thought we prayed the way we should, and Lord, we don't understand. It seemed so right that You should answer—but thank You, Lord. You do love us, we know that. We will keep right on trusting You no matter what happens now." The silence that follows is broken by some hurting "whys."

And Daddy finds no answers. Since this is our story, let's not stop right now. Let's imagine five years have gone by. We are again walking down the lane by those same two farms. The first thing that catches our eye is the freshly painted barn and the new car parked in front of the one farmhouse. Out behind are rolling hills covered with wheat. Let's move up close by the window. There is mom, standing looking robust and strong. Walking around the kitchen and fixing breakfast. The kids are just coming in. They are five years older now, and there is dad taking off his boots after the early morning chores. "Family," he says, "do you know what day this is? This is the fifth anniversary of the greatest crisis that our family has ever gone through. Do you remember that night we prayed? And God heard our prayer, didn't He?" "Dad, wasn't it great? Mom is well now, the farm is all ours, isn't it, Dad?" "That's right; in fact, God has blessed us more than I had ever dreamed. He deserves not only our thanks but also our lives, so let's gather around the table and each one of us tell Him how much we love Him."

What might we find if we stop in at the house down the road? There it is, such a contrast. It looks so run down and the name on the front of the barn has been changed. The family is still there, but they are tenants now. Let's step up closer to the kitchen window. There are the kids coming in along with Dad, fresh from his morning chores. Dad walks down the hall and in a few moments, Dad returns, pushing his wife's wheelchair closer to the kitchen table. Before asking the blessing, Dad turns to the family and asks, "Family, do you know what day this is? This is the fifth anniversary of the greatest crisis our family has ever gone through. Do you remember what happened five years ago?" As they recall that devastating night, the family joins hands and Dad prays, "O God, thank You! Thank You for Your grace and Your goodness. At first that night seemed like such a catastrophe, and yet, O Father, how You have taught us things about Yourself! You have opened the door to a knowledge of You through our suffering we never would have known any other way. God, You're so good."[2]

When I read Needham's story, I didn't say, "This is just a make-believe story, things like this don't really happen." Needham says, "Yes, they do! Stories like this one could be told thousands of times over by Christian steelworkers and shut-ins, students and missionaries, teachers and shopkeepers. Unique stories. Stories only they know about. Yet, woven through it all are threads that lead back to one all-knowing, all-wise, Most High God. Oh, the wonder of the mysteries of our God who knows the end from the beginning."[3]

Needham's story resonates with me since today is the anniversary of our daughter's death. She wasn't healed, even though we prayed with faith and obedience. Not only was she not healed, but she also lived for thirty-one years unable to speak, hear, or care for herself, and then she died. Friends looking at our family might say we were the tomato farmers, but I can tell you in the words of Dr. David Jeremiah that "our God knows the strength of suffering, the hurt of prosperity, the happiness of simplicity, and the success that aris-

Our God knows the strength of suffering, the hurt of prosperity, the happiness of simplicity, and the success that arises from our perceived failures.

es from our perceived failures. He knows the end from the beginning. He sees it all at once, eternally, infinitely. Because He knows it all, we can trust Him even in the darkest times. He never makes a mistake. He never fails us."[4]

I'm beginning to understand that I started with the wrong question. Let me explain my meaning as we consider that God is without equal.

CHAPTER 9

GOD IS WITHOUT EQUAL

When you go through a trial, the sovereignty of God is the pillow upon which you lay your head.

—*Charles Haddon Spurgeon*

The sovereignty of God is the only foundation for worship in the midst of tragedy.

—*David Platt*

Asking the Wrong Question

In the early years following our daughter's accident, I was asking the question: *Where Was God When I Needed Him*? As I examined every nook and crevasse of the Bible, God's blueprint for living, I came to understand that I was asking the wrong question. I already knew the answer to my first question: He's everywhere. Yet, that didn't seem all that helpful when God appeared to be distant when I prayed. The focus of my question was centered on my immediate problem, our needs, and desires. When God didn't respond to my petitions as requested, it caused me to question what I thought I knew about God. What was I missing?

Since I believe that God is present everywhere, at any given time, it also means that He was at the scene of our daughter's accident. He was in three hospitals every day. He was present every moment of her eight-to-ten months of coma. He was there the two years at home when she returned from the last hospital. He was there when a faithful congregation of saints made pleas for her healing. He was there with my wife, Dorene, who lived with a wounded heart as she lived a selfless life, expressing her love in those hospitals. She knew her love alone could not restore Renee to how she once was. He was there when we prayed for some indication that our heavenly Father loved us and cared. He was there during every moment of Renee's final thirty-one years. And He was there when she closed her eyes for the last time only to open them to see what we can only imagine. All of this is an expression of my simple faith that God is present everywhere at any given moment. But, still knowing that God is not limited or restrained by His own creation of time and space, and knowing that He is present as we prayed, why did it appear that He was blind, deaf, and worse, uncon-cerned about our circumstances?

Is it possible I'd been asking the wrong question all those years? Of all people, I should know enough to realize that a "where" question is a bit foolish when you believe that God is present everywhere. The better question may have been "Why"? Why does God allow bad things to happen to good people? Or, as Vaneetha Rendall Risner states, "I wondered why hard things happened when a loving God was supposedly in control?"[1]

God's Sovereignty: A Definition

I discovered two things about God that I had not learned in my formal academic training, or from my more than nearly fifty-four years of study and preaching. It's a confession I am embarrassed to make, since it took me so long. I did not understand the sovereignty and omniscience ascribed to God. I could name all of the attributes of God, and knew a great deal about God. I had an enormous amount of information; yet, through the events of our daughter's accident, God has helped me understand that there is a difference between knowing God and knowing about God.

In the previous chapter we considered His omniscience (His capacity to know everything there is to know). God never needs to learn since He knows everything. This is just one of the many attributes of God. In this chapter, we will examine God's sovereignty. I believe each of these provides clues to the primary question I had: *Where Was God When I Needed Him*? And also, the next one: "Why didn't God restore our daughter when we prayed?"

The word *sovereign* is a biblical word, yet it is often used by countries, world leaders, and currencies to express a certain kind of power and excellence over others. David Jeremiah states, "According to the Bible, there is only One who is truly sovereign, and that's Almighty God....The English word *sovereign* means 'having unlimited power or authority.' It comes from the prefix, *sov* 'over,' coupled with the word *reign*. When it comes to finances and politics, the term *sovereign* has to do with a nation's right of self-determination, of answering to no higher authority, of being an independent power. To say God is sovereign is to simply declare He is God, elevated above the highest authority in all the universe and possessing not only infinite power but infinite right, rule, and reign."[2]

It may be that former Secretary of the Treasury Salmon P. Chase understood there would be no better way for Americans to recognize or express God's sovereignty than by printing "In God We Trust" on our currencies as early as 1864. His decision was prompted by a letter written on November 13, 1861, by the Reverend M. R. Watkinson, a minister from Ridleyville, Pennsylvania.[3]

Gideon: From Doubts to Faith in God's Sovereignty

Based on Scripture, I am confident that David Jeremiah is correct. However, I still find some insight, perhaps comfort, in recognizing other giants in Scripture who have raised questions that sound like mine. This is not intended to excuse my questions, but rather to support the fact I'm a part of the human family. Let's look at Gideon. We find him in the pages of Judges 6:11-8:32. His encounter with the angel of the Lord didn't begin all that well.

In the beginning, Gideon wasn't in the Bible's Hall of Fame, but he stands there today because he finally got on God's side of the issue. The angel of the Lord appeared to him and said,

"The Lord is with you, mighty warrior." (Judges 6:12)

In the next verse, Gideon asked a very logical question,

"If the Lord is with us, why has all this happened to us?" (Judges 6:13)

Had Gideon forgotten the very first words of the angel so quickly? Those words should have settled the matter, right? But Gideon, because of his impossible circumstances, wasn't encouraged by the angel's message. Gideon said,

> Gideon said to Him, "Please Sir, if the Lord is with us, why has all this happened? And where are all His wonders that our fathers told us about? They said, 'Hasn't the Lord brought us out of Egypt?' But now the Lord has abandoned us and handed us over to Midian." (Judges 6:13, HCSB)

Or, my version: "Angel, are you unaware that my clan is the weakest of the bunch, and besides, I'm the least of my family?" (Judges 6:15, Dan Myers Version or DMV). Gideon had a problem in understanding the sovereignty of God. It's not all that difficult to understand Gideon. After all, his less-than-stellar army has been whittled down from thirty-two thousand to three hundred, and then the angel tells him he is about to defeat an army almost without number. Initially, when Gideon heard the angel's instructions, he must have thought, *This angel (with or without wings) is beyond belief.*

We don't ask the Gideon questions when riding the crest of prosperity and living a beautiful life. It's when life goes south, when we suffer, when we lose that special person, when we face oppression or suffering, when we suffer beyond our ability to handle the pain of a tragic event—those are the times when Gideon and his questions come knocking at our door.

What was it about Gideon that enabled him to go from being a frightened and reluctant warrior in hiding, threshing wheat at the foot of a hill out of sight of the enemy, to rise up and completely annihilate that same enemy in battle?

When God gave Gideon his orders, he was fearful. God was asking him to take a stand against his own father and tribe. He feared his own people (Judges 6:27), and so three times he asked God to make His will clear. Gideon put three tests before God:

1. The sacrifice of a young goat and the seven-year-old bull (Judges 6:17-25),

2. The first wool fleece (Judges 6:36-37), and

3. The second fleece (Judges (6:39-40).

As we read his story, it is evident that Gideon came to fear God more than the enemy. Gideon proved to be faithful and obedient because he came to understand that the God of Israel was above all: no one could stand with Him or beside Him. This was a recognition of God's sovereignty

"From Gideon's example we can learn that no matter how great the odds against us may be, our faithful God is sovereign, and He will always see us through whatever battles we face in life, as long as we remain faithful to His calling and obedient to His commands.

> *Trust in the Lord with all your heart and lean not on your own understanding; in all your ways submit to him, and he will make your paths straight. (Proverbs 3:5-6)*

We can also see how God uses ordinary people to accomplish His plans, although with Gideon, the key factor was his willingness to obey God."[4]

Gideon and his army went against the odds that no general in his right mind today would even consider following. Yet, with the sovereign God on Gideon's side, the overwhelming power of the enemy was defeated.

If you have lived very long, the time comes when you ask the question: "Why did this happen? If God is loving and in control, how can I reconcile His love and power with my suffering?" Or, like Gideon, when God appears to have clearly spoken to my confusion and unbelief, how can I be certain it is God who is speaking?

The question becomes even more important and critical knowing that I'm unable to write a book that progresses from one great miracle to another until finally, I'm able to say, our daughter was miraculously and beautifully restored by a loving expression of God's grace. That book would contain such a confirming message, a message gushing with unlimited and overflowing hope. Having said that, I refuse to take refuge in my suffering. I am seeking to understand something from God's Word and His abiding presence that has brought me three things: peace, comfort, and purpose. I am not writing to report the great miracle for which we prayed; yet, I write of God's overwhelming comfort and peace which may be the greater miracle.

I look at Gideon. He had no history of being a great military leader although he had done well. He was a prophet. He was not a General Patton of his day. Because of disobedience, his people had been ravaged by the Midianites, the Amalekites, and foreigners from the east who had destroyed their crops and cattle. They had been unfaithful to God by worshipping the gods of the Amorites (Baal). They had violated God's first commandment:

"You shall have no other gods before me." (Exodus 20:3)

When they realized their sin against the sovereign God, they cried to the one true God, and He sent the angel of the Lord to a less than receptive Gideon. (Judges 6:11-14)

My personal battle may not be against an impossible army, but it may be as hopeless as what Gideon faced: an army of thousands, thick as locusts (Judges 7:12) that waited patiently to grind his pathetic army of three hundred into the dust. Gideon realized he didn't have the wisdom, the resources, or the military might to stand before his enemy. He had every human reason to question the sovereignty of his God. The angel laid out the battle plan. Can't you just hear Gideon? "Angel, wait just a minute. You have already cut my troops from thirty-two thousand to three hundred. Now tell me again, you want me to leave all of our modern weaponry at home? Did I hear you right? You want me to place my three hundred in the hills, each with a trumpet and an empty jar with torches inside, and then you want me to give the command for each to blow his horn, bang on his jar, let the enemy see the burning torches, scare the hell out of them, and shout, 'For the Lord and for Gideon?' No question about it, that sounds like a winner to me. I can see it now, all three hundred of my men dead on the valley floor, clutching their trumpets, empty jars, and burnt out torches."

Truthfully, Gideon may have had such thoughts in the beginning, but he was obedient anyway. And God, the one and only God, would prove Himself to be sovereign. After that, Gideon really got with the plan. He was no longer asking who's going to bury the dead.

I don't know what your challenges are, but let me suggest a couple of hypothetical questions, they may not be so hypothetical. If I pray for my wife with terminal cancer, and she still dies, or I pray for the safety of our youth on their way to summer camp and yet they are killed in a tragic auto accident, or I pray for my friend with brain cancer and he still dies, what am I to do or think? What or who should be the object of my faith? Even though I am challenged and perhaps crushed for the moment, I need to take my place beside Gideon and allow the sovereign Lord to be the object of my faith.

It is helpful to understand that the story of our lives does not end with the death of a loved one. More often than not, we are not able to see why God is able to promise:

> *And we know that in all things God works for the good of those who love him, who have been called according to his purpose. (Romans 8:28)*

Only God is sovereign and all-knowing. Even though I hurt from my loss and have lost a relationship with one I love dearly, I refuse to be destroyed.

Biblical Giants Embrace the Sovereignty of God

Once again, I turn to the examples from Scripture and see how people with great faith were able to place their trust in a living God, their God who is sovereign over all. In some cases, they had not received what God had promised, yet they recognized the Lord as Sovereign.

Habakkuk said,

> *The Sovereign Lord is my strength; he makes my feet like the feet of a deer, he enables me to tread on the heights. (Habakkuk 3:19)*

Abraham expected that God would give him a son and when that heir did not come according to Abraham's expectation, he prayed,

> *"Sovereign Lord, what can you give me since I remain childless and the one who will inherit my estate is Eliezer of Damascus?" (Genesis 15:2)*

Abraham didn't ask the questions *where* and *why*. The Bible says,

> *Abram believed the Lord, and he credited it to him as righteousness.*
> *(Genesis15:6)*

In Isaiah 50, the prophet heard the Lord speak, and then four times Isaiah used the word *sovereign* to identify his Lord.

> *The Sovereign Lord has given me a well-instructed tongue, to know*
> *the word that sustains the weary. He wakens me morning by morning,*
> *wakens my ear to listen like one being instructed. The Sovereign Lord*
> *has opened my ears; I have not been rebellious, I have not turned*
> *away. (Isaiah 50:4-5)*

> *Because the Sovereign Lord helps me, I will not be disgraced.*
> *Therefore, have I set my face like flint, and I know I will not be put to*
> *shame....It is the Sovereign Lord who helps me. (Isaiah 50:7,9)*

Moses was quite clear in his understanding of God's sovereignty when he prayed:

> *"Sovereign Lord, you have begun to show to your servant your*
> *greatness and your strong hand. For what god is there in heaven*
> *or on earth who can do the deeds and mighty works you do?"*
> *(Deuteronomy 3:24)*

Even the psalmist was able to proclaim,

> *I have made the Sovereign Lord my refuge. (Psalm 73:28b)*

A man called Simeon described in Scripture as "righteous and devout," was visited by the Holy Spirit.

> *It had been revealed to him by the Holy Spirit that he would not die*

until he had seen the Lord's Messiah. (Luke 2:26)

When Mary and Joseph took the child Jesus to the temple courts, Simeon was there. Simeon took the child in his arms, praised God, and said:

"Sovereign Lord, as you have promised, you may now dismiss your servant in peace. For my eyes have seen your salvation." (Luke 2:29-30)

The first century church is noteworthy since many were taught by Christ and the rest were less than a generation or two away from personal contact with the Lord. During intense persecution, they were able to proclaim,

"Sovereign Lord," they said, "you made the heavens and the earth and the sea, and everything in them." (Acts 4:24)

Early in Chapter 6, we addressed the problem of false teachers. Peter warned and wrote openly about such teachers who deny that God is Sovereign:

But there were also false prophets among the people, just as there will be false teachers among you. They will secretly introduce destructive heresies, even denying the sovereign Lord who bought them—bringing swift destruction on themselves. (2 Peter 2:1)

King Nebuchadnezzar, the great king of Babylon, had his authority and reign taken away by God because he boasted of his own greatness and denied the sovereignty of God. It wasn't until the king said,

I, Nebuchadnezzar, raised my eyes toward heaven, and my sanity was restored. Then I praised the Most High; I honored and glorified him who lives forever. His dominion is an eternal dominion; his kingdom endures from generation to generation. All the peoples of the

earth are regarded as nothing. He does as he pleases with the powers of heaven and the peoples of the earth. No one can hold back his hand or say to him: "What have you done?" (Daniel 4:34-35)

That was some turn around for this pagan king, but being driven from his people and made to live with wild animals eating grass like an ox, watching his hair grow like the feathers of an eagle and his nails like bird claws, got his attention. This Babylonian king recognized, honored, and glorified the sovereign Lord. His reward? His kingdom was restored and became even more significant than before.

Compare the life experience of these two kings: King Nebuchadnezzar of Babylon and the Pharaoh of Egypt who refused to let God's people go until God crushed him with the final Egyptian plague. The first was also defeated by God, but eventually repented to proclaim the sovereignty of God. Pharaoh, while declaring his own deity, denied the existence and power of God, only to lose his firstborn child and be ground into the dust of history.

All but Pharaoh shared their understanding that God is Sovereign, and the writers of the New Testament were able to observe that from their relationship with Christ. Pharaoh was destroyed for his lack of faith, while many others died a martyr's death to live again *because of their faith* in God's sovereignty.

A Contemporary Embraces God's Sovereignty

I have found help and encouragement from others. Vaneetha Risner is such a person. When she was writing as a freelance writer for "Desiring God," she focused on a single little word. She wrote: "I took comfort in the truth that God was with me and could use my suffering to demonstrate his glory, but when new struggles surfaced, sometimes I would return to that familiar question: *If the Lord is with me, then why did all this happen?*[5] That was Gideon's question, if all he had been told about God being with the Children of Israel, then why was he faced with the arrows of his enemy and why are his army and people about to be destroyed?

If you have lost a spouse, a child, someone you love, or employment, you may have felt abandoned by God. You may have even convinced yourself that if God loved you, why would He allow these things to happen? That was indeed my question. I remember standing on one of my hang-gliding launching sites unable to release the pain of our daughter's loss, wanting to scream like a child, "God, if You love us, why has this happened, or at best, why don't You do something?"

When Vaneetha Risner was raising her own questions similar to mine, she said, "Those questions must have delighted Satan. Satan turns truth into doubt with that little word: *if.* Satan's temptation of Jesus began with the words:

> *"If you are the Son of God, tell these stones to become bread." (Matthew 4:3)*

"Satan and Jesus both knew that Jesus was the Son of God. Everyone at Jesus' baptism knew He was the Son of God. Yet when Jesus was alone in the wilderness, Satan tempted Him to doubt what He undeniably knew to be true."[6]

> *"If you are the Son of God," Satan said, "throw yourself down. For it is written: 'He will command his angels concerning you, and they will lift you up in their hands, so that you will not strike your foot against a stone.'" (Matthew 4:6)*

Finally, Satan said to Jesus after showing him all the kingdoms of the world,

"All this I will give you if you," he said, "if you will bow down and worship me." (Matthew 4:9)

Jesus knew He was the sovereign God, and Satan was soon to learn that testing or tempting *God* in the wilderness would not end like his temptation of *man* in the garden. There was no need for debate. He merely did what He could do because of his matchless power and so,

Satan was soon to learn that testing or tempting God in the wilderness would not end like his temptation of man in the garden

Jesus said to him, "Away from me, Satan! For it is written: 'Worship the Lord your God, and serve him only.'" (Matthew 4:10)

When Jesus won the battle with Satan in the wilderness, Satan knew his days were numbered and that God had moved one step closer to the cross that would seal his fate for eternity. Jesus faced and overcame Satan's testing and challenge by knowing who He is. This is one glorious manifestation of the sovereign God.

How Does a Sovereign God Embrace Us?

But still, for many, the question becomes: *How can I know and be confident of God's love especially when caught in the clutches of suffering?* Once again, we need to place our trust in the promises God has made, not on our feelings. God says in Jeremiah 31:

I have loved you with an everlasting love. (Jeremiah 31:3b)

That is a love beyond our comprehension. Jesus said,

"As the Father has loved me, so have I loved you." (John 15:9)

When you consider what it cost God to prove His love—the giving of His Son so He could do for us what we could not do for ourselves—that becomes a very persuasive argument and more, an actual demonstration of his unrelenting love.

Often the songs we sang as children confirm the truth of God's Word: "Jesus loves me this I know, for the Bible tells me so." How could that get any more straightforward? "'Jesus Loves Me' with its simple, direct message, is one of the first hymns missionaries teach to new converts. It was the favorite hymn of Francis Schaeffer, who recognized that ultimately what intellectuals and children alike need is the simple message of Jesus. Amy Carmichael, the Irish missionary to India, was converted after hearing this hymn at a children's mission in Yorkshire, England."[7] This little song would be meaningless if not supported by the truth of all Scripture as well as the actions of a sovereign God. Because I am assured of God's love and have experienced it, I must reframe my question slightly yet again, *Since I know that God loves me*, then why did this happen?

When I know God loves me, I begin to think differently. I am less absorbed with my own hurt and disappointment. I am starting to look at God as my Father instead of a distant landlord. At the beginning of a crisis, it is not easy to come to the place in which you see your life as what Vaneetha Risner calls, "the result of his love and his presence, not his disfavor or absence."[8]

Through our experience with our daughter, I have come to understand that I never have a *right to insist* that God answer my request according to my desire. My request must be based on His will as determined by His forty-thousand-foot perspective and beyond. And so, I come to one more minor refinement of my question: *What is God trying to accomplish through my suffering?* In the grips of the trial I was not looking for the next great theological lesson, but I had to move from "Where is God?" and "Why did He allow this to happen?" to "What can I learn from this" and "how should I respond?" If I fail in the transition from my pain to embracing a loving, sovereign God, I will be destroyed. But standing with Abraham, the prophet Isaiah, Gideon, the apostles Peter and Paul, the psalmist, Simeon, so many saints of the early church, and even Jesus, I choose to ask, "What does He want from me?"

Before answering the question, it would be helpful to understand how God sees us through His Son. It is easier to understand what He wants in return when we understand who we are, His wonderful creation in Christ.

Kimberly Taylor (on her takebackyourtemple.com website) has provided many references that provides God's standard as found in His Word in answer to the question: *Who am I in Christ Jesus?* The following verses are taken from her site; I did not use the entire list. *There are many more!* Check the whole thing out for yourself at takebackyourtemple.com.[9]

I am Jesus' friend.

"I no longer call you servants, because a servant does not know his master's business. Instead, I have called you friends, for everything that I learned from my Father I have made known to you." (John 15:15)

I am made whole in Christ.

And in Christ you have been brought to fullness. He is the head over every power and authority. (Colossians 2:10)

I am victorious!

I can do all this through him who gives me strength. (Philippians 4:13)

I am fearfully and wonderfully made.

I praise you because I am fearfully and wonderfully made; your works are wonderful, I know that full well. (Psalm 139:14)

I am blessed!

"If you listen obediently to the Voice of God, your God, and heartily obey all his commandments that I command you today, God, your God, will place you on high, high above all the nations of the world. All these blessings will come down on you and spread out beyond you because you have responded to the Voice of God, your God." (Deuteronomy 28:6, MSG)

I am complete in Him who is the Head of all principalities and powers.

And in Christ you have been brought to fullness. He is the head over every power and authority. (Colossians 2:10)

I am set free in Christ!

It is for freedom that Christ has set us free. Stand firm, then, and do not let yourselves be burdened again by a yoke of slavery. (Galatians 5:1)

I am God's handiwork and destined to do good works.

For we are God's handiwork, created in Christ Jesus to do good works, which God prepared in advance for us to do. (Ephesians 2:10)

I am a new creation, God's workmanship, a branch on God's vine, a child of light, bought with a price, and fearfully and wonderfully made!

See 2 Corinthians 5:17, Ephesians 2:10, John 15:5, 1 Thessalonians 5:5, 1 Corinthians 6:20, and Psalm 139:14!

I am the apple of His eye.

In a desert land he found him, in a barren and howling waste. He shielded him and cared for him; he guarded him as the apple of his eye. (Deuteronomy 32:10)

I am chosen by God and holy and dearly *loved*!

Therefore, as God's chosen people, holy and dearly loved, clothe yourselves with compassion, kindness, humility, gentleness and patience. (Colossians 3:12)

I am like a tree firmly planted by streams of water which yields its fruit in season and whose leaf does not wither— whatever I do prospers.

> *That person is like a tree firmly planted by streams of water, which yields its fruit in season and whose leaf does not wither—whatever they do prospers. (Psalm 1:3)*

I am more than a conqueror.

> *No, in all these things we are more than conquerors through him who loved us. (Romans 8:37)*

I am hidden with Christ in God.

> *For you died, and your life is now hidden with Christ in God. (Colossians 3:3)*

I am dead with Christ and dead to the power of sin's rule over my life.

> *What shall we say, then? Shall we go on sinning so that grace may increase? By no means! We are those who have died to sin; how can we live in it any longer? Or don't you know that all of us who were baptized into Christ Jesus were baptized into his death? We were therefore buried with him through baptism into death in order that, just as Christ was raised from the dead through the glory of the Father, we too may live a new life. (Romans 6:1-4)*

I am the righteousness of God in Christ.

God made him who had no sin to be sin for us, so that in him we might become the righteousness of God. (2 Corinthians 5:21)

I am not my own. I am the temple of the Holy Spirit.

Do you not know that your bodies are temples of the Holy Spirit, who is in you, whom you have received from God? You are not your own." (1 Corinthians 6:19)

I am God's workmanship, created in Christ Jesus to do good works.

For we are God's handiwork, created in Christ Jesus to do good works, which God prepared in advance for us to do. (Ephesians 2:10)

I am set apart.

Know that the Lord hath set apart him that is godly for himself; the Lord will hear when I call unto him. (Psalm 4:3, KJV)

I am no longer a slave, but a child and an heir.

Now you are no longer a slave but God's own child. And since you are his child, God has made you his heir. (Galatians 4:7, NLT)

If we confess our sins, he is faithful and just and will forgive us our sins and purify us from all unrighteousness. (1 John 1:9)

I am free from the law of sin and death.

Therefore, there is now no condemnation for those who are in Christ Jesus, because through Christ Jesus the law of the Spirit who gives life has set you free from the law of sin and death. (Romans 8:1-2)

I am a chosen generation, a royal priesthood, a holy nation.

But you are a chosen people, a royal priesthood, a holy nation, God's special possession, that you may declare the praises of him who called you out of darkness into his wonderful light. (1 Peter 2:9)

I'm a servant of God.

"Whoever serves me must follow me; and where I am, my servant also will be. My Father will honor the one who serves me." (John 12:26)

I am a child of God.

You, dear children, are from God and have overcome them, because the one who is in you is greater than the one who is in the world. (1 John 4:4)

For all who are led by the Spirit of God are sons of God. For you did not receive the spirit of slavery to fall back into fear, but you have received the Spirit of adoption as sons, by whom we cry, "Abba! Father!" (Romans 8:14-15, ESV)

I am light.

"You are the light of the world. A city set on a hill cannot be hidden; nor does anyone light a lamp and put it under a basket, but on the lampstand, and it gives light to all who are in the house. Let your light shine before men in such a way that they may see your good works, and glorify your Father who is in heaven." (Matthew 5:14-16, NASB)

This is a pretty impressive list of credentials. God allows us to see ourselves as He sees us. These verses and many more like them become like little computer icons representing what God sees as we receive His love and embrace His Son. When we click on any of these, we get to see ourselves through God's eyes.

In this chapter, we have learned about God's sovereignty. He reigns above all principalities and powers. There is none who stand above Him. Yet, it is impossible for us to know how to please our sovereign Father until we understand who we are according to the truth of God's own words. His truth about us will help us know what our response should be to this God who is above all.

I return to a statement made earlier by J. I. Packer, when he said, "One can know a great deal about God without much knowledge of Him."[10] He also writes, "Yet interest in theology, and knowledge about God, and the capacity to think clearly and talk well on Christian themes, is not at all the same thing as knowing him. We may know as much about God as Calvin knew—indeed, if we study his works diligently, sooner or later we shall—and yet all the time (unlike Calvin, may I say) we may hardly know God at all."[11]

And so, in our quest to please our sovereign God, it is imperative to *experience Him*, and not be satisfied with *merely knowing* a great deal about Him.

As a child coming to know this magnificent Father, our hurts and disappointments are no longer the driving force in our lives. If I disagree with this it is undoubtedly a sign that I need to ask the question: "Do I understand the difference between knowing God, or merely knowing a great deal about God?" When we allow God to take residence in our lives, a bonding takes place like that between a son and his father. A son doesn't have to have a complicated theological statement in order to know and experience his father's love. He knows that by virtue of a loving relationship, and so it is with us as we find ourselves as sons and daughters of our heavenly Father.

This brings me full circle to my last and perhaps the final question: "What does a sovereign God, the God with perfect knowledge, want from me?" Successfully answering this question removes the focal point of my question about God to God's question about me. How can I get there?

In the Old Testament, we have the real-life experience of Daniel and his relationship with the sovereign God. His life is a model for us to observe and follow. From the record, it's clear that Daniel doesn't ask the question, "Where Was God?" Our question probably would be, "God, You want me to casually walk where? Are You serious about that? Two steps and we're dead. Come on, let's sit down and talk this over and come up with a better plan." But when faced with death, he didn't ask, "God, why are You allowing this to happen?" Instead, Daniel had faith to believe that God was sovereign. No matter what the outcome, he rested his case (and his life) in the perfect relationship he had with God. He expressed the same quality of faith demonstrated by Abraham when God told him to sacrifice Isaac, the son of the promise. Great rewards came from the faith and obedience of both Daniel and Abraham.

When reading Daniel, you realize this reveals at least three things about God: His unequaled power, His wisdom, and His ability to demonstrate

His sovereignty as He rules both individuals and nations according to His own will.

Daniel is one of the most graphic presentations of God's sovereignty found in the Bible. When I read it, I declare, like Daniel that I want to know God. I will not be content to simply know a lot of things about God. I want to experience Him, no matter the cost. I would like to believe I have the courage of the three Hebrew children, and that I would face the furnace with full confidence and faith in the sovereign God. From Daniel's experience, I create my own response to God and provide the answer to my final question, "What does God want from me?"

What Does God Want from Me?

In considering this question, I began to write down all that God has a right to expect from me: my praise, thanksgiving, exaltation, obedience, faith, worship, and so much more. The list seems almost endless. While all are desirable, these make my final cut. How I give back to the Father will determine if I believe that He is sovereign over all. It will also make clear whether I know God, or merely know many things about God.

I have narrowed my choice to three things, and each of these in some way encompasses all of the above. God wants the following from me:

- My thoughts must be focused on Him.

- My contentment must be in Him.

- I must be like clay in the Master Potter's hands.

My Thoughts Must Be Focused on Him

J. I. Packer puts forth this proposition quite well. "In the face of the might and splendor *(sic)* of the Babylonian empire which had swallowed up Palestine, and the prospect of further great world-empires to follow, dwarfing Israel by every standard of human calculation, the book as a whole forms a dramatic reminder that the God of Israel is King of kings and Lord of lords, that 'the heavens do rule' (4:6), that God's hand is on history at every point, that history, indeed, is no more than 'His story', the unfolding of His eternal plan, and that the kingdom which will triumph in the end is God's."[12]

Packer speaks of Daniel's lessons for Nebuchadnezzar and Darius and their response: "The central truth which Daniel taught Nebuchadnezzar in chapter 2 and 4, and of which he reminded Belshazzar in chapter 5 (verses 18-23), and which Nebuchadnezzar acknowledged in chapter 4 (verses 34-37), and which Darius confessed in chapter 6 (verses 25-27), and which was the basis of Daniel's prayers in chapters 2 and 9, and of his confidence in defying authority in chapters 1 and 6, and of his friends' confidence in defying authority in chapter 3, and which formed the staple substance of all the disclosures which God made to Daniel in chapters 2, 4, 7, 8, 10 and 11-12, is the truth that 'the most High ruleth in the kingdom of men' (4:25; cf. 5:21). He knows, and foreknows, all things, and His foreknowledge is foreordination. He, therefore, will have the last word, both in world history and in the destiny of every man; His kingdom and righteousness will triumph in the end, for neither men nor angels shall be able to thwart him."[13]

All of this occupied Daniel's mind. We see evidence of this as he prayed to the God of Israel. On one occasion, Nebuchadnezzar had a dream. He was troubled by it and called for his magicians, enchanters, sorcerers, and astrologers. The king promised them great wealth if they could interpret the dream, but if they failed the penalty would be their death. These char-latans, seeking to buy time, asked the king to tell them the dream and then they would interpret it for him. The king realized they were stalling, and so he ordered the execution of all the wise men of Babylon.

Daniel stepped into the unfolding drama of this impending execution and asked Arioch, the commander of the king's guard,

"Why did the king issue such a harsh decree?"(Daniel 2:15)

Daniel asked for a little time so that he might interpret the dream. He returned to his home, sought out his friends Hananiah, Mishael, and Aza-riah, and urged them to plead with the God of heaven concerning the king's dream. Daniel and his three friends were facing death at the hand of the king if they failed, but they prayed. During the night, God answered their prayer and revealed to Daniel the mystery of the king's dream in a night vision.

When Daniel received this life-saving vision, he prayed, offering praise to his sovereign God:

"Praise be to the name of God forever and ever; wisdom and power are his. He changes times and seasons; he deposes kings and raises up others. He gives wisdom to the wise and knowledge to the discern-ing. He reveals deep and hidden things; he knows what lies in dark-ness, and light dwells with him." (Daniel 2:20-22)

Daniel, a careful student of his people's history, must have either read or learned through oral instruction the truth of Joshua 1:

"Keep this Book of the Law always on your lips; meditate on it day and night, so that you may be careful to do everything written it." (Joshua 1:8)

The very language and passion of his prayers convey that he knows God when he prays:

> *"Lord, the great and awesome God, who keeps his covenant of love with those who love him and keep his commandments...Lord, you are righteous...The Lord our God is merciful and forgiving...For the Lord our God is righteous in everything he does...Now, Lord our God, who brought your people out of Egypt with a mighty hand and who made for yourself a name that endures to this day." (Daniel 9:4, 7, 9, 14-15)*

Daniel reveals a personal relationship with God when three times in this passage he refers to God as "our God," and then in verse 15, Daniel speaks of "Your people."

When we pray, do our hearts convey the passion and reverence expressed by Daniel? Like Daniel, do we express a depth of humility, an awareness of God's magnificence, a recognition of His faithfulness, and a willingness to be obedient? Do we allow our thoughts to be consumed with God? If we have little passion for such prayer, and no regular practice of it, any statement that we know God as Daniel knew God is suspect.

My Contentment Must Be in Him

The apostle Paul speaks of a peace known only to those who have an absolute assurance that they know God, and that God knows them. It is the knowledge and this relationship as God's children that gives us the confidence that we possess God's favor in this life, and then through death and eternity. Listen to Paul as he reveals what our complete fulfillment in God produces. There is peace with God, access by faith to receive His grace, and the ability to boast in the hope of God's glory. As Paul teaches, he says:

> *Therefore, since we have been justified through faith, we have peace*
> *with God through our Lord Jesus Christ, through whom we have*
> *gained access by faith into this grace in which we now stand. And we*
> *boast in the hope of the glory of God. (Romans 5:1-2)*

Paul has an interesting take on our suffering. He reveals that pain can
have positive results for God's children:

> *Not only so, but we also glory in our sufferings, because we know*
> *that suffering produces perseverance; perseverance, character; and*
> *character, hope. And hope does not put us to shame, because God's*
> *love has been poured out into our hearts through the Holy Spirit, who*
> *has been given to us. (Romans 5:3-5)*

The kernel of this passage is that we have been justified through faith,
our faith in the risen Lord, and that makes peace between the Father and
us. The apostle elaborates on this in Romans 8:

> *There is now no condemnation for those who are in Christ Jesus...*
> *The Spirit himself testifies with our spirit that we are God's children...*
> *Heirs of God and co-heirs with Christ...We know that in all things*
> *God works for the good of those who love him, who have been called*
> *according to his purpose...And those he predestined, he also called...*
> *If God is for us, who can be against us?...Who will bring any charge*
> *against those whom God has chosen?...Who shall separate us from*
> *the love of Christ?...For I am convinced that neither death nor life,...*
> *neither the present nor the future,...will be able to separate us from*
> *the love of God that is in Christ Jesus our Lord. (Romans 8:1, 16-17,*
> *28, 30, 31, 33, 35, 38-39)*[14]

The late Dr. S. M. Lockridge, the longtime pastor of the Calvary Baptist
Church in San Diego, California, was a much loved and frequent guest
speaker at The King's Place in Lancaster, California, during my years as

lead pastor there. On one such occasion in the early 1980s, Dr. Lockridge was preaching about the three Hebrew youth: Shadrach, Meshach, and Abednego, or in his unsurpassed humor, Your Shack, My Shack, and a Bungalow. That night he was in high gear as he described the contentment of these three young men. King Nebuchadnezzar sent out a poorly devised ultimatum in Daniel 3:16-18:

> *"Now when you hear the sound of the horn, flute, zither, lyre, harp, pipe and all kinds of music, if you are ready to fall down and worship the image I made, very good. But if you do not worship it, you will be thrown immediately into a blazing furnace. Then what god will be able to rescue you from my hand?" (Daniel 3:15)*

Their reply proceeded from their complete confidence in the living God, the contentment they had in knowing their God lives. Listen to these young men in verse 16,

> *"King Nebuchadnezzar, we do not need to defend ourselves before you in this matter." (Daniel 3:16)*

Such confidence! In the next verse, they continue,

> *"If we are thrown into the blazing furnace, the God we serve is able to deliver us from it, and he will deliver us from Your Majesty's hand." (Daniel 3:17)*

Such faith! Then, they close their case by saying,

> *"But even if he does not, we want you to know, Your Majesty, that we will not serve your gods or worship the image of gold you have set up." (Daniel 3:18)*

Such contentment! We are in God's hands, and whatever happens, if we die or live, we rest our case with the Living God, who is sovereign above all.[15]

I believe it's safe to say these three young men engaged in a very dynamic time of prayer before entering the furnace. When the furnace doors were open, they didn't know an angel of the Lord would be waiting inside. What they did know and express was their faith and contentment in their sovereign God. It was merely one evidence of how well they understood and pleased their God.

Being Clay in the Master Potter's Hands

David understood what God wanted when he prayed,

> *You do not delight in sacrifice, or I would bring it; you do not take pleasure in burnt offerings. My sacrifice, O God, is a broken spirit; a broken and contrite heart you, God, will not despise. (Psalm 51:16-17)*

David realized that whatever is broken needs repair. Other writers in Scripture take us back to the very beginning, using the analogy of the clay and potter. Isaiah gives us an understanding of this idea when he declares,

> *Yet you, Lord, are our Father. We are the clay, you are the potter; we are all the work of your hand. (Isaiah 64:8)*

Jill Austin is one of the most brilliantly gifted, allegorical writers of our time. Her book, *Master Potter*, is the story of a young girl moving from brokenness to divine destiny. The main character is Forsaken, a lump of clay, created by God, a beautiful young girl destroyed by alcohol and life. Hopelessly lost, we find her in the field of broken vessels in the Potter's Field (ruined lost lives). It is the final battle for her life. Michael, the archangel, arrives with his unbeatable forces to drive back the satanic horde.

Their assignment has been commissioned by the Father to rescue this lost, broken, young girl. It is at the beginning of this battle that Austin so masterfully describes:

Heaven responds to a cry for help. The groans of prisoners appointed to die never fail to inflame the Father's heart of mercy to bring salvation. The name of Master Potter thunders across the field, releasing His violently passionate love, electrifying the spirit realm. Heavenly portals open and an avalanche of praise and worship roars across the Potter's Field, driving the demonic horde into increased frenzied terror.

Valiant swings his fiery sword and shouts to the angelic ground troops on the Potter's Field, "For the Father, the Son and the Holy Spirit that this Bride may come forth." They move like pillars of fire throughout the damned field, routing out the hidden swarms of evil strongholds. Demonic reinforcements arrive and the battle is fierce and bloody as the sound of war resounds throughout the land. In a flash, Valiant takes an ancient silver shofar from his waist and blows a mighty blast, sounding a war cry to open up the heavens. Michael, the archangel, and his magnificent warriors mount their huge white stallions and descend from the ethereal realms to drive back the screaming satanic hordes. Their assignment is straight from the Father—to rescue this lost, broken soul.

Catching the scent of the battle, the horses charge into the fray, obeying the commands of their riders. Muscles rippling with strength, they strike paralyzing terror in the enemy forces as they carry the splendor and majesty of the Lord's own angelic host. The gusty wind of the Spirit blows like a golden whirlwind around them. Explosions of resurrection power bombard screeching demons as angelic hosts rejoice in the strength of the victory of the Cross. The warriors wield flashing swords and wreak havoc in the Potter's Field. Swirls of fiery glory break the dark fog of oppression holding Forsaken prisoner as the first light of dawn rises in the eastern sky. This power invasion from Heaven annihilates the demonic stronghold in Forsaken's soul. Death screeches in horrendous defeat and throws Forsaken down. Leaving her barely alive, he flees with his evil regiment of dark angels.

Rejoicing, her lifelong guardian, Valiant, catches her before she can hit the ground and gently lays her down. Angels of glory fill the skies, exulting in praise and worship over Forsaken's rescue. A blanket of holy peace fills the atmosphere as a cloud of glory grows with each exalted verse. Blazing with fiery determination, Valiant's great expanse of translucent wings cover her. He lovingly stands guard over the broken little heap. Valiant shakes his head in marvelous wonder at the wisdom of Master Potter (Christ). He lifts his blazing sword and joins the heavenly choruses of high praise.

The atmosphere changes as golden rays of resurrection light pierce the darkness. Death and his entourage are vanquished. Having tasted of this unstoppable power before, they regroup for another day, another battle. Silhouetted against the rising sun, a man appears in this graveyard of broken lives. The desperate cries of Forsaken's lost soul stir His unending compassionate love. "How My heart rejoices to hear her call My name. I deeply feel the pain of your suffering, My precious one. I'm coming."

Still lying with her face to the ground and weeping, Forsaken hears footsteps. Startled, she looks up to see the bloody feet of a man standing in front of her. Her eyes travel from His nail-pierced feet up His bruised legs. Streams of blood and water flow to the ground from a deep gash in His side. His wounded chest has been ripped open by the lashes of a cruel, relentless scourging, leaving bloodied and torn flesh.

Pain and grief are etched into His features. Black and blue swollen mounds exit where soft brown eyes should have been. Patches of His dark curly beard have been violently ripped from his flesh, leaving exposed muscle. His cheeks are caked with dried blood. Forsaken is gripped with compassion that wells up within her heart. Hot tears run down her bruised and bloodied face. His features are so disfigured, she thinks to herself, if He were my own brother, I would not recognize Him.

Streams of blood drip from His brow where a cruel crown of thorns punctures His flesh. Overwhelmed, Forsaken cries, "Who are You? I've never seen a man so battered and beaten! Who would have done such a thing?"

"This is Master Potter," Holy Spirit gently says, "You did, Forsaken! This is the Son of God, who took the punishment for your sins. He was whipped, beaten and put to death so that you could be rescued and reconciled to the Father. You've encountered the crucified Savior who died for you. This is Master Potter, who rescues clay vessels from this field of death."

Master Potter "How can this be Master Potter? My dad said He loved to destroy clay vessels." Master Potter begins to turn away, and she sees a rugged wooden cross beam, which is bound to His outstretched arms. Desperately she cries, "Wait! Come back! Please don't leave me!" He turns, faces her once again and gazes deeply into her tear-filled eyes. Unconditional love pierces deep into the numbness of her soul with convicting revelation.

Forsaken hears a crack within her soul as the lie is broken and the chains of bondage are loosed. She now knows this is Master Potter and realizes that everything her Grandma Pearl had told her was true. He really does love her, and He really did choose to die rather than be without her. Her heart is illuminated by Holy Spirit's light, and she understands her awful sinfulness and desperate need for this humble man standing before her. Only Master Potter can save her soul and make her clean.

"I'm so sorry. Please forgive me," she sobs. "I've made such a mess out of my life! Master Potter, save me! Help me!" Completely broken, she wraps her arms around His bloody feet.

Safe in the Savior's arms Master Potter gently picks up little Forsaken with His nail-pierced hands and placing her head against His wounded chest He holds her close and weeps over her pain. Cradled in the Savior's protective arms, Forsaken responds to His overwhelming sacrifice and compassion for her with deep tears of repentance that wash her sin-drenched soul. Embracing Him tightly, she weeps, "Oh, Master Potter, I love you! Please save me! I've wasted so many years and have done so many horrible things. Please forgive me!"

Born Again! "Forsaken, I do forgive you. I've always loved you and yearned for you to come to Me. I died to save you and bring you out of the Potter's Field. I endured these wounds so that you might be saved and made whole."

Suddenly, her deep repentance causes the fiery seed of eternity to erupt inside her soul! The wonderment! The transforming miracle! Surging resurrection life flows into her being and connects her spirit with His in holy communion for the first time. Forsaken is born again! She's alive—truly alive!

Resurrected Lord! She watches in stunned amazement as His brutal-

ly disfigured features change before her eyes, transforming themselves into a radiant face more lovely than any she's ever seen. He is stunning and radiant—altogether lovely. Once He was her crucified Savior, but now He is also her resurrected Lord.

For a brief and shining moment, white light illuminates off His shimmering clothing, and rays of golden glory shine from His face, hands and eyes. He stands before her, transformed into the Lord of glory. All at once, Forsaken's ears are open, and she hears the glorious singing of angelic hosts. Bathed in white light, she looks down at herself and realizes that she, too, is shining with the light of His glory.

The Humble Potter's ministering angels clothe Him in the soft brown robes of a humble potter, and the glow of glory gradually dims into the rugged and handsome face of Master Potter. Holding her close, He penetrates her knotted muscles with His healing anointing, soothing her painful spasms and calming the horrible effects of alcohol withdrawal. Sweet perfume and fragrance wash over her as she clutches Him tightly to herself.

Such wonder! Such unspeakable grace that He would choose to save one such as her from the grasp of death and the destitution of the Potter's Field. Deep waves of glory continue to heal and cleanse her as He joyfully proclaims to the heavens, the earth and the realms below, "No longer are you called Forsaken. I name you Beloved, the delight of My heart!"[16]

We are all like clay. Will we be shaped and designed by the hands of our Master Potter? He alone creates a miracle of beauty as He shapes our lives. Darlene Zschech wrote about the Potter and the clay in her lyrics included below. Let's finish this chapter by meditating on this beautiful picture.

The Potter's Hand

Beautiful Lord, wonderful Savior
I know for sure, all of my days are held in Your hands.
Crafted into Your perfect plan
You gently call me, into Your presence
Guiding me by, Your Holy Spirit
Teach me, dear Lord,
To live all of my life through Your eyes.

I'm captured by, Your Holy calling
Set me apart
I know You're drawing me to Yourself
Lead me, Lord, I pray

Take me, mold me,
Use me, fill me!
I give my life to the Potter's hands.
Hold me, guide me,
Lead me, walk beside me;
I give my life to the Potter's hand.[17]

CHAPTER 10

CHEAP CLICHÉ OR PRECIOUS PROMISE?

Grace: You know that everything happens for a reason.

Bruce: See, that I don't need. That is a cliché. That is not helpful to me. "A bird in the hand is worth two in the bush"...I have no bird, I have no bush. God has taken my bird and my bush.

—from the movie "Bruce Almighty"[1]

Where Is My Bird and My Bush?

You should not be criticized when you ask, "How could this writer, a pastor, be so conflicted and why has he struggled with this particular promise in God's Word?" The simple answer is that pastors are people, too, and like all of God's children who have received Christ as their Savior and Lord, they too struggle with the hard times in life.

The longer answer that shook, but did not shatter, my faith to the core were the two most devastating events of my life which happened on consecutive days in my history. As mentioned earlier, the first was our daughter's accident on December 2, 1978, and the next day, December 3, 1978, Leslie Long, the young mother in our church family was brutally raped and murdered. When I conducted her service on December 11, standing in the sanctuary before members of her family and a standing-room-only group of friends, I was incapable of finding words that even came close to describing my thoughts and emotions. At her graveside, my own tears ran hot down my face as I thought of Leslie's three little children, all under the age of five. Then there was her young husband who was struggling, endeavoring to be the very best father and husband he could be. Now he was looking at what seemed like a mountain too high to climb.

When I drove out of the cemetery that cold winter day, I knew I would soon be meeting with the family in one of their homes, but first I needed to stop at the hospital. Our daughter, Renee, was in intensive care for the tenth day of her coma, clinging to life. If it had not been for the tubes and specialized equipment, she looked like a sleeping angel, yet, her condition was listed as critical, and the prognosis was not encouraging. Dr. Birsner was there with my wife and me, and he did his best to prepare us for what he said was inevitable. He shared his professional opinion, "Friends, even if Renee lives for some unexplained reason, she will never be able to live a normal or independent life. Her brain stem has simply suffered too much damage, and the stem cannot regenerate itself or allow other parts of the brain to compensate for the damage."

When I walked out of Renee's room, my mind was like mush, and my heart was shattered in a million pieces. Like the guy in *Bruce Almighty*, I wanted to cry, "I have no bird, I have no bush. God (You have) taken my bird and my bush."

When I left the hospital, I immediately went to be with Leslie's families, the Combs and the Longs. As we were sitting in their home, the great-grandmother of Leslie and Jim's babies laid her head on my chest and asked the question, "Pastor, help us to understand what Paul means when he says in Romans, I believe it is in chapter 8." She paraphrased the verse. Let me share the KJV version which was her preference:

And we know that all things work together for good to them that love God, to them who are called according to his purpose. (Romans 8:28, KJV)

Since I was struggling with Paul's promise for obvious reasons, I stumbled through an inadequate response. Her reply was, "I don't know how God will work this out, and I may not live long enough to see it, but I am trusting that God knows this situation from beginning to end, and eventually we will see good come from all of this."

Late in my life, I have been helped in understanding and making peace with Romans 8:28. Something I saw happen in the life of the young woman who stole my car opened a window to God's promise and grace. "All things work together for good," has become quite clear to me now. I can say the same for the Combs and Long families. Through the years in living life with these families joined with our own daughter's struggle for healing and survival, and the miraculous change in the young woman who stole my rental car, I have seen how God used each of these to help me appreciate that the apostle's promise in Romans 8:28 is precisely that—a promise—not a cliché. Some have even gone so far as to say this is one of the most significant promises in the Bible.

These real-life experiences are three of four events that have been most profound in helping me get beyond the minefield of questions and anger. The fourth event I will explore with you later in the chapter.

I confess that I'm without excuse in taking this long, especially when I had all the intellectual and academic tools to have resolved the issue long ago. My problem was that I was dealing with feelings in my heart that short-circuited my mind. My heart was asking questions that created a distance between the Father and myself. This was not a good place for a man who was trying to be faithful in leading God's people through their times of stress and heartache.

Long ago, I learned that when the heart and mind do battle, the heart usually wins. On the other hand, it seemed that my mind was playing a sort of spiritual jeopardy, requiring I find the right answers to questions that would bring clarity to my hurt and pain. This only resulted in further pain and anger.

I knew the ultimate solution was to seek counsel and instruction from God's Word. That was helpful, but not the complete solution. I discovered it is not enough to be instructed by what you learn from the Bible. I also had to be receptive to what God's Spirit was teaching me from what I was reading. Even that was not enough until I became involved in confessing my pain and anger. I had to capitulate, to surrender to the truth of God's Word, allowing God's Spirit to bear witness with my spirit. Admittedly, some consider this blind faith, but for me, I had to come to the place where I was willing to say with Dee Blackburn, the grandmother of Leslie Long, "I don't know or understand how God will bring good from all of this heartache, but I am trusting that He will and that He will keep His promise."

This opened up a conversation with the Lord for me like any open, transparent conversation I might have with a dear and trusted friend. I found that my anger began to disappear and my questions were far less important. Even with this significant step of reconciliation, I still was unable to understand how the events of my life fit into the "all things" of Romans 8:28. However, today there is a major difference.

The change in my heart and attitude for the most part took place after my resignation as pastor of The King's Place. My experiences with those dear people mentioned above became the mortar holding the structure of my life secure. The rebuilding began in those early years.

Rounding Third

Let me digress and go back to 1980-86 to lay a foundation for what has become the final piece as God removed my mental cobwebs related to His promise in Romans 8:28.

In the early 1980s I found myself in what I called the Valley of Spiritual Blahs. I didn't have the same intensity, excitement, and creative drive that had always been a part of who I was. I was known for a very healthy sense of humor, but that too seemed to have flattened out, and frankly, I felt like I was going through the motions.

It was two years after our daughter's accident and my productive, creative energies seemed to be deteriorating, rather than improving. I felt as though

I was slipping into a very dark place regardless of my efforts to connect with the Father of my faith and life. I felt like I was trapped in quicksand. The more I struggled, the more I sensed the inevitable closing in.

After eighteen years with this beautiful group of people, I had to face the one question I didn't want to even contemplate: "Is this the time to submit my resignation?" I didn't have Gideon's fleece to lay before the Lord, but I was trusting that God would answer my question.

Our eighteen years at The King's Place provided some of the greatest spiritual mountaintop moments any pastor and his family could ever experience. It also produced some of the deepest valleys and darkest times due to our daughter's accident and Leslie's death.

My friend, our stewardship consultant, had visited with me about every six months, always with the intention of encouraging me to join him and his company. Once again in 1986, he made the offer to join his firm. I accepted and became part of the company. It was not the same company that assisted our congregation a few years earlier, but he was the consultant when working for a different firm.

The consultant and I had become very close friends. He offered me a position at half the salary I received at The King's Place, but with the promise that I would become a full partner in the company by the end of the first year. That didn't happen.

In the course of my first eighteen months with that company, they increased from four consultants to seven. It was clear that my friend would not be able to fulfill his promise of a full partnership. When my friend chose to take my most substantial contact (one I had developed and signed), and gave it to a newly hired and experienced consultant to put him to work, the handwriting was on the wall. By the end of my second year with the company, I was producing above all the other consultants except the other partner, Doug Laird. I needed to make a decision.

Before moving from a lead pastor's role to that of a stewardship consultant, I never thought of myself as anything but a lead pastor. However, God gifted me in such a way that this became a very successful and fulfilling twenty-seven years of active ministry.

In 1988, I started Master Plan Ministries. In 1996, Dr. Dan Jackson, my associate stewardship senior consultant, joined me, and between the two of us, we worked with more than 326 churches in that twenty-seven year period, helping churches accomplish what they could not do for themselves.

While much of my enthusiasm and heart for the ministry returned as strong as ever, there was still this one little verse: Romans 8:28. I wept when I read it. It seemed like a cliché, but never a promise. There was something more here that I had not completely grasped. I was making progress, but I wasn't quite there.

Several years ago, I was reading from one of my favorite preachers, Charles Haddon Spurgeon, often called the prince of preachers in all of history. He wrote something that grabbed my attention and shook me to my core as he commented on Romans 8:28.

Everything that happens to you is for your own good. If the waves roll against you, it only speeds your ship toward the port. If lightning and thunder comes, it clears the atmosphere and promotes your soul's health. You gain by loss, you grow healthy in sickness, you live by dying, and you are made rich in losses. Could you ask for a better promise? It is better that all things should work for my good than all things should be as I would wish to have them. All things might work for my pleasure and yet might all work my ruin. If all things do not always please me, they will still benefit me. This is the best promise of this life.[2]

While I have read what seems to be every commentary on Romans 8, I have been helped most from the writings of Robert J. Morgan, especially from his book, *The Promise: God Works All Things Together for Your Good*, first published in 2008. It is from this book that I have borrowed the title for this chapter. Robert Morgan's writings have provided my fourth source of help.

Everyone will have good days and bad. That's an undeniable fact. I smile when I remember the boast I once made that I never took so much as an aspirin until I reached the age of thirty-two. I had never visited a hospital except to visit with my parishioners. My medical bills were nearly non-existent. And then at the age of eighty-one, I entered the hospital for a triple-bypass. After heart surgery, my life changed dramatically. I now keep what appears to be a biweekly calendar for visits to doctor's offices for checkups and medication management. I am well informed on each of my meds: when they need to be ordered, and when not to order too soon so my insurance will contribute their part of the cost. Yes, long lost are the days of my boasting about no prescriptions in my life.

Robert Morgan wrote, "No, clichés are not helpful. Instead, these are soul-bracing realities that flow from a central truth of Scripture succinctly stated in Romans 8:28: 'We know that all things work together for the good of those who love God: those who are called according to His purpose.' It is arguably the most powerful promise in the Bible. Cliché and platitudes are temporary bandages, but Romans 8:28 gives complete and ultimate healing to both our souls and our situations."[3]

So far Morgan hadn't said anything that most Christians will challenge. He does help us differentiate between a cliché and a promise, but he has not yet provided us with the substance of the promise. Before we get to what Paul declares is the heart of Romans 8, here's another Morgan quote that still sounds a bit preachy, yet it provides a platform for the good stuff that follows. Listen to Morgan as he raises some important questions:

> *But consider this: What if you knew it would all turn out well, whatever you are facing? What if Romans 8:28 really were more than a cliché? What if it was a certainty, a Spirit-certified life preserver, an unsinkable objective truth, infinitely buoyant, able to keep your head above water even when your ship is going down?*
>
> *What if it worked? What if it always worked? What if there were no problems beyond its reach?*
>
> *Would that make a difference to you? If you really believed it, would it shore up your spirits? Brace up your heart? Gird up your strength? Beef up your attitude? Put a bounce in your step? Put the sparkle back into your eyes?*
>
> *Romans 8:28 is all-inclusive, all-powerful, and always available. It is an as omnipotent as the God who signed and sealed it. It's as loving as the Savior who died to unleash it. It can do anything God can do. It can touch any hurt and redeem any problem. It isn't a mere platitude but a divine promise.[4]*

Morgan's books came sometime after the change began to sprout within my own soul. I began to take a serious inventory of the events in my life. It ended well but didn't have the greatest beginning. Was there something for me to learn from God's hand in my own life? Almost immediately I remembered my flight to Des Moines, Iowa.

The day before that flight, I was in Sacramento, California, working with one of the churches in that area. I was enjoying a working lunch with a subcommittee of the Master Committee. The restaurant setting was beautifully poised on the banks of the Sacramento River, and we were enjoying perfect seventy-five degree weather, sitting on a patio cantilevered over the water.

The next morning, I boarded my flight in Sacramento headed for Des Moines, Iowa. My itinerary called for a plane change in Denver. The plane was delayed about thirty minutes in Denver because of weather conditions in Des Moines. When we lifted off from Denver, I was working on something and not paying much attention to the pilot's status report. While the conditions in Des Moines were becoming increasingly severe, I was not concerned. I had probably landed or taken off on snow and ice more than a couple hundred times before. Fifty miles out of Des Moines, the captain spoke again to report that we were being diverted to Cedar Falls because of an incident at the Des Moines airport. He didn't provide any details. We learned later that one of the larger jets had slid off the runway, causing a temporary closing of the airport. That night I was to be in Boone, Iowa, fifty miles north of Des Moines. This was going to present a severe problem since Cedar Falls was 105 miles northeast of Boone. My first of two sessions was to begin at six thirty that evening.

So far on this travel day, the "all things" were not working all that well. We landed in Cedar Falls in a blizzard. I walked up to the car rental counter to arrange for my car. The counter employee asked me where I was headed, and I told him Boone, Iowa. He answered, "We are here to rent cars, but this may be a day to find a room and ride this out." I explained that if it were at all possible, I needed to get to Boone where I had two training sessions scheduled to begin at six thirty. He said, "Let me give you a car with brand new snow tires, and take this candle and matches as well." The candle was about eight inches tall and four inches in diameter.

The state highway from Cedar Falls to Boone was only two lanes, so he told me, "As you drive, you will see several vehicles that have slipped off the road into the ditch. If that should happen to you, don't leave the car! Light the candle and wait for help. When the snow stops, and it begins to freeze, the candle will create enough heat inside the car to keep you from freezing when the temperature starts dropping."

In my twenty-seven years of "flying the friendly skies," United proved to be just that. During those years I did not miss a single appointment or calendar event due to weather or mechanical failure caused by United. I was determined this would not be the first. I drove that 105 miles on ice-and-snow-covered roads. I don't recall seeing a single snowplow.

I drove into Boone, and carefully made my way to the church. The parking lot was hardly recognizable. The lot was covered with three or four feet of recent snow, and in the parking lot, you could see snow piled up to ten feet from previous storms.

I walked up to the entry just outside the offices. I was met there by one of the custodians. He greeted me and said, "Dr. Dan, it's good to see you, but how did you get here? Are you aware the meetings for tonight have been canceled?" He said, "The pastor and co-chairpersons felt it was too dangerous for more than a hundred of our people to be out on the streets this evening." We each had a good laugh considering I had flown from Sacramento and been in the air or on the road driving through one of Iowa's most difficult storms to get there, only to find the meetings had been canceled. Maybe these Hawkeyes were not as hardy as I thought, but perhaps more intelligent than this consultant.

Again, it crossed my mind: these "all things" the apostle Paul is talking about, really? How do all these things of the past twenty-four hours fit in this promise?

I began to recall the events of that day and realized my flight from Denver to Des Moines could have created an incident far worse than diverting to Cedar Falls. I could have slid off the highway while driving to Boone and possibly even froze to death. What I was unable to know or understand is what was to happen in the life of that church because of those canceled meetings.

We rescheduled our two meetings, and instead of doing them on one night, we set aside the next two nights. That gave me more time to challenge and teach. Those two nights set the stage for one of the most successful capital stewardship programs ever. That may be the closest I've come to a break-out revival. That congregation raised more than five times their annual budget income over the next three years. This happened because the people seriously allowed their hearts to be moved and their minds to be shaped by the teaching of stewardship found in the New Testament.

On the final Sunday of that program, I preached. When I concluded, the retiring lead pastor, Paul Williamson, stood before his people and said, "I have a confession to make. You know I was not sympathetic with this program in the beginning, but I will tell you that in all my years in ministry I have not seen the power of God move the hearts of folk as He has among us. These past three months will be the capstone of my ministry." There was what I call a holy hush among his people, but he was not through. He continued, "We have prided ourselves in the beautiful craftsmanship of this altar that stretches across the front of our sanctuary. In my years with you, I have never seen a single person come forward at any time to kneel and pray before the Lord. I would like to see that change. This morning at the end of this extraordinary hour, I'm inviting those of you who wish to come and kneel, thanking God for what He is doing in your life and in the life of our church." The people moved forward; they knelt and prayed, many with tears flowing down their faces. It was a prayer time that lasted well over an hour. God was doing something very special among His people in the heartland.

"All things" were beginning to look more than encouraging all because of a diverted flight, a dicey drive in the snow and ice, and canceled meetings. These were God's people who loved their Lord, and who were called according to His purpose, and He was doing a work in their lives which they could not produce, yet they received it by His grace.

When beginning a program with a church, that first visit is very intense. I would usually arrive on a Friday evening, preach at the weekend services, then teach a Sunday afternoon session designed to motivate and help the people appreciate what they could expect and achieve. Sunday evening and Monday was always set aside for the enlistment of the Master Committee. This was a group I would train, a very committed group that would assist me in providing leadership to the rest of the congregation. The Master Committee always became the heart of any capital stewardship program. The lead pastor and I, along with a few key staff members, determined two couples we wished to invite to become campaign codirectors in every program.

I was beginning to work with St. John's United Methodist in Davenport, Iowa, for the third time. The enlistment of the Master Committee had gone very well and according to schedule. Twenty-eight couples and four single people had agreed to serve. One of the couples we wanted to invite as co-chairs were out of town and would not be returning until the following Friday afternoon. That created a bit of a problem since I was holding return flight tickets for that Friday morning. Back in those days, United was a bit more relaxed with their business flyers who flew more than a hundred thousand miles a year. They agreed to reissue my Friday tickets for the same flights on Saturday instead.

I was a bit irritated over the delay in returning home. It meant I would have less time with my wife before I had to leave again. I treasured every day at home. They were like precious nuggets. I smiled privately when I remembered my recent conversational prayer with the Lord over Romans 8:28: "Lord, I believe we're making progress. While You have said, 'all things' work together for good, I have at least moved to a place where we can say 'some things' are working for the good."

And so it turned out, because of the delay, we were able to recruit one of the finest and most competent couples as co-directors, and it also appeared that I would soon sign a contract with a wonderful congregation on the other side of the Mississippi in the Quad-Cities, all as a result of my schedule change. Of course, I reminded God that I was still not too happy about losing time with my wife at home.

After doing some work on my computer, I retired rather early on Friday evening, knowing that I had a very early call for that first flight out the next morning. I caught that first flight, since my plane was probably already on the ground from the last flight the previous night.

I arrived at the airport, checked in my rental car, and picked up the morning paper. A front-page article and all the TV monitors were describing the details of the tragic accident the night before between USAir Flight 1493 and SkyWest Flight 5569 at the Los Angeles International Airport. The USAir flight was a Boeing 737-300, and the SkyWest flight was a small two-engine Metroliner turboprop. Air traffic had not been that heavy at the time, yet the local controller had been distracted, and the SkyWest crew was told to taxi into the takeoff position while the USAir flight was landing on the same runway. When the crew of the USAir sighted the smaller plane on the very spot they were landing, it was too late. The little plane was crushed beneath the larger aircraft. All twelve people in the smaller aircraft were killed; and twenty-three of the eighty-nine on the larger plane died, mostly from asphyxiation in the post-crash fire. You can imagine my additional grief when I read that the pilot of the small plane was my neighbor who lived just four doors from our home. (This crash led to the National Transportation Safety Board's recommendation on using different runways for takeoffs and landings at LAX.)

This was one of the most significant events of my life—and I wasn't even there. My life would have ended on February 1, 1991, if my schedule had not been changed. I was scheduled to catch commuter flight 5569. Through an experience which I had grumbled over inwardly that was riddled with personal inconvenience, God allowed me to lose a couple of days with my wife and son, and gave me years to replace that time in return. Any irritation I felt melted into gratitude.

In my case, the "all" in "all things" of Romans 8:28 was looking enormous. My delay had been caused by the unavailability of this couple. If it had not been for that delay, I would have perished with all the other passengers and crew of flight 5569, the flight for my original ticket. God had my attention.[5]

Syncing the Heart and Mind

The question of this book: *Where Was God When I Needed Him?* is more a plaintive cry for help rather than for information of God's whereabouts. For the non-believer the cry might be, "God, if You really exist, why don't You present yourself and do something about my suffering?"

For those of us within the family of God, we know the answer to the question. God is everywhere present at any given moment in time. We call this God's omnipresence. He cannot be limited by what He created: time and space. The truth that God is present right here in this moment as I write. He is present with you wherever you are as you read too. He is present with the mother giving birth. He is present with the soldier taking his last breath. God is always there and here. We may not acknowledge His presence, but our acknowledgment or lack of it does not change the reality of God's presence. God's power, God's sovereignty, God's love, or anything else about God is always present.

It is not a secret that I have struggled with Romans 8:28:

And we know that in all things God works for the good of those who love him, who have been called according to his purpose. (Romans 8:28)

Clearly, I have made incremental steps in reconciling my heart with the truth of this passage. How do any of us do that when faced with circumstances that seek to destroy us? All of the moving illustrations of others will be helpful and encouraging, but there is only one source of help that provides a final solution, God's Word.

Romans, the Jewel of the New Testament

Again, Morgan wrote, "Romans is the greatest theological treatise ever written. It's the sixth book of the New Testament, containing sixteen enriching chapters that can rightly be called the spinning core of Scripture. More than any other book in the Bible, it systematizes and articulates what the gospel of Jesus Christ is all about."[6]

About Romans 8:28, David Martyn Lloyd-Jones wrote, "This statement…is probably more packed with doctrine and comfort than any other in the whole realm of Scripture."[7]

The book of Romans, a jewel within the New Testament, was written by a man who was once the enemy of Christians. Saul of Tarsus was on his way to Damascus with the intent of gathering up Christians to return them to Jerusalem in chains. While on the Damascus road, he had a personal visitation with the Lord which resulted in his miraculous conversion. Not only did Saul receive a new life when he accepted Christ, but he also received a new name, Paul, and was to become perhaps the greatest apostle of all.

Before his time of seclusion and preparation, he returned to Jerusalem to be introduced to a very suspicious and hostile group of believers. Barnabas personally took him to the apostles and told them about Paul's conversion experience on the road to Damascus. That went well with his new Christian friends, but those who were once his friends had now become his enemies, and on several occasions sought to kill him. Paul is often referred to as the apostle to the Gentiles. The focus of his ministry was in the Middle East and Asia Minor; later he moved into Eastern Europe, Europe, and Greece. Everywhere he went, he endeavored to preach first to the Jews, and when rejected, focused on the Gentiles, planting churches while preaching the good news of Christ. When Paul finished his third missionary journey, he returned to Jerusalem. He wanted to make careful plans for his fourth tour to spread the gospel even further west in Spain. Paul was hoping the church in Rome would assist him in that effort.

Acts 20 gives us a wrap on Paul's third missionary journey. Paul had a special friend, Gaius, who lived in a little villa just outside Corinth. The three months he was there provided him with some rest and relaxation from the tour now just ended. It also offered him the opportunity to orchestrate his plans to take the gospel to Spain. Perhaps his most celebrated letter, the book of Romans, is believed to have been written in AD 56 (Acts 20:2-3; Romans 16:23). What Paul wrote while Gaius's guest would one day become the basis for Martin Luther's break from the Roman Catholic church. In Romans, Paul, inspired by the Holy Spirit, wrote an explicit and systematized presentation of the doctrine of justification which comes from faith, not works.

Paul was aware the Jews were plotting against him, so he was diligent in the event they were successful. His explanation of the gospel would be permanently secured and passed down through the ages until the end of time. In writing to the Christians in Rome, Paul was placing his mark for Christ in the center of the empire. Could he have made a better choice?[8]

Perhaps there is no greater explanation in Scripture of just how God did what only He could do: make us acceptable for unconditional communion with Him. We call this justification. When we respond with confession and repentance of sin made possible by God's gift of Christ, we call that salvation.

The word *justification* appears several times throughout Romans. Before moving on to the biblical narrative, an illustration is helpful to understand what justification does. My friend Lou owned a printing business before current technology replaced typesetting. He explained that *justify* to printers means that type is set precisely in such a way that all of the full lines are of equal length and flush both left and right. When printers are successful, the printed lines are in a perfect relationship with the page they're printed on and with each other. Frederick Buechner, when thinking about printers of the past, said, "The religious sense of the word is very similar to what printers once did." He explains that being justified means a person is brought into a proper relationship with God.[9] In Romans 5:1, Paul says that being justified means having peace with God. Paul uses the noun *justification* and explains that it is the first step of salvation.

Paul was on his way to Damascus to clear out those pesky Christians when suddenly he heard the voice of Jesus Christ, whose resurrection he had discounted as an ugly rumor. Paul might have expected the voice to say, "Just wait, I will have the last word." But the voice said, "I want you on my side." Paul never got over that moment, but lives through eternity because of it, and so do millions of his spiritual offspring who embraced his message.

This voice, the Lord, only wanted two things; First, for Paul to believe He meant what He said, and second, to do what He was telling him to do. Paul did both.

When Paul had no reason to believe what he just experienced, he was overwhelmed by the idea that no matter who you are or what you've done, God wants you on His side. There isn't anything you can do to earn God's favor. It's on the house. It goes with the territory. It's all up to God. God is the One who "justified you." He is the One who lined you up, making certain you are in perfect alignment with Him.[10] That, my friend, is justification.

The theme of Romans is stated in its prologue, Romans 1:1-17, especially in verses 16 and 17:

> *For I am not ashamed of the gospel, because it is the power of God that brings salvation to everyone who believes: first to the Jew, then to the Gentile. For in the gospel the righteousness of God is revealed—a righteousness that is by faith from first to last, just as it is written: "The righteous will live by faith." (Romans 1:16-17)*

Paul dedicated the first eight chapters of Romans to make clear that man just doesn't have the ability to make himself acceptable to God. Romans would be devastating if Paul ended it there, but thankfully he does not.

People often say: "There are many roads to finding God, right?" Paul says, "Sorry, my friend, there aren't. There's only one." Man alone will never be righteous before God, no matter how many good things he does. There is only one way to reach God, and that is through the merits of Jesus Christ.

And who was this Christ? He was the Son of God, the perfect Man and perfect God, who lived without sin and became the perfect sacrifice. Because of His perfection, He was able to satisfy God's demand for our justification and enable us to stand before the living God, just as if we had never sinned. This is why what Christ did on the cross is called *substitutionary* atonement. He became *our substitute*, standing in our place before God, a place where we had no previous standing. Amazing! Christ removed forever the wall that prevented us from having fellowship with the Father. As you read the first eight chapters of this magnificent letter, you will see that Paul is a master at presenting God's plan for our salvation.

It is helpful to observe that Romans comes after the four Gospels and Acts. These books are historical and chronological, telling the story of Christ, the cross, the reason for the crucifixion, the resurrection, and the beginning of the church. The letters, or epistles, which follow provide color, and the theological explanation for what we read in the first five books. While the entire book of Romans is critical for our understanding, the first eight chapters provide the foundation, the theological structure for the rest of Scripture and Christianity. Romans 1-8 are essential for reading and comprehension. In my pursuit to sync heart and mind, and find the answer to my question, I came to realize my effort could not succeed until I made peace with Romans 8:28. The following exposition is my effort to reconcile my heart and mind with this great verse, a verse that shines like a gem in what may be Paul's most celebrated epistle.

- Separation (Romans 1:18-3:20)

Following the introduction, Paul presents the nature, loss, condition, and hopelessness of all humanity. The cause of this complete separation from the Father is sin, man's conscious disobedience. If one is separated from the holiness and perfection of God, he is left with the impossible task of trying to live a life that pleases God. Such a person cannot make himself righteous since he does not possess the tools to recreate himself.

> *Therefore no one will be declared righteous in God's sight by the works of the law; rather, through the law we become conscious of our sin. (Romans 3:20)*

• God's Offer (Romans 3:21-31)

In these eleven verses, Paul explains that God was the only One able to offer us grace. During the Old Testament generations, man tried to please God by endeavoring to keep His law, an effort that was a total failure. God's grace was expressed through a person who could communicate with us, but more importantly, who died for us:

> *But now apart from the law the righteousness of God has been made known, to which the Law and the Prophets testify. This righteousness is given through faith in Jesus Christ to all who believe. There is no difference between Jew and Gentile, for all have sinned and fall short of the glory of God, and all are justified freely by his grace through the redemption that came by Christ Jesus. God presented Christ as a sacrifice of atonement, through the shedding of his blood—to be received by faith. (Romans 3:21-25a)*

• Abraham the Example (Romans 4)

In this chapter, Paul realizes there will be questions about his teachings, and so he addresses them before they are even asked. Since justification (acquired by faith instead of by man's attempt at keeping the law) is a whole new concept, Paul knew they would ask: "Who is this Paul and by what authority does he speak?" Paul returns to the Old Testament to illustrate his point. Here he helps his readers understand that his authority is found in the Old Testament, a point that would not be lost among the Jewish members of the church in Rome. Paul explains that the principle of justification by grace and faith goes back to the very first book of the Bible. He is referring to Abraham when he writes:

> *What does Scripture say? "Abraham believed God, and it was cred-*
> *ited to him as righteousness."...The words "it was credited to him"*
> *were written not for him alone, but also for us, to whom God will*
> *credit righteousness—for us who believe in him who raised Jesus our*
> *Lord from the dead. He was delivered over to death for our sins and*
> *was raised to life for our justification. (Romans 4:3, 23-25)*

• Standing (Romans 5:1-11)

Winning an all-day pass to Disneyland or a lottery that pays seven thousand dollars per week for the rest of our life pales in comparison to Paul's outline of the benefits we receive from God's gift of grace and justification. Get this! When God offers His gift of justification (salvation), and we accept it, we are immediately ushered into God's presence. Additionally, we receive an inheritance that provides us with every benefit and privilege of His grace. This is our ticket that transcends time and lasts without end:

> *Therefore, since we have been justified through faith, we have peace*
> *with God through our Lord Jesus Christ, through whom we have*
> *gained access by faith into this grace in which we now stand. And we*
> *boast in the hope of the glory of God. (Romans 5:1-2)*

• Death Destroyed (Romans 5:12-21)

In these ten verses, Paul is speaking of the Old Adam and the New Adam. When Adam fell from his perfect state into sin, thereby infecting all humanity, we were forced from the presence of God. The Old Adam was overwhelmed by sin bringing death. The New Adam removed the sting of that death and offered life. Once we have been forgiven, we are no longer the children of the original garden inhabitants, but we are now justified and have become the descendants of the New Adam, the second Adam, the Lord Jesus Christ. We stand with Him before the Father having inherited His righteous nature:

> *For if, by the trespass of one man death reigned through that one man, how much more will those who receive God's abundant provision of grace and of the gift of righteousness reign in life through the one man, Jesus Christ! (Romans 5:17)*

• Sanctification (Romans 6-7)

Paul has done a remarkable job in explaining how God has provided for our redemption and justification, but he is careful to warn us that bits and pieces of our old nature yet prevail. He introduces a concept or teaching called sanctification. The very idea of sanctification makes clear we do not become perfect just because we have now confessed faith in Christ. We have been saved from the consequences of sin, but we are not perfect. Sanctification is that process by which believers grow as they follow Christ. "He treats this subject in three parts: (1) freedom from sin's tyranny (Ch. 6), (2) freedom from the law's condemnation (Ch. 7) and (3) life in the power of the Holy Spirit (Ch. 8)."[11]

As with the experience of salvation, Paul understands we need a supernatural presence of God's Spirit to help us with the challenging moments of life, and so He provides the presence of His Spirit to guide us along the way.

After reading the first part of Romans in which Paul lays out the state of humanity and what God has done to make us right, how could we come to Romans 8:28 with ambivalence, questions, or lack of faith? Suddenly my own question: *Where Was God When I Needed Him?* seemed disrespectful in light of the cross, our justification, His tenderness in bringing us back to Himself, and His gift of His Holy Spirit who is a constant Companion and Guide to help us through the hard times in life.

My question was clearly not crafted well. It revealed an inadequate understanding of God's sovereignty and His ability to be everywhere present at any given moment. We call that the omnipresence of God. In chapters 8 and 9, we examined God's sovereignty and omniscience.

If my question is the wrong question, then what do I do about my confusion and frustration? We can find no better solution than that found in Romans 8.

Making Peace with Romans 8:28

Even though we find Romans 8:28 difficult to reconcile with the way a natural man thinks and reasons, it is one of the greatest promises in the Bible and leaves no misunderstanding concerning the presence and work of the Holy Spirit in our lives.

We are not only set free from sin and its consequences, but the Spirit of the Living God actually dwells within us.

In the first part of Romans we learn of mankind's fall and demise as well as God's recovery plan. Chapter 8 teaches about living our lives with the presence and power of God's Spirit. We are not only set free from sin and its consequences, but the Spirit of the Living God actually *dwells within us.* We understand that the Spirit of the Living God and the Spirit of Christ are one and the same.

God made a choice to shape us in the image of His Son. It is our destiny to be "little Christs." He now dwells within us. God is committed to producing in us all the beautiful qualities of His Son: love, joy, peace, kindness, patience, long-suffering, goodness, and gentleness. Therefore, we can claim his purity, holiness, and grow in attitudes that honor our Father God.

The first seven-and-a-half chapters of Romans provide faith and confidence in our Father who is sovereign. Warren Wiersbe explains that when we suffer, we can be confident that He is at work in the world, and He has a perfect plan.

> *"God has two purposes in that plan: our good and His glory. Ultimately, He will make us like Jesus Christ! Best of all, God's plan is going to succeed! It started in eternity past when He chose us in Christ (Ephesians 1:4-5)."*[12]

The question of this book was a plaintive cry from a broken heart. Our Father in heaven is also in our lives. He is a gentle Father who understands our pain. He comes to us in our confusion, hurt, and anger, lifting us in His celestial arms, even praying on our behalf when the hurt is so severe that we are unable to speak coherently. Paul speaks of those times when we are weak,

> *And the Holy Spirit helps us in our weakness. For example, we don't know what God wants us to pray for. But the Holy Spirit prays for us with groanings that cannot be expressed in words. And the Father who knows all hearts knows what the Spirit is saying, for the Spirit pleads for us believers. (Romans 8:26-27, NLT)*

Fred Fisher makes the point that "Verse 28 does not teach that all things are good. It teaches that God combines all life's experiences 'for good' in the Christian life. The 'good' is defined in verse 29; it is being 'conformed to the image' of Christ (RSV). This happens only when we meet the experiences of life with love for God; it is not true automatically."[13]

When we try to understand the phrases "all things" and "God works for the good," we are made strong in the faith that not only does our God know, He also He cares. By praying on our behalf when life has crushed us, He shows that. When I began to understand the context of verse Romans 8:28, the Father helped my complaints become smaller and smaller until they were finally non-existent.

I understand that I am not writing the final word on the truth of God's Word as found in Romans 8:28, but I invite you to take a grammatical journey with me in these next three paragraphs that reveal one of the methods God used to move me from confusion to confidence, from anger to joy, from despair to hope, and from doubt to faith.

Here's the technical understanding of Romans 8:28-30 that I found online: The "all things" in papyri manuscript P46 has "God" as the subject of "working together." It is even grammatically possible that the *subject* of verse 28 is "the spirit" (see verse 27). This verse also relates to "the sufferings" referred to in verses 17-18; and the "groanings" of verse 23. There is no such thing as luck, fate, or chance in relation to believers.

"To work together for good" is in present active indicative. This is also a compound with "syn" (verse 26). Therefore, it literally means "all things continue to work in cooperation with one another for good." (In a world of evil and suffering, this is a difficult subject to understand. Two helpful books on this are *The Goodness of God* by John William Wenham and *The Christian's Secret of a Happy Life* by Hannah Whitall Smith.) The *good* here is defined in verse 29 as those "conformed to the image of His Son." Christlikeness, not prosperity, fame, or health is God's unalterable plan for every believer.

"To those who love God, to those who are called according to His purpose": These are two present active participles. These are two conditions which continue to allow the believer to view life, *regardless of the circumstances*, in a positive light (see verse 15). Again, notice the twin covenantal aspects of human freedom ("love") and God's sovereignty ("called").[14]

This may be seen all too complicated to believe especially if one doesn't possess a working knowledge of Koine Greek and the details of the English language. You might find yourself hopelessly lost in the effort to understand the essence of Scripture. If you are caught in such a crevice, let me share Pastor Chris Noland's simplified outline of the "Eight Benefits of Justification by Faith" from Romans 5:1-11. According to him, God has given us:

- Past Justification
- Peace with God
- Access into His grace
- Joy in tribulation
- The indwelling of His Holy Spirit
- His unconditional love
- Deliverance from future condemnation
- Present reconciliation with God[15]

When absorbing the abundant provisions of the Father that Paul describes so eloquently in Romans 1:18-8:27, is it any wonder that my questions and anger have been replaced by faith and love?

The Harvest from Romans 8:28

In the next chapter I write about finding hope. You will note that my hope is focused on the young lady who had stolen my rental car. This was such a profound experience that it began to provide me with some balance and understanding of what may be one of the grand statements and promises found in God's Word. This young woman was at the very bottom of life, addicted to drugs, charged with several felonies, convicted of a serious crime, and now a seven-year resident of the state correctional facility for women. Her demeanor when entering that facility was not open to any kind of help. However, when that change took place, which was a gracious act on the part of God the Father, she was presented with another promise from the Bible:

> *Therefore, if anyone is in Christ, the new creation has come: The old has gone, the new is here! (2 Corinthians 5:17)*

The *New King James Translation* gives us:

> *Therefore, if anyone is in Christ, he is a new creation; old things have passed away; behold, all things have become new. (2 Corinthians 5:17, NKJV)*

In this passage, Paul is dealing with the eternal significance of our new life. He is helping us understand that the old creation that defined who we were before being made new would not stand before God who is both holy and just. That old nature could never live with Him eternally. The word Paul used to make his point is *reconciliation*. Paul is dealing with the forgiveness of sin and replacing our old sin nature with the new one God gives us as we become reconciled with Him through Christ. This is precisely the meaning of verse 19,

That God was reconciling the world to himself in Christ, not counting people's sins against them. (2 Corinthians 5:19)

If you personalize Paul's teaching by replacing *world* with your name, the thought may have greater meaning. *Reconciliation* was first used in English in the fourteenth century. It has many meanings, and usually focuses on being restored relationally. How does the Word of God define it?

Dr. Michael L. Williams provides help with his question. He writes this in his article titled "What Is Reconciliation? How Does the Bible Define It?"

In the Old Testament, the word reconciliation is the Hebrew word kapar, pronounced kaw-far. This is one of the most theologically significant words in the Bible. In addition to reconciliation, kapar is also translated into English words such as forgive, purge away and merciful as well as a few others. By far, the most commonly translated word for kapar is the English word atonement.

When the word "atonement" is broken down to its historical parts (a-tone-ment) it means a condition without tension. When Christ died on the cross for us, He removed the tension between us and God (Romans 5:10; 2 Corinthians 5:16-21). His shed blood, reconciled the conflict between us and the Father. With this in mind, reconciliation has its Biblical foundation in the atonement of Christ.[16]

Paul is not promising that all the consequences of the old nature would be eliminated. Donna, the young lady who stole my car, is now paying the consequences for her old nature's lifestyle. Even though she is forgiven by God and has a new eternal nature, she is still responsible for the penalties caused by her sinful actions. The good news is that because of her new life, the sting of death has been removed because of Christ.

When she stole my rental, Donna was not concerned or even aware of what the apostle Paul wrote in Roman 8:28. She didn't love the Lord, and had no idea that she was "called according to his purpose." Once in a relationship with Jesus Christ, she could not automatically claim this verse as a ticket to get out of Dodge. When she received a new nature and life, the fact remained that she was serving out the penalty of her former life, even though the old nature had been replaced with the new. The new nature has both present and eternal significance; the old nature no longer does. Her new state enables her to be content with her current confinement. The eternal promise provides her with reconciliation with her Creator and an eternity with the Father.

Today my young friend is not asking the questions I did. Her only knowledge of God at the time was rather limited. She used His name in profanity, but she was not wondering where He was. Neither was she concerned about His existence. Now that she is a believer with a new nature, she has the good sense to understand that her new nature is not like a Disneyland pass. It's much better than that—it's a promise of life for eternity. She may have never known peace with the Father had it not been for the "all things": the events that transpired the day she stole my car.

Many years ago, when I was a very young pastor right out of seminary, I was serving on staff in a beautiful congregation in southeast Los Angeles. In the congregation, was an exceptional man. He was much older than me. He had one of the most effervescent joyful expressions I have seen. As a young pastor, he took an extraordinary interest in me, wanting to do anything possible to make sure I would have every opportunity for growth. He always reminded me that God's hand was on my life and he simply wanted to encourage me. On several occasions, he would give me a call and say, "Dan, let's go fishing." Usually, he had already made reservations for us to go out of San Diego, 120 miles south of our home. We would board a boat that could accommodate about twenty-five, find a bunk and head out to sea; the next morning we might hopefully find the big bluefin albacore tuna. Those were great moments of my life when John, an older saint, poured from his life into mine, producing some of the great building blocks for my later life and ministry.

The day finally came when John entered the UCLA Medical Center. My friend would not return home. He was suffering from a chronic case of lung cancer. He was dying from a physical condition caused by his earlier life of chain smoking. Even though he became a new person in Jesus Christ, utterly unafraid of facing death, the habits of his earlier life eventually exacted their due. He truly was reconciled and forgiven by God. He became a new person in Christ. He had the hope and promise of an eternity with God, but he suffered the temporary loss of this life because of his previous lifestyle.

John, as a young man, felt that God had placed a special calling on his life to preach, yet because of his excessive smoking when young, he was denied that calling. His ability to teach and preach was lost. When faced with the results of his cancer, John like many struggled with Romans 8:28. For a time he seriously wondered how "all things" really worked. How could this situation bring about good? Yet John was to be a servant in God's kingdom and invested his life into mine as well as several young men who would do what John was never able to do. My friend John had found his birds and I was one of them.

CHAPTER 11

FINDING HOPE

Tough circumstances are no match for the kind of
inner strength fueled by hope.

—*Ray Johnston*

A Hope Specialist

Ray Johnston is a gifted communicator of God's truth. He is the lead pastor of one of America's mega churches, Bayside, in Granite Bay, California. He is also the creator and dynamic force behind Thrive Communications. Thrive is designed for pastors, church leaders, and anyone else who wants to be inspired and recharged in their faith. A promotional piece states, "Our goal at Thrive Conferences is to make you feel appreciated, loved, encouraged and motivated. We strive to connect us all more closely with the one who is the ultimate source of inspiration and power."[1] Thrive, an annual conference held in different cities around the country, offers hundreds of breakouts covering topics for most any interest or need. In 2020 Thrive goes international with the first Thrive Pastor's Conference in Havana, Cuba. A major full blown Thrive for both Cuban pastors and laity is planned for 2021. See the Thrive page at the back of the book.

Ray has written an encouraging book from which hope simply cascades called *The Hope Quotient: Measure it, Raise It, You'll Never Be the Same*. It should be in every correctional facility, university, seminary, church, and home.

An Unforgettable Alumni Reunion

By now you may be wondering if I am interested in something more substantial than flying a hang glider and if there are any solutions when you feel hopeless and when God seems to have a deaf ear to your cries for help.

This chapter will help you appreciate that hope is not only possible, it's available. In a later chapter, we will experience through others what happens when faith, hope, and love replace hopelessness. In my final chapter, you can journey with me when you lift your heart over the bar and find sense out of what seemed so senseless.

Jumping in our alumni time machine, I find myself in the San Diego airport heading for my sixty-fifth high school reunion. Flights were late, and I missed my connecting flight out of San Francisco, and traffic out of Portland was worse than anything I'd ever experienced in southern California. I finally arrived two hours late for the Wednesday afternoon Laurelwood Country Club event in Eugene, Oregon.

Our reunion committee had determined that this sixty-fifth reunion would be our last major reunion. With that news, I decided to attend, thinking this could well be the last opportunity to see many good friends. On Thursday morning I decided to revisit some of the homes we lived in during my high school years. Because my father was a general building contractor, we moved often. I even enjoyed a visit to the site where the church of my youth once stood on 13th Avenue in Eugene.

After my nostalgic visit to the many places that helped shape who I am, it was time to head for my reunion. It was now elven thirty in the morning, and I was having some difficulty finding the place. I knew it was on Franklin Boulevard, but I couldn't remember exactly where. I was on Franklin, so I stopped at Trap Town Pizza located across from the Matthew Knight Arena to get directions for the Roaring Rapids Pizza Parlor. The Matthew Knight Arena was built with the contribution of millions by Phil and Penny Knight of Nike fame.[2]

My car rental had one of those push buttons located on the dash: you push it and the engine started or stopped. I pushed it thinking I had turned the engine off. Unfortunately, my push wasn't adequate for the engine to disengage. I jumped out, ran about ten feet to the other rear side of the car, opened the front door of the pizza place, and called out, "Where can I find the Roaring Rapids Pizza Parlor?" The fellow yelled back and said, "It's just down Franklin almost to Springfield, on this same side of Franklin." I said, "Thanks."

The next five seconds were unreal. I turned to get back in my car, and I noticed someone had just jumped in. My first thought was, *How come that car is where I left my mine?* My second thought was, *That is my car! Why is someone in it?* My brain was missing in action. It took but a fraction of a second for my internal computer to reboot, helping me realize someone was trying to steal my car.

My next decision could have been fatal. I thought if I stood in front of it nobody would run over me to steal it. Wrong! I stood directly in front of the right front headlight. The person in the car hit the gas and knocked me about fifteen feet through the air where I landed on the asphalt drive. A bit dazed, I was still able to see my car moving west on Franklin Boulevard, tailpipes hot with exhaust.

There was a couple I'd never met also driving west on Franklin who saw everything. In fact, they had to brake hard to miss my car as it veered into traffic again. They called, "Are you OK?" I said, "I think so." They immediately pursued the car. These people were twenty-first century good Samaritans. They called 9-1-1. The operator patched these exceptional citizens in with other police units who arrested the suspect on the other side of Eugene.

The suspect was trying to hide in one of the supermarket parking lots, but when she saw seven police SUVs moving in her direction, she decided it was time to make a run for it. The officers in two of the SUVs did a pincer move on her forcing her into a giant concrete light post. So the suspect was apprehended, the rental car was totaled. Because of the people who called it in and the remarkable efficiency of the Eugene Police

Department, the thief was arrested within about twelve to fifteen minutes from the time she stole the vehicle.

Meanwhile crumpled on the driveway of the first pizza place, I thought, *My cell phone was on the right front seat. My life is in that thing.* That's not really true, but that's what I thought at the moment. *I can't call my wife; I can't even call anyone who will be at the reunion to let them know I won't be able to make it.* Apparently, I was in shock. If my mind had been clear, I would have realized that the cell phone did not matter and that if I had been only a few more inches toward the middle of the car, the driver may have killed me.

The officer helping me was very kind and competent. After the medics from the fire department bandaged me up and put me back together, Officer Mac asked, "How can I help you now?"

I said, "What do you mean?"

He said, "Would you like me to take you to the car to retrieve any of your belongings, or the emergency room, or would you like me to take you to your reunion?"

I said, "Let's go to the car." When we arrived, it was a bit overwhelming. My car that had less than seventeen-hundred miles was completely destroyed. The officer took me around the car so I could look inside, and there on the right front floor was my cell phone, smarter than me, surrounded by little pieces of broken glass and other debris. I picked it up and pressed one of the buttons. Immediately the screen flashed on, and a delightful woman's voice said something like "Good morning, Dan! How can I help you? Here are some things you can ask me."

I put the phone in my pocket, placed one hand on the car top, and the other on the right front door, which was open. In the middle of the chaos,

I prayed, "Thank You, Father, for my life. Father, how is it possible to help this desperate woman who finds herself in such a pit?" The officers had already removed her from the scene. Later I discovered she was on both methamphetamine and heroin, and had both in her possession at the time of the crime. Initially, she faced seven felony charges. Several of those were reduced or dropped. However, she is currently serving a seventy-two-month prison sentence without the benefit of early parole.

Standing there next to my rental I felt a tap on my shoulder. It was my attending officer. He said, "It's time. It's time for us to get you to that reunion." On our way, we had several minutes to discuss the events of the previous hour. I was not asking to see the accused, but I wondered what I might say to her if that were to happen.

We finally arrived at the Roaring Rapids Pizza Parlor. My classmates took one look at me and my bandaged arm and asked, "Dan, what brings you to the reunion, chaperoned by one of Eugene's finest? The flashing lights are impressive, but what in the world happened?" When I explained, some looked at me with skepticism until they remembered the flashing lights and the officer. I simply smiled remembering this was our sixty-fifth high school reunion, perhaps our last, and some of my dear friends might be a bit confused.

When it came time to say goodbye, my mind was racing with thoughts of the young woman in the car. However, my immediate concern was making arrangements for a replacement vehicle since I had to drive back to Portland the next morning. I left the reunion early, feeling overwhelmed with those and other questions.

The next morning before my flight back to San Diego, I wrote a rough letter that I later sent to Donna (fictitious name). The letter calmed my mind and provided the opportunity for correspondence with her that continues to this day. This is the letter:

Dear Donna,

We have never met, but I did get a quick look at you as you were in the process of stealing my car, that is, before I did the flying nun thing, make that flying monk.

Some people, knowing they had come within inches of killing another person might feel some remorse and say, "I can't tell you how badly I feel. Can you ever forgive me?" Forgiveness could well be offered, but nothing can ever change the consequences of the decisions each of us made in those two seconds: your decision to steal my car and my foolish decision to step in front of the vehicle. The consequences for me are insignificant, but I can only imagine the consequence the courts will impose. Forgiveness can be given and received, but in many cases, the consequences remain.

Many years ago, I finally came to where I was able to forgive the intoxicated woman who struck the car causing the death of our beautiful fourteen-year-old daughter, forgiveness, yes, but the loss and pain remain for the rest of life.

It is not in my nature to condemn people; quite the opposite, my life has been committed to helping people who have lost their way, people who know little about love, or folk who don't believe there is such a thing as love, or a God who cares.

By now you may have figured out that I'm not a banker, lumberman, or business owner. But I'm not unlike many of these people. I'm an ordinary clergyman who loves people, even people who screw up. If someone else were writing this, I would be in the group of screw-ups.

During my life, I have seen hundreds (perhaps thousands) of people changed when they found themselves in a hole so deep they couldn't climb out, people who for the first time came to know the Author of us all and the Creator of love. They have come to the end of themselves and embraced the One who said, "I am the Way the Truth and the Life, no man/woman comes to the Father God except through me" (John 14:6). Those are the words of Jesus Christ, but that's only part of the good news.

The apostle John said of Christ, "If we confess our sins, He is faithful and just to forgive us our sins and purify us from all unrighteousness. But if we claim we have not sinned, we make him out to be a liar, and his word has no place in our lives" (1 John 1:9-10).

It is not my intention to preach, and I would not want to be presumptuous, but perhaps I am, and I may have already done so. My sense is you might appreciate the good news from God if only you knew what it was.

Donna, if you are inclined to be open for help, I will offer you the same book I gave to my granddaughter who at the time was a resident of the Washington State prison system. She found The Hope Quotient *by Ray Johnston to be helpful. This book helped change the way she perceived life. If you wish something better in life, if you desire life, it can help you as well. I won't tell you I love you, only because I don't know you, but I know Someone who does. I spoke with Him yesterday morning, standing beside the car you had taken. I will see that you receive a copy of the book I mentioned above if you like.*

There is hope, a better way. Are you up for that?

Donna, I pray that you might find peace, purpose, hope, and love.

Dr. Dan G. Myers

A Friend

All the law enforcement agencies in the Eugene community knew Donna well. She had a very long list of drug violations and arrests. Donna lived in the shadows of society. Her life was controlled by drug use, and her uncontrollable addiction meant her primary source of revenue was stealing. Donna was hopeless; the word *discouragement* doesn't seem to come close to the despair she was in.

The late Howard Hendricks, one of the esteemed Dallas Theological Seminary professors, gave one of the most compelling definitions of discouragement: "Discouragement is the anesthetic the devil uses on a person just before he reaches in and carves out his heart."[3] Ray Johnston, my friend, responding to that quote said, "He's right. When people lose hope, they lose their ability to dream for the future. Despair replaces joy. Fear replaces faith. Anxiety replaces prayer. Insecurity replaces confidence. Tomorrow's dreams are replaced by nightmares. It's a lousy way to live."[4]

Donna knew a lot about discouragement and hopelessness, and only a little about love. I'm happy to report that Donna has moved from chaos to hope. Her life is not where it once was, but she is on a journey where faith, hope, and peace are now possibilities for her.

After Donna took my rental car and was found guilty, she was sentenced for seventy-two months in the Oregon State Correctional System. I did not attend her trial but if I wanted to press charges the invitation was extended by the court. I said I did not. There were already many felony charges against her. If found guilty of all, she would spend a good deal of her remaining life in prison. I did ask for the privilege of corresponding with her once incarcerated. The court agreed.

The beginning of that first contact did not go all that well. However, over time she seemed to relax when she realized that I intended to help rather than take advantage of her. The breakthrough seemed to happen when I sent her a copy of the book I referred to earlier: *The Hope Quotient: Measure It. Raise It. You'll Never Be the Same.*

Before having the book sent to her, I had pulled a few thoughts from it to give her some interest in hope, something that had not been a reality for her. I mentioned a promise that Johnston makes and calls the seven factors that sustains hope. My question to her was, "Would you like to know what these seven factors are?" She said she would; and so, I sent some of Johnston's quotes with the hopeful expectation that she might be encouraged to find a better way.

> *When spouses lose hope, they give up on their marriages. Parents give up on their children. Teens and young adults give up on their parents. Healthy emotions like contentment and peace are replaced with toxic feelings of confusion, shame, worry, and disappointment. The bottom line, it's impossible to be spiritually, psychologically, emotionally, or relationally healthy when we're gripped by discouragement.*

> *Some wise person said that we can live about forty days without food, about three days without water, about eight minutes without air—but not a single second without hope. And that is why...*

- *the greatest gift parents can give their children—hope.*

- *the greatest gift coaches can give their athletes—hope.*

It's also why . . .

- *the greatest gift you can give your family—hope.*

- *the greatest gift you can give your friends—hope."*[5]

- *the greatest gift you can give those where you are—hope.*

- *The truth is that the greatest gift you or I can give anyone is hope.*

Think hope doesn't make a difference? Let's get real for a second. Two people are walking in your direction. One of them is the most encouraging person you know. The other is the most discouraging person you know. Which one do you want to spend time with? That is true in every setting.

The truth is that the greatest gift you or I can give anyone is hope.

Picture what happens when a person of genuine hope comes into your life. All it takes is one. In a flash, the whole atmosphere changes. The impossible starts to look possible (think Steve Jobs). Defeat starts to look like it could be turned to victory (think Peyton Manning). Difficult things begin to look like they might be possible (think Nelson Mandela). Courage replaces fear, and strength chases away powerlessness. Drugs are no longer the crutches that unsuccessfully seek to prop up a failing life.

Yes, hope is that important! It's a big deal.

Imagine two lives with identical circumstances, except one person faces those circumstances with hope and confidence, and the other person does not. How differently would those two lives turn out from one another?

My observation after working with people for more than sixty-five years provides evidence that this holds true. The presence of hope and confidence creates eleven significant differences. You will:

- *have more satisfying relationships,*
- *be more productive,*
- *be less affected by stress,*
- *be more successful,*
- *feel more satisfied,*
- *be more compassionate,*
- *be more willing to help people in need,*
- *be physically healthier,*
- *hold to higher moral and ethical standards,*
- *be more likely to assume responsibility and*
- *be more likely to see God as loving, caring, and forgiving.*[6]

Let me ask you a question. Do you understand that rising hope can change everything for you as well? God doesn't ask us where we came from. He couldn't care less about your color, job, education, or lack of knowledge. Where you are right now is of no concern to Him. He merely wants to know if you are interested in, and receptive to, a hope that only He can give. If you are it will change your world from hope-lessness to hope.

To some, hope can seem like cotton candy, which tastes good at first, but there's nothing of substance to it. Real hope is a deep and powerful force when it is anchored in the seven factors that sustain it.[7]

I was hopeful that Donna would see that the HQ (Hope Quotient) may be as important as her IQ (Intelligence Quotient). Clearly, I wanted Donna to ask the question, "What are those seven factors?" I was thrilled to receive her response, and immediately had the book sent to her.

Finding Your Balance in Hopeless Situations

One of life's significant challenges is knowing how to find a balance when coping with hopeless situations. Any person who tells you he has never dealt with a desperate problem is just not dealing with reality. Age makes no difference; impossible situations can come at any time in life. There are times when they catch us by surprise, and sometimes they come from a well-developed history of our ignorance and lifestyle. Bill Cottringer in his blog, "Staying Happy in Hopeless Situations" outlines many things that may cause people to lose their balance:

- *"Being born with a serious disability.*

- *Being terrorized by school bullies out to destroy you.*

- *Getting in trouble with the law that ruins your relationships, job, and finances, or being stuck in a miserable marriage, while having too many reasons to stay (like children).*

- *Losing everything in a natural disaster.*

- *Being the best parent you can be and ending up with a son or daughter on drugs, in jail or dead or in the hospital from a suicide attempt.*

- *Caring for a loved one who is dying and is an awful burden with a worse attitude.*

- *Hating your job, boss or coworkers but not being able to afford to quit.*

- *Or anything else as equally bad that you just don't deserve or want to cope with."* [8]

A person need not be in prison, convicted of a serious crime, or even addicted to drugs in order to find God's hope, peace, and love. The aspiring young professional, the teenager trying to find his way, the young house-wife: all may struggle for love and hope. Sarah Ortiz was such a young mother who like so many cried out,

> *There was a season in my life when I was filled with hopelessness. My life was falling apart, and I woke up every day with what felt like the weight of the world on my chest. I had two small children at the time, an infant and a toddler, and every day felt like a steep, uphill battle. I was exhausted and raising them alone, overwhelmed with the situations swirling around me. I'm normally a very outgoing person, but I remember sitting down every night, rocking my baby to sleep and wondering when it would ever get better.*

> *I knew it would, eventually. It had to. But when you're so deep in that pit of sadness, it's hard to see how God will bring you out. People would tell me 'this too shall pass,' but in the middle of hopelessness, there's little anyone can say or do to make you feel better.*

> *By God's grace, I'm now six years removed from that dark season. Yet I still look and see people I know and love fighting through their own hopelessness: the wife who is losing her husband to cancer, the single mother with no food and three days until payday, and the young woman fighting daily anxiety attacks. Yet, even in the midst of these dark times, where it seems there is no way out, God's Word reminds us that with Him, there is always hope.*

> *Maybe you feel hopeless today. You are in a dark place, over-whelmed by the situations you are facing and wondering when it will ever get better. In times like these, explore the hope of God's Word.[9]*

Ray Johnston gives us a very practical list of what hope and confidence creates. Bill Cottringer in his blog provides a list of things that may be the reason for losing one's balance, and Sarah Ortiz provides solutions from God's Word when facing tough times or impossible circumstances. See if they make sense for you; they have for Donna and for Sarah.

- The pain won't last forever.

He will wipe every tear from their eyes. There will be no more death or mourning or crying or pain, for the old order of things has passed away. (Revelation 21:4)

- Praise God, even when it's hard.

Why are you cast down, O my soul? And why are you disquieted within me? Hope in God; for I shall yet praise Him, the help of my countenance and my God. (Psalm 45:3, NKJV)

- Give your burdens to God.

Come to me, all you who are weary and burdened, and I will give you rest. (Matthew 11:28)

- When you are weak, God is strong.

But he said to me, "My grace is sufficient for you, for my power is made perfect in weakness." Therefore I will boast all the more gladly about my weaknesses, so that Christ's power may rest on me. (2 Corinthians 12:9)

- Keep your eyes on Jesus.

I sought the Lord, and he answered me; he delivered me from all my fears. Those who look to him are radiant; their faces are never covered with shame. (Psalm 34:4-5)

- God will strengthen you.

But those who hope in the Lord will renew their strength. They will soar on wings like eagles; they will run and not grow weary, they will walk and not be faint. (Isaiah 40:31)

- Don't stop praying.

Be joyful in hope, patient in affliction, faithful in prayer. (Romans 12:12)[10]

After I was thrown by the car and was lying on the pavement I admit that my first thought was not, *How can I keep my balance in this hopeless situation?* I was dazed. My first thought was, *What just happened?* I didn't know if the thief was a male or female, until I found a driver's license and several credit cards the driver had dropped in their rush to get away. The photo on the license was for an older man. Later we discovered that the thief had stolen these cards too. As I sat inside the pizza place waiting for the police to arrive, a lot of questions popped through my mind, questions that didn't seem to have answers. Dazed and in shock, not much made any sense. All those questions were answered and resolved with time, but regaining my sense of balance didn't happen in an hour, a day, a week, or even a month. The puzzle came together a piece at a time.

To begin the process, an alumni friend offered to help me get another rental car. I was thankful for their help in filling out all the paperwork for the stolen vehicle and in securing a replacement vehicle so I could get back to Portland. Eventually, the rental car company and my insurance company worked out all the details to pay for that vehicle that would never again kiss a freeway. Even though I had been thrown by the car, my injuries proved to be minimal, and my recovery required no further care. I was beginning to find emotional, mental, and physical balance.

At the time I knew nothing about the young woman who had taken my car. However, when the details of the day were aired on TV and published in the *Eugene Register-Guard* that evening, I had questions about this young woman. She had a long rap sheet with a history of theft and drug-related charges. I couldn't help but wonder what conditions caused such a hopeless situation. Was she from a broken home? Had she been abused as a child? What caused her to escape reality with drugs? Had she ever known a loving relationship? Those questions and more occupied my mind when flying back to San Diego.

Almost immediately the Eugene Municipal courts contacted me to gather more information. They were most helpful and suggested how I could reach out to Donna, assuming she was found guilty and served time.

Since I am writing this exactly one year after the incident, I can now ask a different set of questions about Donna. What at first looked like a tragic event turned out to be something entirely different, which demonstrates the power of a loving God. If you had stood above me while I was lying there in that driveway, and said, "Dan, I've got good news for you. Listen to this:

And we know that in all things God works for the good of those who love him, who have been called according to his purpose. (Romans 8:28)

What do you think of that now?"

I would have answered, "Are you crazy? That lady came within inches of killing me! What possible good can come from this?"

Is it possible to mine a valuable nugget from the commission of a crime? I remembered that conviction of an alleged crime brings inevitable consequences. Some might say, "Lock her up, throw the key away, she deserves what she got. That's a good thing." The truth is that one day she will be released. That is supposed to be the positive result of fulfilling the requirements of the law. By then she should be rehabilitated enough to create a proper balance in her life.

However, there is a far more significant result that has come from this crime. Consider the timeline of Donna's life from the moment of her crime. She stole the car, was arrested, tried in court, and is now serving a sentence. If she had gotten up that morning and made different decisions, she would not have stolen my car, would not be in prison, and would not have received or read Ray Johnston's book about hope. But most significantly, she probably would never have heard or experienced anything about God's grace and salvation through His Son Jesus Christ either. She may have never heard about God's love by reading the Bible or from friends. If these are not positive results born out of a great mistake, then I don't understand the meaning of positive.

Remember it was a whole series of crimes that put Christ on the cross. God, because He is sovereign, wrapped the sins of His accusers and the sins of humanity to His cross to help us understand the words of the apostle Paul when he said,

> *And we know that for those who love God all things work ogether for good, for those who are called according to his purpose. (Romans 8:28, ESV)*

What happened to Christ was not the result of *His* sin. It was the result of *our* crimes, *our* sin. Christ was providing a final solution to evil and sin when there was absolutely no recognition, confession, or repentance on our part.

Without being guilty of blasphemy, when facing a hopeless situation, it might be well for us to repeat the words and heart of Christ when He spoke from the cross:

"Father, into your hands I commit my spirit." (Luke 23:46)

Christ in the midst of His circumstances cried out from the cross,

"Yet not my will, but yours be done." (Luke 22:42)

When God created the cross, He didn't do it to provide us with a perfect understanding of all things. You may struggle with "all things working together for good," especially when you feel you are in a hopeless situation. Those are the times when we take consolation in trusting God's Word.

The cross is the doorway to life. When we choose Christ, we choose life. Our choice is available because of Christ's victory over sin and death. Satan's power over man was broken through the death and resurrection of Jesus Christ. Like Christ, there are times when we realize that balance and purpose only come from a surrender to the will of the Father. The Son of God is not a bad example to follow.

Donna, while sitting in her cell, without benefit of bond, might have cursed her luck in being caught, causing her to believe that her life was hopeless. After her conviction, she may have felt like all was lost. When she walked through the gates of the prison, she could have even contemplated suicide. After writing the first draft of this chapter many months ago, I discovered that is exactly what did happen. She did feel hopeless, as though her life had no purpose. In her mind there was no longer a reason to live. In an attempt to take her own life, she threw herself off a prison balcony, but God had other plans. Her head injuries were severe. God appeared to be using very difficult events to get her attention. Eventually she was released from the hospital to find my first letter. It was the beginning of hope for a young woman who had given up on snatching hope and love from a pit of hopelessness.

The fact that she can find forgiveness as a result of her criminal act is fantastic. She is now free from drugs, living with a new and wholesome purpose in life, ready to make a difference in the lives of others, and most important, dedicated to becoming a mother for her two young daughters and son, the mother they have never known. She is finding her balance and purpose from a life that was hopeless, and so can you.

Human suffering is not what we wake up for in the morning. We don't say, I'm going to take sixteen ounces of suffering in order to make my day. Yet, suffering can come in many forms. It came on that morning when my car was stolen. Yet, my moment of pain was minor compared to Donna's when she was eventually arrested, convicted, and incarcerated. Even though she continues to serve time for her crimes, those who knew her before and after she espoused faith in the living Christ, declare God has worked nothing short of a miracle in her life. Clearly, the whole tragic experience was meant for evil, but became a transformational moment when God, through His miraculous grace, made something lovely from brokenness and strife. Gloria and Bill Gaither express God's miracle beautifully in this song:

Something Beautiful

Something beautiful, something good
All my confusion He understood
All I had to offer Him was brokenness and strife
But He made something beautiful of my life.

If there ever were dreams
That were lofty and noble,
They were my dreams at the start;

And the hopes for life's best
Were the hopes that I harbor
Down deep in my heart;
But my dreams turned to ashes,
And my castles all crumbled,
My fortune turned to loss,
So I wrapped it all
In the rags of my life
And laid it at the cross![11]

CHAPTER 12

THE PRIG WHO STAYED HOME

Be careful not to mistake insecurity and inadequacy for humility! Humility has nothing to do with the insecure and inadequate! Just like arrogance has nothing to with greatness!

—C. Joy Bell

Definition of a Prig

A friend looking at the title of this chapter immediately penciled a line through the word "prig." He thought it was a typo and meant to be "pig." Actually, the title was correct. It was taken from a sermon I preached many years before. The intent of that sermon was to see two prodigal sons, each loved by their father, but each expressing a different face of rebellion. In it there is a lesson in helping me find an answer for my question.

When Jesus speaks of the older brother, the "prig," he seems to have far less patience with him than with the prodigal. Some may dismiss the prodigal simply because we find little in his lifestyle with which we can identify. And when it comes to the older brother, our own priggishness makes it nearly impossible to say, "Hey, that's me." Yet, if we are able to achieve a better self-awareness, we might want to ask: "What is a prig and how does such a person relate to others?"

H.W. Fowler's *Modern English Usage* provides a pretty reasonable definition of a prig:

> *A prig is a believer in red tape; that is, he exalts the method above the work done. A prig, like the Pharisee, says: "God, I thank thee that I am not as other men are"—except that he often substitutes Self for God. A prig is one who works out his paltry accounts to the last farthing, while his millionaire neighbor lets accounts take care of themselves. A prig expects others to square themselves to his very inadequate measuring rod and condemns them with confidence if they do not. A prig is wise beyond his years in all things that do not matter. A prig cracks nuts with a steam hammer: that is, calls in the first principles of morality to decide whether he may, or must, do something of as little importance as drinking a glass of beer. On the whole, one may, perhaps, say that all his different characteristics come from the*

combination, in varying proportions, of three things— the desire to do his duty, the belief that he knows better than other people, and blindness to the difference in value between different things.[1]

The sin of the older, priggish brother was his display of self-righteousness which caused him to be condescending toward his younger brother.

My Search for a Simple Answer Is Nearly Over

I considered many things about God and little about my attitudes in my quest for an answer to my big question, *Where Was God When I Needed Him?* In my own mind I had developed a theology that had God perfectly compartmentalized, but my theological understanding of God wasn't working as I expected when I went to the compartment that suggested I could pray for my daughter's healing and get timely results. When I prayed expressing faith, Renee was not healed; in fact, it seemed as though God had deserted me. Whatever line of communication I once had seemed to be broken.

Could it be I had become like the older brother with the mistaken idea that I could negotiate with God? Was I confusing my faithfulness in service to the Father with a bargaining chip that I could cash in when I needed Him to do as I wished? I didn't like what was happening to me. Like the priggish older brother, my obedience was turning to anger and frustration, leaving me with an attitude that challenged my faith. In earlier chapters I have explained the course I set to find an answer, with the hopeful expectation that my anger and confusion would be replaced with faith and love.

You know my history; I had been the pastor of two incredible congregations, and during those years I had learned a great deal about God. Could it be there was a major difference between knowing *about* God and *knowing*

God, knowing Him as a Father, my Father? Even though I had preached hundreds of sermons and taught college and seminary classes about the God of my faith, it became apparent that I didn't allow Him to sit on the throne of my life. How could I change that? How could I take the little faith I had and allow that faith to be internalized in my soul?

Even though I had preached hundreds of sermons and taught college and seminary classes about the God of my faith, it became apparent that I didn't allow Him to sit on the throne of my life.

I sought an answer in knowing God's greatness, in the fact that He is all-knowing, without equal, and true to His promises. I have now realized my personal need for humility, the antithesis of that sometimes silent arrogance and pride I took in knowing many facts.

Unlike the Prodigal Son, I never demanded an early inheritance from my earthly father. (My father had none to give.) I wasn't selfish, desiring wealth; I just wanted to see my daughter healed. I never squandered what I had after I left my father's home. I can't recall doing anything that would dishonor my father or bring embarrassment to my family. On the contrary, I chose to follow my calling as a minister of the gospel. I didn't hate anyone, and alcohol and drugs were never an issue in my life. In those earlier years I didn't consider myself better than anyone else. I was simply blessed to be in God's presence.

My father and mother were simple people. During World War II they struggled to raise a family of three children, sacrificing to see that we had the best they were able to offer. They provided us with a godly standard that would help us live our lives as they had—loving God, others, and especially each child.

My life experience, which included both our family, the church family, and my eventual decision to serve God by serving people, set me up to think of myself unconsciously as privileged. It was not long until I realized that being the apple of God's eye did not mean that I was privileged to receive any request. Perhaps I had been influenced by the "name it and claim it" group that taught their disciples they could simply name the desire of their hearts, claim it, and have faith to receive it. I don't know what the apostle Paul would have done with that theology when it came to his thorn in the flesh.

Something Happened while Doing Good

I will not say many, but some, ministers develop a persona of near perfection when it comes to the interpretation of God's Word. This creates a kind of subtle arrogance. It's a very easy trap to fall into. After all, our source of knowledge and information, God's Word, is the embodiment of God's revealed truth. When we allow the Holy Spirit to bear witness with our spirit that produces confidence. Without God's assistance, no matter how bright we might be, we may become arrogant.

When I considered my blessed past, and my best efforts to be a faithful communicator of God's truth, I stumbled over the hurdles the enemy placed before me. It was subtle. At times I was pretentious and pompous. I didn't mean to be. If anyone had described me thus, I would have felt offended. Yet, there was a bit of smugness, and I did feel a bit entitled above others because I had been chosen by God to share and communicate His Word. I had been faithful in doing good for many people. I wasn't seeking to develop my own brand, but I had high expectations that God had a responsibility to come through when I really needed Him. Why? Because I had served him faithfully, and because I was His son. In my subconscious mind I was beginning to act like a prig. This created a problem I was blind to at the time, a problem which caused me to ask a stupid question: *Where Was God When I Needed Him?*

Jesus' parable of the Prodigal Son (Luke 15:11-32) is like looking in a mirror. It is usually considered a parable about *one* prodigal, but I think it is actually a parable of *two* prodigals and one loving father. The younger prodigal became lost when he prematurely left his father's home. He immediately fell in with the wrong crowd and squandered his birthright to the point of wallowing with pigs. He was hired to feed pigs, yet not allowed to even eat the slop he was feeding them. Floundering in such a mess got his attention. Then there is the older son. The older prodigal was lost in his own arrogance, pride, selfishness, and lack of love. What can we learn from them?

In the midst of my questioning as to where God had hidden Himself, I saw that I was more like the priggish, older son than like the thoughtless, younger one. This self-disclosure didn't come until later in life when I faced my greatest challenge, a challenge that caused me to ask whether or not I could put my faith and confidence in what I had always believed to be the truth of God's Word, especially when my expectations were not being met.

It is critically important to understand who God is, what He has promised, and how He desires that we be the beneficiaries of His love. Of equal importance is the need for self-awareness. Are we like King David, who committed what many believe was the ultimate sin with Bathsheba? I say "ultimate" because that sin brought with it a whole family of further sins and deaths. David saw Bathsheba bathing from his balcony. Despite the fact she was married to a loyal warrior in his army, a strong defender of the king and nation, David sent for Bathsheba and had sex with her. She later bore a child from that affair. David tried to cover up his sin by commanding that Bathsheba's husband be positioned in the frontlines so he would die. He was and Uriah perished. David's further sins were many, all stemming from that one transgression. Even so, he is referred to by God as:

> *I have found David son of Jesse, a man after my own heart; he will do everything I want him to do. (Acts 13:22)*

I suspect there were moments when the king displayed arrogance, proclaiming his rights as a king, and the results were sin. However, he demonstrated a soft, contrite heart in confession of his sin, evidenced by the many psalms he wrote.

The priggish prodigal also assumed entitlement. In his own eyes, he had remained faithful and obedient to his father. He had not demanded an early inheritance, like his heedless brother. And he feels justified in his anger when the lost son, his brother, returns. His father calls for a fancy robe, a ring, shoes, and a feast, and that is more than the older brother can handle. The father declares:

> *"'For this son of mine was dead and is alive again.'" (Luke 15:24a)*

and

> *"'He was lost and is found.'" (Luke 15:24b)*

All this seemed like a slap in the face to the older brother's "faithfulness" to his father.

How did the older brother respond? To camouflage his own anger he thought: *Why should my unfaithful, wasteful, sinful brother receive such a reception by our father?* The older brother is so angry that he refuses to go inside and join the party. Their father hears about this and sits down with him. We soon discover that he is not just angry with his brother, he's angry with his father too. He tells his father how he'd never disobeyed his commands. He goes on to complain that his father had never given him so much as a young goat to throw a party with my friends.

The older brother paints a picture, contrasting himself with his brother. He reminds his father just how corrupt this young brother is. He tells him that his younger, faithless brother has:

"devoured thy living with harlots." (Luke 15:30, KJV)

The older prodigal points to how this profligate wasted a third of the estate, and then counters the father's response in killing "the fatted calf" to celebrate his homecoming. (The fatted calf was the best, most tender and delicious animal they had—specially raised to be that way.) I can hear him say, "Dad, you must be insane." The older brother sees this difference in treatment as a gross injustice toward him and he cannot control his anger toward his father.

This reminded me of the first night of the crusades in Kerala, India. That night when God healed so many by the power of His Spirit, especially the young girl whose eardrums had never heard a sound before and yet were miraculously opened, I felt a little like the older brother. Earlier I wrote about how I was conflicted on the long ride back to my hotel. I knew it was God who healed, but why would He use me in the healing of that young girl, and not heal my own daughter? It seemed like God was rubbing his finger in my eye. What was I to make of this?

I had preached about the (younger) Prodigal Son many times, but never about the older one. Many years after the Indian crusades, I was studying this parable again. Little did I know that God would provide another part of the answer to my ongoing question.

The story of the prodigals became like windows allowing the light of God's love to penetrate what had become a very dark place. The parable caused me to examine my own life carefully. I knew I wasn't like the lost son, but my likeness to the priggish one was becoming disgusting. Had I become so insensitive to our Father's love? Had I been expressing a spiritual contempt for others who had a different point of view, or perish the thought, a different interpretation of God's Word? Because of my advantages as a minister, I expected God had some sort of a divine obligation to answer my prayers and requests, according to my wants and understanding. Like the older prodigal, had I become angry with God when I saw how He in His love and mercy blessed those with sinful lifestyles and passed me by?

Perhaps the young men that had visited me in my office were partly right. They said God couldn't or wouldn't heal my daughter because of sin in the congregation and sin in my life. They may have identified a sin in my life I could not see: arrogance. But I knew that they were wrong in their point, not because I did not sin but because God doesn't require perfection before He heals. James does instruct us to confess our sins to one another when praying for the sick (James 5:16), but there are many examples of healing in the New Testament where confession of sin is not mentioned.

Finding an answer to my question was a process. But no matter the need, request, or praise, like King David and the lost son, I needed to have a contrite heart.

There is something very compelling about the younger prodigal. When he is still hardly within eyesight, the father sees him; and because of his compassion for this son who was lost, he runs to him, hugs him, and kisses him. This is a world away from the humiliating reunion the son might have expected based on his insulting treatment of his father. The son has his scripted speech memorized for his father, but he manages to get out only the first couple of parts. In the New American Standard Bible, we hear this son say:

> *"'Father, I have sinned against heaven and against you. I am no longer worthy to be called your son.'" (Luke 15:21)*

But before he can say the third part, before he can ask to be treated as a servant instead of a son, the father interrupts and takes the interview in a very different direction. Rather than treating this son as a servant, he turns to the actual servants and orders a celebration.

Here's a question for you: Which son pleased the father more? That may be difficult to answer. The father had reasons to be disappointed by both: the rebelliousness of the younger brother, and the arrogance, selfishness and lack of love displayed by the older brother.

The younger brother teaches us that we can be a genuine son of the Father and still be "lost" through sin. Yes, this son teaches us all about sin and where it leads, but he also teaches us that we can return to the Father and be accepted by Him with great joy and celebration. The Father being spiritually alive received him with open arms. The younger son, though lost because of his own disobedience, came to himself, and returned to his father's home with humility and confession, hoping only to be received as a servant. Instead he was restored in his relationship with his father. How good was that?

The older brother, the prig, is described as faithful. Yet he was jealous, smug, and proud, with a sense of entitlement. The younger brother, while he blew it, eventually returned to his father, confessed his sin, and was completely restored as a son. Nothing is said about the final state of the older brother. We don't know if he felt privileged because of being eldest.

Did he believe his father had to treat him differently because of his position in birth? Probably. Because of his earlier faithfulness and obedience to his father, was he confident the father was somehow obligated to provide him with whatever he wanted?

These are questions I began to ask of myself. Did I have the right to "name it and claim it": to demand the healing of our daughter? It seemed like an arrogant stance, an expression of little or no faith in my all-knowing, omnipresent, sovereign Father. Not only does He know my circumstances, He has the perfect knowledge to handle both the one who made the request and the request itself.

For more years than I like to admit, I kept asking that first question: *Where Was God When I Needed Him?* Over time, I saw that there were attitudes in me as well as a lack of faith and love that needed reconciliation. It was at this time that I realized how unimportant my question was. It sounds immature in my own ears.

Today I no longer ask that question. I know where God is, He is everywhere, unlimited by time and space. He is in every corridor of my soul. I need not raise that question again, but I still wanted to understand the meaning of "all things" in Romans 8:28, the final piece in my understanding.

I was reading something Robert Morgan wrote in his book, *100 Bible Verses*. He was speaking of a verse in Ephesians 1:

> *In him we were also chosen, having been predestined according to the plan of him who works out everything in conformity with the purpose of his will. (Ephesians 1:11)*

Morgan suggests this may be a duplication of Romans 8:28.

> *And we know that all things work together for good to those who love*

God, to those who are called according to His purpose. (Romans 8:28, NKJV)

Morgan thinks it is from an "above" perspective. These two verses provide different perspectives of the same truth. Romans 8:28 tells us that here on earth all things work together for good. This is *man's* perspective. Ephesians 1:11 is from *God's* perspective. Here He tells us that all things work together in conformity with the purpose of His will in order that we might be for the praise of his glory (verse 12).[2]

This is not the answer one looks for (or expects) when standing in an emergency room, hearing a doctor tell you that your daughter will not live to see the morning. At that moment, I was not thinking that "all things" will work together in conformity with the purpose of His will in order that we might be for the praise of his glory. But God was in that emergency room. He was in all three hospitals every day for the next thirteen months. He was with Renee and every member of our family as we struggled to find our way. She is now with God and God is still with us.

CHAPTER 13

WEATHERING THE STORMS OF LIFE

Those people who influence us most are not those who buttonhole us and talk to us, but those who lived their lives like the stars of heaven and the lilies in the field, perfect, simply, and unaffectedly. Those are the lives that mold us.

—Oswald Chambers

Lessons from Early Life

As a student in high school, I admired my woodshop teacher, Mr. Mickelson, and everything he taught me about working with wood. He was a very short man. He walked with a considerable limp because one leg was about four inches shorter than the other. One of his shoes was built up to make his limp less obvious. He may have had a limp, but his smile was something you never forgot. Of all my high school teachers, Mr. Mickelson was at the top of my list.

I made a beautiful redwood cedar chest for my mother, a coffee table for a friend, turned a couple of lamps on the lathe, and crafted a toboggan for fun. The toboggan was the most challenging since it required heating the individual slats in boiling water. Once they were wet and pliable, it was possible to shape them around a small steel barrel. Clamps were placed, allowing them to cure. In about forty-eight hours, I could remove the clamps and complete this little masterpiece. That toboggan provided an unlimited amount of fun for my brother and his friends long after I left for college. Our friends always sought out Dan's toboggan to enjoy the perfect ride down snow-covered slopes close to home.

I knew little if anything about boats. As a boy, I had never taken a lesson in the proper operation of a typical ski boat and certainly knew little about those beautiful boats with sails, but I was interested.

Because of my apparent success in those first woodworking projects, I decided to build an eighteen-foot ski boat. I spoke with Mr. Mickelson and asked if that were possible. Would it be beyond my abilities? He was more than encouraging and promised he would help me, assuring my success. He even offered to help me after regular school hours. Mr. Mickelson and I sent away for dozens of plans for the type of boat I had in mind. We finally decided on an inboard design that would not only be beautiful on the water but have the power to tow four-to-five skiers at a time.

As a sixteen-year-old student, my excitement was high. I was fortunate since my father was a small building contractor, which meant I had his experience and tools with which to work. Early on, we realized the project was too large to be assembled in the school shop, so we made the decision to prefab the boat and assemble it in another location. Remember, this was in the early 1950s before fiberglass boats. When I endeavored to create my masterpiece, boat construction was very different compared to present-day construction. Each era of construction had their lines of beauty unlike the other. I remember how proud I was in the accomplishment and charm of that significant effort when we placed it in the water for the first time. My mother suggested we name it *Danny Boy* after me.

It would have been very easy to move from motor ski boats to making those beautiful sailing racers. However, that was not to be. I had sold *Danny Boy* to help pay for college, as I pursued my call in the ministry. To this day, I know very little about sailing, but when I see a book describing a great sailing adventure, my imagination is always captured. I see myself at the helm of such a fantastic boat dancing across the open sea.

The Mike Plant Story

Julia Plant has written such a book, an excellent book about the life of her brother and his boat building and sailing adventures: *Coyote Lost at Sea: The Story of Mike Plant, America's Daring Solo Circumnavigator*. From her book and others, I have learned significant lessons about the integrity of those magnificent vessels. I've also learned about the discipline, commitment, and sacrifice of those who risk their lives when preparing for around-the-world competitions. This is a story that has been told perhaps thousands of times. In 1994, Gordon MacDonald recalled the story of Michael Plant in his book, *The Life God Blesses: Weathering the Storms of Life That Threaten the Soul*.[1]

In Michael Plant's final adventure, he sailed out of New York harbor on his way to Les Sables-d'Olonne, France, for the starting line of the next great race. There Michael would join about twenty other ships for a solo competitive circumnavigation. The object was to see who could sail around the world as a solo yachtsman in the shortest amount of time. Plant's boat, the *Coyote*, was a thing of beauty, the latest in design and technology, considered to be one of the greatest racing boats ever to sail. It was the top of the line. Plant was not only the one who would sail this beautiful boat, he also was a significant craftsman in the construction of the *Coyote*.

On his way to compete in his second Vendee Globe and fourth single-handed circumnavigation aboard *Coyote*, a powerful Open 60 sloop, something went terribly wrong. Two weeks out of New York his radio signal went silent. Authorities began to search the vast expanses of the North Atlantic. Commercial and search pilots listened for emergency signals; boats in the area were also vigilant in looking for Plant and *Coyote*. Thirty-two days after Plant departed from New York, *Coyote* was discovered adrift by a passing French tanker about seven hundred miles southwest of Ireland. Airplanes and ships from four nations had been involved in the search.[2]

When the *Coyote* was finally found she was "turtled": without the eighty-four-hundred-pound lead bulb. The bulb had been attached to the keel by six stainless steel bolts. When the storm came (or whatever the cause of the tragic loss was), the ballast was lost, and there was no way for the *Coyote* to sail with stability and remain upright.[3] The term "turtled" describes a sailing vessel that had entirely turned upside down with the sail pointed to the bottom of the sea. The bottom of the boat is now floating on the surface with the keel and lead bulb no longer attached. Consequently, it looks like the shell of a turtle. Did the ballast bulb hit a sunken ship, a whale, or did it get torn off because those six bolts could not weather a storm? Since the *Coyote* was considered by many to be the very finest within its category of racing sloops, reasons for the missing bulb remain a mystery to this day. Plant was never found. While we know the date of his birth, we do not know the exact time of his death. On September 6, 2002, ten years after Plant's death, he was inducted into the Single-Handed Sailing Hall of Fame in Newport, Rhode Island.[4]

What do Mike Plant's final tragic moments have to do with my responsibility in understanding God and where He might be? The beauty of Plant's magnificent vessel was what you saw above the waterline, but the most important, the critical part of the boat was below the water, the bulb keel. A boat can survive without a sail, rudder, or navigation system, at least for a time. But it can't recover from a storm without that unseen ballast beneath the surface, which provides the boat's stability against storms. Once it becomes detached from the boat, the racer and his boat are doomed. The same was true for me.

David Jeremiah draws an excellent analogy from the story of Mike Plant. He makes the point that when considering the ballast for our lives, the in-depth character-building stuff that comes from God's grace must be present. What we need to see in Plant's tragic story is the necessity of building our lives with strength and character *below* the waterline. That strength will provide the integrity to support what people see above. No matter how beautiful the vessel, if there is not adequate strength below, the ship will not survive. If the ballast in our lives is inadequate or flawed, we will suffer eventual defeat. When we rely on the Spirit of God and His Word, we allow God to be our Encourager. He becomes our strength and stability. He provides our faith, virtue, and knowledge. These three enable us to navigate the most difficult storms in life.

What others see is far less important. What counts is that you and God together know what's going on. What God provides is the stuff we build in the quiet places of our lives. It happens when nobody is looking. It occurs, when on our knees, we find ourselves in the solitude of our closets in sweet communion with the Father. It happens when we open our Bibles to learn, asking God to help us become what we arc not. When we are in the storm, this is the unseen part of our lives, supported by God's Spirit, enabling us to chart our course through any storm.[5]

This kind of ballast is what rendered my original question immature; it also gave me reconciliation with the "all things" in Romans 8:28.

In 2019, David Jeremiah preached a series that I suspect will become a book. Called "Everything You Need," he taught from 2 Peter 1. Four of the nine sermons in that series were about godliness, self-control, perseverance, and brotherly kindness. In the ninth and final message, he serves as a master communicator of God's Word revealing just some of the spiritual components that make up the ballast for our lives:

- Godly maturity (2 Peter 1:8; 2 Peter 3:18)

- Growing productivity (2 Peter 1:8)

- Greater clarity (2 Peter 1:9)

- Grateful memory (2 Peter 1:9)

- Genuine stability (2 Peter 1:10)

- Guaranteed security (2 Peter 1:10)

- Glorious eternity (2 Peter 1:10-11).[6]

The answer to my question came much earlier than Dr. Jeremiah's series from 2 Peter. However, he has provided exceptional teaching and confirmation for what is needed as we face the challenge of any storm.

Not only have I found the answer to my question, I have also discovered my responsibility in allowing God to support the very core of my life. This enables me to weather whatever storms life brings.

I found the answer to my question, I have also discovered my responsibility in allowing God to support the very core of my life.

In the next chapter I will share the lives of five extraordinary people. Each, in different ways, demonstrates strong character and integrity, the ballast for living. Each, under very different circumstances, has weathered the storms of life while making compelling contributions to others.

CHAPTER 14

GIVING LIFE

You give but little when you give of your possessions. It is when you give of yourself that you truly give.

—*Kahlil Gibran in his book,* The Prophet

The Archbishop and the Cross

Most young ministers have had many mentors from which they have gained invaluable insight and experience. One of my mentors was the late Dr. L. Doward McBain, former president of the American Baptist Convention. He also served as one of my seminary professors, and continued in a unique mentoring role until his death in 1999.

When he was serving as president of the American Baptist Convention, he invited me to serve on our denomination's planning committee for our national convention. That committee invited the late renowned Catholic Archbishop, Fulton Sheen, to deliver the keynote address at the American Baptist Churches USA Cincinnati Biennial Convention in the early 1970s.

When the bishop addressed the convention, he told of his visit to a leper colony in Ādīs Ābeba, Ethiopia. He intended to give a silver cross to each of the five hundred lepers. The ravages of leprosy grotesquely disfigured the first man he saw. The sight repulsed the bishop. The man's left arm was eaten off at the elbow, and his extended right hand was unspeakably corrupted. Unable to touch him, the bishop held the cross above his palm. He accidentally dropped it, where it was swallowed in the decaying flesh.

The bishop was grabbed by an eternal moment when he realized what he had just done with the cross, the sign and symbol of God's great love. Overcome with remorse for his own revulsion, Bishop Sheen dug his fingers into the man's leprosy to take up the cross, and then carefully placed it into what was left of the man's right hand. And so, with each of the other 499 lepers, gently touching each hand, he lovingly placed a cross in each.

The bishop's time with the lepers is a beautiful picture of God's love in stark contrast to the beheadings we see today. The tie that bound the bishop to those lepers was his focus on the cross and on those five hundred lepers who needed him. The question for us is: Would we be willing to give such a gift of love, knowing there was no way the recipients could reciprocate?

Frederick Beuchner gives an excellent definition of a sacrificial gift in his book *Wishful Thinking*: "To sacrifice something is to make it holy by giving it away for love."[1]

"To sacrifice something is to make it holy by giving it away for love."

A Mother's Gift of Love and Life

On November 27, 1989, Teri Smith, then twenty-nine, donated a portion of her liver to her twenty-one-month-old daughter Alyssa. The surgery took place at the University of Chicago Medical Center. It was the first liver transplant ever attempted, and was performed by a team of specialists.

In the recovery room following these two surgeries, a rookie reporter was allowed a few minutes with Teri, the mother of little Alyssa. Apparently, the reporter was tentative and feeling less than comfortable. Finally, she asked, "What was it like to donate a part of your liver to your little daughter?"

Alyssa's mother replied without hesitation, "Once you've given someone a big piece of your heart, it's easy to throw in a little bit of liver."[2]

Terri Smith was later asked about the pain of the surgery, and she said, "The pain for me is minor compared to the possibilities for Alyssa's full life." As you can appreciate, this surgery changed Alyssa's life. She graduated from high school in 2006, and from Meredith College in Raleigh, North Carolina, on May 9 (Mother's Day). Alyssa graduated magna cum laude with a bachelor's degree in social work.[3]

Today, Alyssa is passionate about her future and plans. She envisions a place for children where they can feel comfortable and relaxed as they wait for surgery. They will be able to meet others who are experiencing the same thing. It will be a place where parents with big questions may share with one another without the technical language of the medical profession.

Giving and sacrifice was no stranger to Bishop Sheen, Teri Smith, and later Alyssa. We too will continue to support one another when we look outward in love, when we look at the hurt around us, and when we seek to meet the needs of others. We will soon discover that our wants grow smaller in comparison to the joy we experience in helping others.

In the early nineteen hundreds in New Jersey, there was once a hat dying firm that came up with an interesting sales jingle. They used a play on words to make their clever point: "We dye to live, and we live to dye; the more we dye, the more we live; and the more we live, the more we dye." In their own way, this firm makes the point that Jesus made in Matthew 16:

> *"For whoever wants to save their life will lose it, but whoever loses their life for me will find it." (Matthew 16:25)*

A heart of compassion comes only after our hearts have been flooded by the love and mercies of God.

A New Life Begins

On July 31, 2009, we had friends in our home for a meal just to enjoy our friendship with one another. It was such an enjoyable evening, and the exceptional culinary gifts prepared by Renee's mother made for a wonderful evening. When our friends left, we began to prepare for a restful night. That was not to be.

A midnight call came from Renee's home, the Shepherd's House located in Montclair. The long journey was over. At first, her caregiver reported that paramedics had taken Renee to the hospital. I remember asking, "Is she still alive?" There was a long pause, and then the answer we expected, "No, Dr. Myers, she was gone by the time they reached the hospital."

> *We were beginning to learn,*
> *The wisdom of dying, not doing;*
> *To give to have;*
> *To let go to keep.*
>
> *—Anonymous*

It had been a long journey since her accident. We lay there in bed, silently weeping, but at the same time, there was a sense of quiet release, knowing that only a few moments before Renee had transitioned from impossible captivity to perfection. When the apostle Paul writes in 2 Corinthians 5:8 and speaks about being absent from the body is to be present with the Lord, in our imagination she was now singing and dancing and speaking a mile a minute—all of the things she had not been able to do for years since the accident. How could we not be grateful? Even so we struggled with our own sense of loss. As I write, more than three decades later, I still weep—not for sadness but because I know that moment gives meaning to my struggle with "all things."

At two in the morning we received a second call. This one was from One Legacy. The caller explained they were a group that made arrangements for body gifts so that others might live or enjoy an enhanced quality of life. The lady apologized for a call in the middle of the night, but explained that there was a narrow window of time in which to act. I could sense the tenderness in her voice when she said, "If your precious daughter is to help anyone, your decision must be made before six this morning."

We agreed for our daughter's remains to be harvested. Dr Birsner's recommendation in the emergency room the night of the accident was now becoming a reality. Renee's gifts made it possible for many to receive skin grafts, in some cases saving their lives. Others received sight, and a host of others live or benefit today from the gifts of her body that ironically refused to serve her well for the remaining years after the accident.

The Renee Scholarship for Physically Challenged Students

At the encouragement of friends, we established the Renee Myers Scholarship Endowment at Vanguard University, the place where her mother and I met many years before. The scholarship is the first of its kind to assist physically challenged students, students that would find it difficult or impossible to secure a college education without help. The scholarship was created in 2009, and in December of 2012, we received the exciting news that the endowment had reached the required threshold, meaning that in 2013 students would begin receiving scholarships, not only in 2013 but also until the end of time.

The First Scholarship Recipient

I served on the Vanguard Alumni Board for seven years and was president of the board for the last three. I was very familiar with the scholarships mostly created by alumni or friends of alumni. Once an endowment was established, a select committee managed it. That committee determined the amount and number of scholarships granted each year determined by the investment portfolio's performance of the previous year. All of the scholarships were invested with a professional group that had been secured to handle the Vanguard University investments. This committee also made the selection of alumni scholarship recipients based on need and the specifications of each scholarship.

Every year the university provides a unique dinner program where all scholarship donors and new scholarship recipients are invited. The tables are set so donors and their scholarship awardees are seated at the same table. It is always a delightful time when donors get to meet exceptional students and students experience the love of those who have created the scholarships. Many students report that they just would not have been able to follow their dream for education without assistance from these scholarships.

There have been several award recipients since the scholarship was created. Alyssa Rossi was the first to receive assistance from Renee's scholarship. Alyssa was a junior music major with an emphasis in voice studies. She served as a worship leader with the Spiritual Formation Department and performs with the Concert Choir. She intends to pursue a career as a choir director, vocal coach, or music therapist. Alyssa has excelled as a blind student and has made a significant impact on the Vanguard student body. This was the information provided us before the reception so we would have a little preview of our new friend.

In our table discussion, we discovered that Alyssa's home was in Palmdale, California, only a few blocks from the site of Renee's accident. Alyssa had also been a student and graduated from the Family Learning Tree, a school we created in 1977 during the time I served as the lead pastor of The King's Place. We knew nothing of Alyssa's past since I had resigned from The King's Place long before Alyssa attended the school.

Alyssa was such a gracious, loving young lady. She wanted us to share a portion of her note. "Thank you for caring about Vanguard students—this is a huge blessing for me!"

Another young student we met on that first reception evening was Richard Hicks. Richard was sitting next to Alyssa that night, and it was evident that he was very attentive to every concern Alyssa might have. Richard was a guest that night and not a scholarship recipient. He was Alyssa's guide to help her around the campus. Alyssa had been blind from birth. Richard had begun to hold more than Alyssa's hand too; he was starting to catch her heart as well.

Shortly after their graduation, they were married and continue to do exceptionally well as they bless many with their ministry. Both Richard and Alyssa are quality young people living out their faith in Christ. When Alyssa was named as a candidate for the Renee Scholarship for Physically Challenged Students, the university published the following piece:

ALYSSA ROSSI

Religion major, member of Concert Choir

She wouldn't let a natural condition keep her from pursuing her dream.

When Alyssa Rossi decided to attend Vanguard University after hearing Vanguard Singers and Band perform at her church, she faced challenges a bit more formidable than a typical student's. Born with a condition called Leber's congenital amaurosis, she could detect light and darkness, but otherwise, was totally blind. "It's my way of life," she says. "I'm very happy with it."

As a religion major and member of the Concert Choir, Alyssa has committed herself entirely to minister to people through worship and teaching after graduation. She is given assistance in reaching this goal through the Vanguard University Counseling Center, which communicates with her professors and provides textbooks and technology to accommodate her needs. The support goes beyond the classroom: in the concert choir, she learns the songs by sound and participates in concerts and tours; she has flourished under the mentorship of professors; and she and her guide dog, January, have enjoyed Vanguard's social community. And Alyssa is aware of the powerful force that's helping write her story at Vanguard. "I felt God's Spirit here and thought, how could you do any better than this? Why go anywhere else?"

Some might look at Alyssa, her blindness, and question the "all things" of Romans 8:28. It just might be that those who look at this precious young lady that way are the ones that are blind. Alyssa, like so many who face a difficult life challenge, exceeds most of us in making a difference in the lives of others.

The Puzzle Comes Together

William Sangster was a man who could have stumbled over the "all things" before the end of his life and ministry. Robert Morgan speaks of this faithful servant of God:

In 1939, William Sangster assumed leadership of Westminster Central Hall, a Methodist church near London's Westminster Abbey. During this first worship service he announced to his stunned congregation that Britain and Germany were officially at war. He quickly converted the church basement into an air raid shelter, and for 1,688 nights Sangster ministered to the various needs of all kinds of people. At the same time, he somehow managed to write, to preach gripping sermons, to earn a Ph.D., and to lead hundreds to Christ. He became known as Wesley's successor in London and was esteemed as the most beloved British preacher of his era. Sometime after the war, Sangster was diagnosed with progressive muscular atrophy. For three years he slowly died, becoming progressively more paralyzed, finally able to move only two fingers. But his attitude didn't falter, for when first learning of his illness, Sangster made four rules for himself. Many people have rules for living. Sangster composed four rules for dying, "I will never complain. I will keep the home bright. I will count my blessings. I will try to turn it to gain."[4]

Sangster under incredible odds accomplished all of this in doing good for his people while being a faithful servant of the Lord. He found a way to translate the apostle's "all things" for the benefit of those he served, including the unrelenting invasions of the enemy and an illness that eventually took his life.

God takes the B,
the A,
the D
And turns them into GOOD

We don't know how He does this thing,
Or even why He should.
It never fails
For those whose hearts are true;
All things may be against us,
but Christ makes all things new.

He takes the S,
the A,
the D,
And turns them into GLAD
Through it may take a while to see
How good can come from bad.
Don't falter, then,
Or faint or fail,
Just search His Word and rest;
Though it may differ from our own
His plan is always best.[5]

CHAPTER 15

HEART POWER

If you lift your heart over the bar, the rest has to follow.

—*Dick Fosbury*

Lifting Your Heart over the Bar

Dick Fosbury won the high jump gold medal in the 1968 Summer Olympics. During his college years at Oregon State University, he popularized and perfected a new high jumping technique, the Fosbury Flop. After winning the gold medal, Fosbury and his new jumping style captured the attention of jumpers around the world. It wasn't long until the Fosbury Flop became the dominant jumping style, and it remains so today. Before Fosbury, most elite jumpers used the straddle technique, Western Roll, Eastern cut-off, or even scissors jump to clear the bar. Given that landing surfaces had previously been sandpits or deep piles of matting, high jumpers of earlier years had to land on their feet or at least land carefully to prevent injury. When deep foam matting replaced the harder surfaces, high jumpers were able to be more creative and adventurous in their landing styles.[1]

You can appreciate Fosbury's jumping style if you visualize the flop. He approaches the bar at maximum speed, and then propels himself up. In his ascent, his body begins to twist. The eyes are looking at the sky while the head is the first to clear the bar. The back is now facing the bar as it passes over the bar drawing the legs and feet to complete the jump.

Each year in the community where I once served, we celebrated the accomplishments of our young athletes. Fosbury was the invited speaker one year. His communication skills were second only to his accomplishment in high jumping. With every eye focused on him that evening, he concluded his presentation with these words, "One of my great lessons for life came from my years of jumping. I discovered once you lift your heart over the bar, the rest will follow."

That night I heard Dick Fosbury speak to accomplished and young aspiring athletes, encouraging them to be successful in any sport and life, letting them know that you must have passion, and you must have a heart. Passion and heart had become the two casualties in my life. I found myself simply going through the motions. When I attended the banquet that night I was not expecting a major insight for my question. Help comes from unexpected places. What Fosbury said that night encouraged and helped me when I needed it most.

Help comes from unexpected places.

Making Sense Out of the Senseless

It was during the Christmas season, our pastor preached a sermon titled, "Making Sense Out of What Seems Senseless." He reminded us of those first moments when Gabriel visited Mary. He asks the question, "What was Mary to think?" His teaching helped me deal with the fact that I could not always understand or explain the ways of God. See if you agree:

When Gabriel came to Mary and announced she would become a virgin mother of God's Son, everything changed in a moment for that young Jewish girl. Who in their right mind could believe her story of being impregnated by God? Try explaining that one to your family, friends, and community. Try telling that to the man you are engaged to, when he knew he was not the father-to-be. Oh yes, her life changed, not only for the moment but also for her lifetime. She knew that the penalty in Jewish Law for a woman betrothed (engaged) caught in adultery was death. How was she to convince anyone of this angel from God and his story that God had impregnated her without the benefit of a man? Can't you just hear the talking heads on this one? The truth would only be seen as fake news. Yes, her life changed never to be the same again. It's most fortunate that Planned Parent-

hood didn't have a chapter nearby to give Mary the better part of their wisdom. I'm confident she would have continued to abide by the message from the angel.

Our pastor listed three things we could learn from Mary when dealing with life-changing events that inevitability shape our lives, one way or the other. I find them to be very instructive. First, rely on God's peace, which is stronger than our fears. Second, embrace our future, so we don't get stuck in the past. One can't drive forward if he keeps looking back. There is a good reason why the rearview mirror is much smaller than the front window. And finally, when we are able to release the past, we can invite God to do something new through us. That was true for Mary, and it can be right for us. Like each of us, Mary in the very beginning didn't have any answers nor did she understand what God was doing, or how He would work it all out, but she put her past where it belonged and trusted God for the future. Jesus was to have a mother of great faith.[2]

A Father's Fantasy of Faith

Some may consider this a contradiction, but you will see that while every line that follows is not precisely historical, yet they speak of the reality of our faith. In one sense these thoughts are similar to a parable. The writer of Hebrews helps us to understand that:

Now faith is confidence in what we hope for and assurance about what we do not see. (Hebrews 11:1)

I started with a fantasy which soon turned to faith because God's Word gave me the assurance for something I could not yet see. Hopefully, you will indulge me for a moment of memory from the past and faith for the future. This is what makes looking ahead with hope possible, instead of looking back in defeat and rage.

Following our daughter's death, friends suggested that God finally answered our request. They would say things like, "She is free, free at last." Who couldn't be happy about that? The fact remains that God didn't answer our prayers according to our request. However, I've finally come to the place where I'm not so concerned about what God did or didn't do. Instead I'm confident that God will fill in the blanks one day. He is the One with perfect knowledge, not me.

As a young boy, I raced to our county fairgrounds to watch the car races and the Joe Chitwood Hell Drivers Thrill Show. I didn't have the money to buy a ticket so we would watch our mini Indianapolis 500 through the knotholes in the fence. As a result, our vision was severely limited to the flash of a single car as it zipped by. We couldn't see the beginning to the end. Life is a series of knotholes, but one day we will see and understand it all from God's unlimited perspective.

A Night Visitor

And so, for me, you can imagine my delight when I welcomed my unique nighttime visitor. I believe he said his name was Gabriel. He helped bring some clarity to my questions. His perspective is much better than mine: he sees our lives from the beginning to the end. He views the race of life from above. I call it, perhaps incorrectly, a fantasy; yet it speaks of truth, based upon the promises of God's Word and faith. He speaks openly and with authority, declaring: "You may not comprehend every word now, but ponder the promises of my Father!"

God is our refuge and strength, an ever-present help in trouble. *(Psalm 46:1)*

When he calls to me, I will answer him; I will be with him in trouble;
I will rescue him and honor him. (Psalm 91:15, ESV)

I can do all this through him who gives me strength.
(Philippians 4:13)

A Special Letter

Gabriel continues, "For you, my friend, I bring this airmail special delivery letter. It comes from a very faraway place, yet present at the same time. You will recognize the One who sent it." When I opened the letter, this is what I read:

My Faith

Dear Mom and Dad, Dana, and Theron,

My faith, it was a simple thing. After reading my story you can see that I was pretty young when my life took a turn. I didn't live long enough to become confused with a lot of "religious" ideas and what other people thought.

What I did know is that even at my young age, I needed something or Someone to place my hope and faith in. It seems that Dad was preaching this all the time, not only at church but at home as well. Man, Dad, you were a trip. I couldn't always understand what you were talking about, but I did make a connection between what you were saying and the little song we sang in Sunday school,

Jesus loves me this I know,

For the Bible tells me so;

Little ones to Him belong,

They are weak, but He is strong.

Yes, Jesus loves me!

Yes, Jesus loves me!

Yes, Jesus loves me!

The Bible tells me so.

Jesus loves me! He who died,

Heaven's gate to open wide;

He will wash away my sin,

Let His little child come in.

Yes, Jesus loves me!

Yes, Jesus loves me!

Yes, Jesus loves me!

The Bible tells me so.

Pretty neat, I believed that. I can't tell you I saw flashing lights or had an extraordinary vision, and I still had some questions about sin. Were some bigger than others, and just how did Jesus handle them? What did He do with them?

My faith actually began from my early days as a child, but I remember that specific moment when I said, "Yes, Jesus, I want You in my life." I remember it was at our breakfast table when you and Mom prayed with me. It was a few weeks before Easter. When Easter arrived, Dad baptized me in our church. That was quite a day. I never forgot that.

I remember when Dad had that class for all of us who were to be baptized. He said, "All the water in the world would not make anyone a Christian if he weren't one already." He added, "If you baptize a frog, that frog is a frog when he goes under, and Mr. Frog is still a frog when he comes up." I kind of smiled when he said this: "When we finish, you're going to be either very wet without faith, or a very wet person excited to tell everyone about your faith in Jesus."

I remember that he helped us understand something one of those men said in the Bible: "When you are placed under the water, you are identifying with Jesus in His death." At first, that sounded a little funny. How could that be? Back then I hadn't died, so how could I identify with Jesus and His death? Then my dad said, "When they took Jesus from the cross, they buried His body in a tomb. When you are baptized, that becomes a beautiful picture of what Jesus did for each of us." At first, I didn't understand, but finally, this is how I realized what Dad was talking about. You see the stuff in all of us that isn't good, gets buried, just like Jesus was buried. Dad called that sin, but good things are put in us by Jesus, and we receive His life. That's what all that going down and coming up out of the water is about: Resurrection! I took that to mean that something got buried that God didn't like, but on the other hand, I received a new resurrected life because of my faith in Jesus. Man, that's pretty neat! You can't go wrong with that deal. The truth is that it got me to where I am. I started to say, it got me to where I am today, but here we don't have days or time, and since we don't have time, there is no end. I know that may be hard for you to understand.

Now don't get me wrong. I didn't become the perfect preacher or Jesus kid after I got baptized. While I got pretty wet, I didn't become a little celestial saint, but I can say that I began to think differently, even though I still liked boys, especially one.

Well, that's about it for my story of faith. After my accident, I completely lost the ability to decide what I would do with my life, or even how I would live. For the rest of my life, those decisions were pretty much made for me by others, but I do remember the hundreds of times when Mom and Dad would hold me, and we would pray. Even though I could not speak, God was able to hear my heart. My parents always seemed to have this quiet calm. I know it was hard for them, but God always seemed to meet with us in those times when we prayed together. We didn't always get what we prayed for—until now.

I'm not going to try to tell you what it's like here; if I did you would have difficulty believing me. It's not that I can't explain; the problem is you can't understand, but you'll find out soon enough. I definitely recommend this place. I hope you will join me."

With love,
Renee Myers.[3]

EPILOGUE

Where was God? He was in the very same place He was in when His Son said,

"Father, into your hands I commit my spirit." (Luke 23:46)

ENDNOTES

Chapter 1

1   Kiefer, James E. "Nate Saint and Other Martyrs of the Ecuador Mission." anglican.org. Accessed October 7, 2019. http://justus.anglican.org/resources/bio/74. html.

2   Cole, Stephen J. "Psalm 57: Singing In The Cave." Psalm 57: Singing In The Cave | Bible.org. Bible.org, 1993. http://www.bible.org/seriespage/psalm-57-singing-cave

Chapter 3

1   Zelley, Henry J. "He Brought Me Out." timelesstruths.org. Accessed October 7, 2019. https://library.timelesstruths.org/music/He_Brought_Me_Out/.

2   Admin. "Gutenberg Castle in Balzers – Liechtenstein." Tourist Spots Around the World. Tourist Spots Around the World, September 9, 2013. http://www.touristspots.org/gutenberg-castle-in-balzers-liechtenstein.

3   Magee, John Gillespie. "High Flight." High Flight - John Gillespie Magee, Jr. arlingtoncemetery.net. Accessed October 8, 2019. http://www.arlingtoncemetery. net/highflig.htm.

4   Lincoln, Joseph Colville. Soaring for Diamonds. Flagstaff, AZ: Northland Press, 1972.

5   Ibid.

Chapter 4

1   Webb, Barry G. The Message of Isaiah: on Eagles Wings. Downers Grove, IL: InterVarsity Press, 1997.

2   Campbell, Mike. "Meaning, Origin and History of the Name Dan (1)." Behind the Name. Accessed October 8, 2019. http://www.behindthename.com/name/dan-1.

3   Campbell, Mike. "Meaning, Origin and History of the Name Saul." Behind the Name. Accessed October 8, 2019. http://www.behindthename.com/name/saul.

4   Campbell, Mike. "Meaning, Origin and History of the Name Paul." Behind the Name. Accessed October 8, 2019. http://www.behindthename.com/name/paul.

Chapter 5

1   Anderson, Matthew Lee. "Book Review: Beyond the Bible - Mere Orthodoxy: Christianity, Politics, and Culture." Mere Orthodoxy | Christianity, Politics, and Culture, August 7, 2005. https://mereorthodoxy.com/book-review-beyond-the-bible/.

2   "What Were the Original Languages of the Bible?" Bibleinfo.com. Accessed October 15, 2019. http://www.bibleinfo.com/en/questions/original-language-bible.

3   Keil, and Delitzsch. "Isaiah 53." Isaiah 53 Keil and Delitzsch OT Commentary. Biblehub. Accessed October 15, 2019. https://biblehub.com/commentaries/kad/isaiah/53.htm.

4   Ibid.

5   Constructed from the biblical narratives found in 2 Kings 18-20, Isaiah 36-39, and 2 Chronicles 29-32.

Chapter 6

1   de Voragine, Jacobus. "The Mystery of the Trinity." Our Lady of Mercy. Accessed October 15, 2019. http://www.olmlaycarmelites.org/reflections/mystery-trinity.

2   Barker, Kenneth L. Zondervan NIV Study Bible: New International Version. Grand Rapids, MI: Zondervan, 2008.

3   Gill, John. "1 Corinthians 2 Commentary - John Gill's Exposition on the Whole Bible." StudyLight.org. Accessed October 16, 2019. https://www.studylight.org/commentaries/geb/1-corinthians-2.html.

Chapter 7

1   Buechner, Frederick. Wishful Thinking: a Theological ABC. New York (osv.): Harper & Row, 1973. 40.

Chapter 8

1   Jeremiah, David. The God You May Not Know: Take the Journey from Knowing about God to Knowing God. San Diego, CA: Turning Point, 2012.

2   Needham, David C., and Larry Libby. Close to His Majesty. Eugene, Or.: Wipf and Stock, 2005. 67-70.

3   Ibid.

4   Jeremiah, David. The God You May Not Know: Take the Journey from Knowing about God to Knowing God. San Diego, CA: Turning Point, 2012. 173.

Chapter 9

1   Risner, Vaneetha Rendall. "If God Is with Me, Why Did This Happen?" Desiring God. Desiring God, October 17, 2019. http://www.desiringgod.org/articles/if-god-is-with-me-why-did-this-happen.

2   Jeremiah, David. The God You May Not Know: Take the Journey from Knowing about God to Knowing God. San Diego, CA: Turning Point, 2012. 176.

3   "U.S. Department of the Treasury." History of 'In God We Trust', July 17, 2019. http://www.treasury.gov/about/education/Pages/in-god-we-trust.aspx.

4   GotQuestions.org. "Who Was Gideon in the Bible?" GotQuestions.org, December 12, 2009. https://www.gotquestions.org/life-Gideon.html.

5   Risner, Vaneetha Rendall. "If God Is with Me, Why Did This Happen?" Desiring God. Desiring God, October 17, 2019. http://www.desiringgod.org/articles/if-god-is-with-me-why-did-this-happen.

6   Ibid.

7   "Jesus Loves Me - Lyrics, Hymn Meaning and Story." GodTube. Accessed October 19, 2019. http://www.godtube.com/popular-hymns/jesus-loves-me.

8   Risner, Vaneetha Rendall. "If God Is with Me, Why Did This Happen?" Desiring God. Desiring God, October 17, 2019. http://www.desiringgod.org/articles/if-god-is-with-me-why-did-this-happen.

9   Taylor, Kimberly. "Encouraging Scriptures: Who I Am in Christ: Take Back Your Temple: Christian Weight Loss." Take Back Your Temple | Christian Weight Loss, March 20, 2019. https://www.takebackyourtemple.com/who-i-am-in-christ/.

10   Packer, J. I. Knowing God. Downers Grove, IL: InterVarsity Press, 1973. 21.

11   Ibid. 22.

12   Ibid. 24-25.

13   Ibid. 25.

14   Adapted from a similar list found in Packer, J. I. Knowing God. Downers Grove, IL: InterVarsity Press, 1973. 26.

15   From a clipping in my file.

16   Austin, Jill. Master Potter: Chronicles of Master Potter. Shippensburg, PA: Destiny Image, Inc., 2011. 66-70.

17   Zschech, Darlene. "The Potter's Hand Lyrics ." FlashLyrics. Accessed October 19, 2019. https://www.flashlyrics.com/lyrics/darlene-zschech/the-potters-hand-71.

Chapter 10

1   "Jim Carrey's Best Lines." The Telegraph. Telegraph Media Group, January 17, 2015. https://www.telegraph.co.uk/culture/film/11225801/Jim-Carreys-best-lines.html?frame=3104177.

2   Morgan, Robert J. The Promise: God Works All Things Together for Your Good. Nashville, TN: B & H Pub. Group, 2010.

3   Ibid.

4   Ibid. 3-4.

5   "Los Angeles Runway Disaster." Wikipedia. Wikimedia Foundation, October 6, 2019. https://en.wikipedia.org/wiki/Los_Angeles_runway_disaster.

6   Morgan, Robert J. The Promise: God Works All Things Together for Your Good. Nashville, TN: B & H Pub. Group, 2010. 18.

7   Ibid. 31.

8   Adapted from Morgan, Robert J. The Promise: God Works All Things Together for Your Good. Nashville, TN: B & H Pub. Group, 2010.

9   Adapted from Buechner, Frederick. Wishful Thinking: a Theological ABC. New York (osv.): Harper & Row, 1973. 48-49.

10 Ibid.

11 Barker, Kenneth L. Zondervan NIV Study Bible New International Version, Fully Revised. Grand Rapids, MI: Zondervan, 1985. 1753.

12 Wiersbe, Warren W. The Bible Exposition Commentary. Wheaton, IL: Victor Books, 1989. 541.

13 Fisher, Fred. Teacher's Bible Commentary. Edited by H. Franklin Paschall and Hershel H. Hobbs. Nashville, TN: Broadman Press, 1972. 715.

14 Utley, Bob. "Romans 8:28-30." You Can Understand the Bible - Romans 8:28 - 8:30. Accessed October 19, 2019. https://bible.prayerrequest.com/9087-utley-bob-you-can-understand-the-bible-study-guide-commentary-series-nt-13-vols/romans/8/28/8/30/.

15 Noland, Chris. "8 Benefits of Justification by Faith – Romans 5:1-11." Pastor Chris Noland, February 4, 2014. https://chrisnoland.org/2014/02/04/8-of-justification-by-faith-romans-51-11/.

16 Williams, Michael L. "The Ministry of Reconciliation." flyingwagners, February 15, 2017. http://www.flyingwagners.wordpress.com/2017/02/15/the-ministry-of-reconciliation.

Chapter 11

1   "Thrive Leadership Conference 2019." Bayside Church. Accessed October 19, 2019. https://www.baysideonline.com/event/thrive-leadership-conference-2019/.

2   "Phil Knight." Wikipedia. Wikimedia Foundation, October 13, 2019. https://en.wikipedia.org/wiki/Phil_Knight.

3   Johnston, Ray. The Hope Quotient: Measure It, Raise It, Youll Never Be the Same. Nashville: Thomas Nelson, 2015.

4   Ibid. 4.

5   Ibid. 4-6.

6   Adapted from Johnston, Ray. The Hope Quotient: Measure It, Raise It, Youll Never Be the Same. Nashville: Thomas Nelson, 2015. 6-7.

7   Ibid.

8   Cottringer, William S. "Staying Happy in Hopeless Situations." AuthorsDen. Accessed October 21, 2019. http://www.authorsden.com/categories/article_top.asp?catid=35&id=63737.

9   Ortiz, Sarah. "7 Bible Verses for When Life Seems Hopeless." American Bible Society, February 24, 2015. https://blog.bible/bible-blog/entry/7-bible-verses-for-when-life-seems-hopeless.

10 Adapted from Ortiz, Sarah. "7 Bible Verses for When Life Seems Hopeless." American Bible Society, February 24, 2015. https://blog.bible/bible-blog/entry/7-bible-verses-for-when-life-seems-hopeless.

11 Gaither, Bill, and Gloria Gaither. "Something Beautiful Lyrics ." Something Beautiful lyrics by Bill Gaither - original song full text. Official Something Beautiful lyrics, 2019 version | LyricsMode.com, February 4, 2013. https://www.lyricsmode.com/lyrics/b/bill_gaither/something_beautiful.html.

Chapter 12

1   Fowler, H. W. "Prig." Wikipedia. Wikimedia Foundation, July 18, 2018. https://en.wikipedia.org/wiki/Prig.

2   Adapted from Morgan, Robert J. 1000 Bible Verses. Nashville, TN: B & H Publishing, 2010. 29.

Chapter 13

1   MacDonald, Gordon. The Life God Blesses: Weathering the Storms of Life That Threaten the Soul. Nashville, TN: T. Nelson Publishers, 1997.

2   Lloyd, Barbara. "Solo Sailor Is Presumed To Be Dead." The New York Times. The New York Times, November 26, 1992. https://www.nytimes.com/1992/11/26/sports/solo-sailor-is-presumed-to-be-dead.html.

3   Ibid.

4   "Mike Plant." Wikipedia. Wikimedia Foundation, September 18, 2013. https://en.wikipedia.org/wiki/mike_plant.

5   David Jeremiah, "The Blessing." Shadow Mountain Church, July 21, 2019.

6.   Ibid.

Chapter 14

1   Bucchner, Frederick. Wishful Thinking: a Theological ABC. New York (osv.): Harper & Row, 1973. 83.

2   "First Living-Donor Liver Transplant Recipient Graduates from College May 9." UChicago Medicine. UChicago Medicine, May 6, 2010. http://www.uchicago-medicine.org/forefront/news/2010/may/first-living-donor-liver-transplant-recipient-graduates-from-college-may-9.

3   Ibid.

4   Morgan, Robert J. The Promise: God Works All Things Together for Your Good. Nashville, TN: B & H Pub. Group, 2010.

5   Ibid.

Chapter 15

1   "Fosbury Flop." Wikipedia. Wikimedia Foundation, October 1, 2019. https://en.wikipedia.org/wiki/Fosbury_Flop.

2   Sharon, Gerald. "Sermon." Sermon. December 14, 2014.

3   "My Faith." Renee Myers Endowment. Accessed October 23, 2019. http://www.reneescholarship.net/?page_id=73.

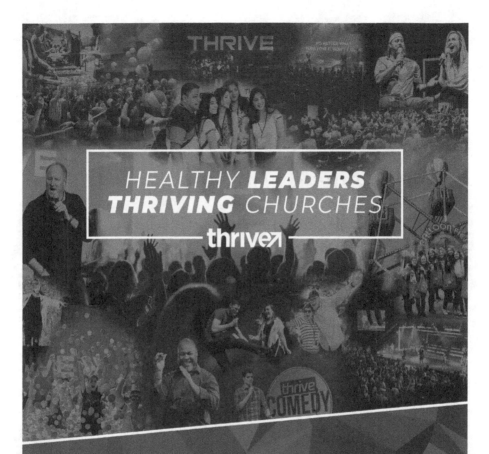

Certificate of Appreciation

from the

HEALTH RESOURCES AND SERVICES ADMINISTRATION

This certificate is presented in honor of

Renee Myers

Who gave "Gifts of Life" to others.

Elizabeth M. Duke, Ph.D.

Administrator, Health Resources and Services

September 14, 2009

Go to vanguard.edu/reneemyers to contribute your "Gifts of Life" to others.

VANGUARD UNIVERSITY

The Renee Myers Endowed Scholarship
A Celebration of a Cherished Life
for Physically Challenged Students

Go to Renee's Life to view video on Kindle and ebooks

Go to vimeo.com/49623284 to view video

The scholarship was established by Vanguard University alumni Dan and Dorene Myers and friends in memory of their daughter Renee. The endowment is awarded each year to Vanguard University students. This scholarship is unique, the first of its kind at the university.

To support the Renee Scholarship please click **Renee Alumni Scholarship**, or if reading from a book, go to vanguard.edu/reneemyers. If you need assistance, call 714-966-5442 and ask for a secretary in the Office of Advancement.

For additional information including blog posts, photos and testimonials visit www.wherewasgod.org or www.reneescholarship.net

WHERE WAS GOD WHEN I NEEDED HIM? THE QUESTION EVERYONE'S ASKING

(www.wherewasgod.org)

If you're a fan of this book, will you help me spread the word?

There are several ways you can help me get the word out about the message of this book…

- Post a 5-Star review on Amazon.

- Write about the book on your Facebook, Twitter, Instagram – any social media you regularly use!

- If you blog, consider referencing the book, or publishing an excerpt from the book with a link back to my website. You have my permission to do this as long as you provide proper credit and backlinks.

- Recommend the book to friends – word-of-mouth is still the most effective form of advertising.

- Purchase additional copies to give away as gifts at www.wherewasgod.org.

The best way to connect with me is by email at dm@wherewasgod.org.

amazon   BARNES&NOBLE

You can order more books from these book sellers or where ever you purchase your favorite books.